Studying Cultural Landscapes

Studying Cultural Landscapes

Edited by

IAIN ROBERTSON
School of Environment,
University of Gloucestershire

and

PENNY RICHARDS
School of Humanities,
University of Gloucestershire

A member of the Hodder Headline Group
LONDON
Distributed in the United States of America by
Oxford University Press Inc., New York

First published in Great Britain in 2003 by
Hodder Arnold, a member of the Hodder Headline Group,
338 Euston Road, London NW1 3BH

http://www.arnoldpublishers.com

Distributed in the United States of America by
Oxford University Press Inc.,
198 Madison Avenue, New York, NY10016

British Library Cataloguing in Publication Data
A catalogue record for this book is available from the British Library

Library of Congress Cataloging-in-Publication Data
A catalog record for this book is available from the Library of Congress

ISBN 0 340 76267 5 (hb)
ISBN 0 340 76268 3 (pb)

1 2 3 4 5 6 7 8 9 10

Typeset in 10/12pt Sabon by Phoenix Photosetting, Chatham, Kent
Printed and bound in Great Britain by MPG Books Ltd, Bodmin, Cornwall

What do you think about this book? Or any other Arnold title?
Please send your comments to feedback.arnold@hodder.co.uk

Contents

Acknowledgements

We would like to acknowledge the enthusiasm and input of all our students, past and present, who have studied the course Symbolic Landscapes with us at the University of Gloucestershire. We would also like to thank the University of Gloucestershire for the support it has given this collection of essays.

We would also like to thank Jessica Munns at the University of Denver for help all along the way, and our editors at Arnold, especially Liz Gooster who has been a steady and helpful presence throughout.

Our contributors also have their own acknowledgements, which follow.

Iain Black would like to thank Mr Edwin Green, Ms Sara Kinsey and the HSBC Group Archives, London, and Ms Margaret Lee and the Hongkong Bank Archives, Hong Kong, for their help and advice in connection with his research into the Hongkong Bank's building programme in the Far East in the nineteenth and twentieth centuries. Figures 1.1–1.13 inclusive are reproduced with the kind permission of the HSBC Group plc. He would also like to thank Dr Alan Baker for his very helpful comments on an earlier draft of this essay. Any remaining errors are his own.

W. Scott Howard would like to thank DC Comics, New York, NY, for permission to reproduce 'The Song of Orpheus: Chapter Three' (p. 187) and 'The Song of Orpheus: Epilogue' (p. 198) from *The Sandman* Vol. 6.

Catherine Brace would like to thank the following for permission to reproduce the figures listed below.

- Figure 6.1: *Abroad*, reproduced with the kind permission of Diane Baylis; grateful thanks to her for her help and co-operation.
- Figure 6.2: *Legacy of England*, reproduced by kind permission of Mrs G. Master and B.T. Batsford Ltd.
- Figure 6.3: *St Just*, reproduced by kind permission of Mrs Sheila Lanyon.

Some of the research discussed in Chapter 6 was funded in part by the British Academy, grant number APN30343, and by the Q Fund, Cornwall County Council, to whom thanks are also due.

Keith Halfacree would like to thanks Alan Lodge ('Tash') for permission to reproduce his photograph of the Stonehenge Festival, 1983 (Figure 7.3).

List of contributors

Iain S. Black is a Lecturer in Geography at King's College London. He has written widely on the historical geography of money and banking in Britain, including the economic, social and architectural transformation of the City of London between 1750 and 1950. More recently, his interests have focused on reconstructing the historical geography of British imperial and colonial banking, with particular reference to the design and building of bank branch networks in the Caribbean, West Africa, Egypt and the Far East between 1850 and 1950. Iain's recent publications include the following.

Black, I.S. 1999: Imperial visions: rebuilding the Bank of England, 1919–1939, in Driver, F. and Gilbert, D. (eds), *Imperial Cities: Landscape, Display and Identity*. Manchester: Manchester University Press, 96–113.

Black, I.S. 2000: Spaces of capital: bank office building in the City of London, 1830–1870. *Journal of Historical Geography* **26** (3), 351–75.

Black, I.S. 2002: Reordering space: British bank building overseas 1900–1940, in de Graaf, T., Jonker, J. and Mobron, J. (eds), *European Banking Overseas, 19th–20th Centuries*. Amsterdam: Aksant, 77–108.

Catherine Brace is a historical geographer at Exeter University whose work is informed by the links between cultural geographies and critical historical geographies. Her research interests include landscape, national identity and regional identity, cultural geography, historical geography and history of geographic thought. Her research focuses on how landscapes and representations of those landscapes worked in the formation of English national identity in the first half of the twentieth century. Recent work includes the following.

Brace, C. 1999: Finding England everywhere: regional identity and the construction of national identity 1890–1940, *Ecumene* **6** (1), 90–109.

Brace, C. 1999: Cornish identity and landscape in the work of Arthur Caddick, *Cornish Studies* **7**, 130–46.

Brace, C. 2001: Publishing and publishers: towards an historical geography of countryside writing, c.1930–1950, *Area* **33** (3), 287–96.

Andrew Charlesworth taught at the University of Liverpool for 21 years before moving to Gloucestershire to become Reader in Human Geography at the then Cheltenham & Gloucester College of Higher Education. Having pioneered the study of historical geography of rural protest in Britain, he began to be drawn to the study of Holocaust landscapes. He is currently undertaking an Economic and Social Research Council project on Oswiecim, the town within whose boundaries lies the former camp of Auschwitz. Recent publications include the following.

Charlesworth, A. 1992: Towards a geography of the Shoah: a review essay, *Journal of Historical Geography* **16** (4), 464–9.

Charlesworth, A. 1994: Contesting places of memory: the case of Auschwitz, *Society and Space* **12**, 579–93.

Charlesworth, A. 1995: Teaching the geography of the Holocaust: the Liverpool experience. *Immigrants and Minorities* **15**, 33–45. (Republished in Millen, R.L. (ed.) 1996: *New Perspectives on the Holocaust*. New York: New York University Press.)

Leah Garrett is an Assistant Professor of Judaic Studies and English Literature, having previously been the Director of the Westside Yiddish School, New York, and held a Fulbright Fellowship, at Tel Aviv University, Department of Hebrew Literature, for 1997–98. She has published numerous essays on Yiddish literature and her first book is *Journeys Beyond the Pale: Yiddish Travel Writing in the Modern World* (Madison: University of Wisconsin Press, 2003). Leah's most recent work includes the following.

Garrett, L. 2001: Shipping the self to America: the perils of assimilation in Glatshteyn's and Shapiro's immigration novels, *Melus* **26** (3), fall, 203–29.

Garrett, L. 2001: Trains and train travel in modern Yiddish literature, *Jewish Social Studies: History, Culture and Society*, **7** (2), winter, 67–88.

Garrett, L. 2002: The Jewish Robinson Crusoe, *Comparative Literature* **54** (3), summer, 215–28.

Keith Halfacree is a Lecturer in Geography at the University of Wales Swansea. His research interests are in rural studies (especially cultural representations of the countryside and land access), population migration and radical anti-capitalist praxis (especially DIY culture and its spatiality). Recent work includes the following.

Boyle, P. and Halfacree, K. (eds) 1998: *Migration into Rural Areas. Theories and Issues*. Chichester: Wiley.

Halfacree, K. 1999: 'Anarchy doesn't work unless you think about it': intellectual interpretation and DIY culture, *Area* **31**, 209–20.

Halfacree, K. (in press): Constructing the object: taxonomic practices, 'counterurbanisation' and positioning marginal rural settlement, *International Journal of Population Geography*.

Andrew Horton is the Jeanne H. Smith Professor of Film and Video Studies at the University of Oklahoma. He is an award-winning screenwriter, and the author of 16 books and numerous articles. Recent work includes the following.

Horton, A. 2000: *The Films of Theo Angelopoulos: A Cinema of Contemplation*, Princeton: Princeton University Press.
Horton, A. 2001: *Make A Joyful Noise* (screenplay).
Horton, A. 2003: *Screenwriting for a Global Market*. Berkeley: University of California Press.

W. Scott Howard teaches at the University of Denver, where he is Assistant Professor of English. His research interests include sixteenth- and seventeenth-century English literature and culture, Shakespeare and Milton, poetics and historiography, twentieth-century American poetry and small press literatures. He has essays forthcoming in *Speaking Grief in English Literary Culture: Shakespeare to Milton* (Duquesne University Press), *Grief and Gender, 700–1700* (St Martin's Press) and *The World in Time and Space* (Talisman House). Scott is currently completing a book manuscript: *Fantastic Surmise: 17th-century English Elegies, Elegiac Modes and the Historical Imagination from Donne to Philips*.

Jessica Munns teaches English at the University of Denver. She is editor of the journal *Restoration and Eighteenth-century Theatre Studies* and has recently co-edited a multi-play volume of dramas for Ashgate Press, based on the Aphra Behn novella *Oroonoko*. Recent works include *The Clothes That Wear Us: Dressing and Transgressing in Eighteenth-century Culture*; co-edited with Penny Richards (University of Delaware Press, 1999) and *A Cultural Studies Reader*, co-edited with Gita Rajan (Longman, 1996). Jessica has also produced numerous essays in books and journals, and an edition of Thomas Otway's play *Venice Preserved* (2001).

Penny Richards lectures in the School of Humanities at the University of Gloucestershire. She has written book and journal articles on early modern France and on English history, and is currently working on a book on the house of Guise in sixteenth-century Europe. Recent publications include the following.

The Clothes That Wear Us (University of Delaware Press, 1999), with Jessica Munns.
Richards P. 2000: A life in writing: Elizabeth Cellier and print culture, *Women's Writing* 7 (3), 411–25.
Power Gender, and Privilege in Early Modern Europe with Jessica Munns (Pearson Education, 2003).

Iain Robertson lectures in Human Geography at the University of Gloucestershire. He has published extensively on the historical geography of social protest in the Highlands of Scotland but, more recently, has turned his attention to questions of heritage, most specifically to the memorialisation of illegality in the form of public art sculptures on the Hebridean island of Lewis. His recent publications include the following.

Robertson I. 1997: The role of women in social protest in the Highlands of Scotland, c1880–c1939, *Journal of Historical Geography* **23** (2).

Robertson I. and Hall T. 2001: Public art and urban regeneration, *Landscape Research* **26** (1).

Robertson I. 2001: 'Their families had gone back in time hundreds of years at the same place': attitudes to land and landscape in the Scottish Highlands after 1918, in Harvey, D. *et al.* (eds) *Celtic Geographies*. London: Routledge.

Gillian Rose is a lecturer in Geography at the Open University having previously taught in London and Edinburgh. Her current research engages with the debates about visual culture by thinking about the spaces in which visual images are displayed. This work makes particular reference to the spaces produced by the display of family photographs in middle-class homes. Her recent work includes the following.

Rose, G. 2000: Practising photography: an archive, a study, some photographs and a researcher, *Journal of Historical Geography* **26** (4) 555–71.

Rose, G. 1997: Spatialities of 'community', power and change: the imagined geographies of community arts projects, *Cultural Studies* **11**, 1–16.

List of Figures

amongst others, by Raymond Williams, that all landscapes are cultural products.

In his groundbreaking work, *The Country and the City* (1973), Raymond Williams analysed four centuries of English writing on the rural and the urban in terms of the ways that they express a range of political attitudes and arrangements. In his discussion of Ben Jonson's poem *To Penshurst* (1616), for example, Williams notes its celebration of 'old' wealth. He draws attention to its insistence on 'traditional' and reciprocal contacts between landowner and peasants. At Penshurst the walls were '. . . reared with no man's ruin, no man's groan' (46–7), and it offered an idealised representation of the relations between poet and patron, and patron and monarch. The approach taken by Williams has been further advanced by John Barrell is his now classic *The Dark Side of the Landscape: The Rural Poor in English Painting, 1730–1840* (1980). Barrell discusses what he defines as the 'contradiction' of aristocratic living. This is the desire simultaneously to 'acknowledge by their display no limits to their income' and thus encourage rural representations that suggest leisure and ease, but also 'to preserve and pass on their wealth with their title from generation to generation', which involved 'ruthlessly prudent management of their estates' (1980: 11). Pictorial art, he argues, was increasingly under pressure as agricultural enclosure and cultivation, and the capitalisation of farming, increased to show 'workaday actuality' without also showing workaday rural misery. As he puts it, 'as the rustic figures become less and less the shepherds of French or Italian Pastoral, they become more and more ragged, but remain inexplicably cheerful' (1980: 16). Anne Bermingham has discussed the art of a similar period to that studied by Barrell in her book *Landscape and Ideology: The English Rustic Tradition, 1740–1860* (1987). For both authors this is a key period for change in the economics of landowning, and the resultant change in the depictions of landscapes. As Bermingham writes in her Introduction, 'Nature with its various representations . . . became a supreme social value and was called on to clarify and justify social change' (1987: 1). Following and adapting these ideas, we can view later representations of landscape in political terms. We can, for instance, note in Thomas Hardy's Wessex, depicted in the age of the locomotive, a nostalgia for labour relations in a pre-industrial England, and, indeed, also in Tolkien's idealised 'Shire' of 'Middle Earth', home of happy Hobbits whose rural way of life is threatened by an evil actualised as factories. It is, to say the least, ironic that this celebration of a long-gone (if it ever existed) rural England has recently been filmed in New Zealand.

We can, however, trace relations in power and the conditions of labour not only in works of art but in the very land around us. W.G. Hoskins (1955) showed how much of England is a created landscape that can be understood in terms of the various social and economic arrangements existing in particular places and times. Indeed, landscapes can often be viewed as a palimpsest in which we note first in the village green, pond and stocks the economic and social needs and disciplines of medieval England. We can then trace in the (now disused) railway station the nineteenth-century incursion of town into country, and in the carefully restored and pristine cottages the second-homeowners of the twentieth and twenty-first centuries.

Stocks, railway station and cottage are all, therefore, highly symbolic landscapes and are themselves constituent parts of an equally symbolic and national landscape icon. Essentially much of the basis of the symbolic landscapes approach, as outlined in the 1980s,[1] comes from the view that landscape is not nature but nature transformed by humanity. In this view, all landscapes carry symbolic meaning because all are products of the human appropriation and transformation of the environment, whether physically, as in the draining of marshes or in the extraction of oil and gas, or in the meaning we give to landscapes such as the Grand Canyon or the World Trade Center. Moreover, this recognition of symbolic meaning in landscape leads to a consideration of the political dimensions of the world/land we see around us and inhabit; and because the symbolic approach recognises this political dimension and extends also to landscape meanings, then landscapes in this view extend to encompass the mental as well as the material.

As nature is transformed, it is the dominant element in society who will seek to write their own landscapes in their own image, in accordance with their own view of the way in which the world should be organised. Landscape projects and communicates that view to the remainder of society who accept that view as *natural*. One of the principal ways in which this is done is through the symbols written into the landscape. These can be both obvious, such as a country church, and more obscure, such as a new type of gate depicted in a piece of landscape art. Whichever it is, the effect is the same: landscape is one of the principal ways by which the powerful in society maintain their dominance through a process of imposition and naturalisation. Landscapes, then, reveal, represent and symbolise the relationships of power and control out of which they have emerged and the human processes that have transformed and continue to transform them. Landscapes are, therefore, cultural images that often hide the processes that have made them – social, political, economic, spiritual – behind a placid and familiar surface. The 'symbolic method' investigates below the surface to reveal the politics, processes and symbolic qualities written into it.

From the layout of a city through to the design of individual houses, from a rural region through to its individual field boundaries, those with power impose their view on the majority through the landscapes they create. It is, however, important to recognise that in the same way that the meanings and values of the dominant group are visible in the landscape, then the meanings and values of resistance and of alternative cultures can also be so written. The identities of landscapes are, in short, multiple and complex. In London, for instance, it is possible to find representations of power and control in a medieval context; we can also identify icons of national government, of empire and of the global city, but also landscapes of difference. Each of these registers, and there are many more, has left an imprint on the city.

There is, therefore, a dynamic and interactive system at work within any landscape and it is important to realise that the cultural processes that shape the landscape are also themselves in turn shaped by landscapes. Let us consider, for instance, the drystone walls that adorn much of upland Britain. These have many different and dynamic meanings. The majority of these walls, particularly those built in seemingly endless straight lines without regard for topography, are products of eighteenth- and nineteenth-century agricultural enclosure. As much as the eighteenth-century landscaped parks written about so eloquently by Williams (1973) and Pugh (1988), enclosure walls symbolise the processes surrounding the introduction of capitalism into the countryside, a fact only enhanced by their disregard for topography. At the same time, however, they symbolise resistance to that process and are in turn directly affected by it. Enclosure walls were frequently destroyed as protestors sought to overturn enclosure and loss of common rights. In some areas, moreover, the continual destruction of walls meant the ultimate amelioration of the policy of enclosure. Today, of course, these walls are venerated as a crucial component of Britain's national heritage landscape and we fear for their disappearance as the socio-economic wheels take another turn and upland farming becomes increasingly unviable.

Recognition of the politics of landscape representation and of the fact that landscapes on the whole manifest the worldview of the dominant group is the beginning of the process of reading and decoding the landscape in order to reveal the deeper processes that have made it and upon which the symbolic method rests. The principal analytical device underlying this decoding is one borrowed, as discussed by Iain Black in Chapter 1 of this volume, from art history, that of iconography. Critically, this symbolic methodology does not deny the visuality of landscape but seeks to reveal the values and meanings written into these visual images by a culture group. Building on, paralleling, but at the same time diverging from, the iconographical method, has led some commentators (Duncan, 1990, for instance) to view the landscape as a text, as a social and cultural document to be read in order to reveal the layers of meaning and processes written into it.

This brings us to the point at which the culturally informed analysis of landscape was in the early 1990s. More recently, two new trends have emerged. The notion of text has been expanded to include that of inter-textuality (Duncan and Duncan, 1997). This is the incorporation into the landscape reading of the acceptance that an already existing body of material and other readings has inevitably influenced the current reading. In this context, it is important to be clear that whilst writers have always made their influences and prior knowledge obvious, intertextuality does this in a more proactive way. Today, therefore, the culture of the interpreter – the readers of this Introduction as much as the writers of this Introduction – is seen to be of significant influence in the interpretation.

The second more recent trend has been a critical one. For some feminist commentators in particular, the fact that virtually all the initial work on landscape iconography focused on class relationships was much too one-dimensional. Reflecting the postmodern concern for polyvocality (allowing many 'other' voices to speak), attention is now also being given to the complexity of images written into the landscape, and emphasis placed on 'polyvisual' interpretations (Kinnaird *et al.*, 1997; Seymour, 2000). Thus a single landscape may well either (or both) be subject to a range of interpretations dependent on the cultural position of the interpreter or be viewed 'simultaneously in a variety of ways' (Seymour, 2000: 194). It is, nevertheless, important to note in this context that whilst it may have been articulated only recently, this is not necessarily a 'new' idea. The eighteenth-century labouring-class poet Mary Collier, for instance, wrote a poem, *The Women's Labour* (1739), in response to what she felt was Stephen Duck's erasure of women from the working landscape in his poem *The Thresher's Labour* (1736). She lamented that he '. . . let our hapless sex in silence lie. Forgotten and in dark oblivion die' (1739: 39–40). One of the most important contributions to this developing kaleidoscopic approach to landscape interpretation has come from Gillian Rose. Working with one of the most frequently cited landscape representations, Gainsborough's *Mr and Mrs Andrews* (*c*.1748–50), Rose (1992) views this from the perspective of gender. She argues that not only does the painting itself represent a gendered landscape but subsequent interpretations also perpetuate the gendering process. Rose returns us here to Berger's (1972) analysis in which he emphasises the energy of the painting. For Rose this emphasis is as much the product of a masculine gaze, as is Mr Andrews' over his estate.

Critiques such as these – and we should also mention here the work of Alison Blunt (1994) and, as already suggested, Bermingham (1987) – have done much to add new layers of sensitivity to the analysis. There is, however, one critical theme that is somewhat less sympathetic to the cultural standpoint. This is the view, expressed most directly in the work of Richard Muir (1998), that the cultural approach leads to an unhelpful separation between mental and material landscapes. Indeed, Muir goes as far as to identify a mutual incompatibility between the two. This is, perhaps, a rather too extreme view and since we would wish to stress the material basis of cultural products (physical and mental), we prefer the idea of a constant dyadic shuttle between ideas and materials thereby allowing the more dualistic and interactive aspects of landscape to emerge. This can be seen in the work of Olwig (1996), who argues for a landscape that is both 'substantive' and partly constituted by representations of it. More persuasive, however, are the views that rework landscape not as cultural product but as cultural process.

2 Landscape as cultural process

In cultural geography this view is most closely associated with the work of W.J.T. Mitchell (1994), who attempted to move our understanding away from seeing landscape as a static text to seeing it as part of a 'process by which . . . identities are formed' (1994: 1). In this view, landscape is active and dynamic, it – to borrow a phrase from Don Mitchell (2000) – 'does work' in both the mental and material senses.

Whilst we can recognise within cultural geography a 'shift from textual interpretation of the working of these texts to an interpretation of these texts in popular cultural practice' (Crouch, 2000: 70) it is within the fields of archaeology and anthropology that the notion of landscape as cultural process finds its most consistent expression, although it has to be acknowledged that in both fields landscape has been too often taken as a given rather than seen as a problematic. Nevertheless, where landscape is considered, the way in which it is understood is often based upon a phenomenological stance, the 'key issue' in which 'is the manner in which people experience and understand the world'. In this view, then, the physicality of landscape is seen as critical and as the setting in which humanly created locales occur. This leads commentators such as Ingold (1993) to reject the notion of landscape as a cultural or symbolic construct as it falsely separates mental and material worlds. Instead, he proposes a temporality to landscape in order to incorporate 'the processes of social life' (1993: 157). This is a term that allows Ingold to see landscape as part of and as product of the dynamic process of dwelling in which it, the landscape, 'is never built . . . is perpetually under construction . . . is always in the nature of "work in progress"' (1993: 162).

For Ingold, landscape derives from the 'taskscape', the life-cycle processes which, via a series of interlocking cycles, build themselves into the landscape and which the landscape embodies. These processes are dwelling 'tasks', the concrete practices of *work*; and the whole array of tasks forms the taskscape, which, according to Ingold, relates to landscape as music does to painting. In the same way that painting can be seen as a frozen form of music, then landscape can be '*understood as the taskscape in its embodied form*' (Ingold, 1993: 162; original emphasis), as activities collapsed into fixed features, although this is not taken to imply stasis.

Ingold's notion of taskscape is recognised as an important, if not universally accepted, meditation on landscape. Tilly (1994), for example, agrees with Ingold that it is unhelpful to think of the world in terms of a binary nature/culture distinction, although this does not lead him to wholly reject the Cosgrove/Daniels thesis. Furthermore, Tilly is critical of Ingold's attempts to see as a sequence people's practical activity in the world and their cultural knowledge of it. Tilly argues instead for the recognition that the cultural construction of the environment is 'both "prelude" *and* "epilogue"' (1994: 24; original emphasis).

For Tilly, as for Ingold, the landscape is never complete. It is always already fashioned by human agency and is constantly being added to. Life activities are the medium through which landscape is experienced and that occur in relationship with the visual and physical forms of the landscape.

Tilly then goes on to develop a sophisticated understanding of landscape, which draws in 'the spirit of a place . . . the social and individual times of memory' paths and narratives, in order to conclude that 'a landscape is a series of named locales' (1994: 26, 34). Critically, however, Tilly's landscape is multivocal in which there is a place for the symbolic through which the social is reproduced and transformed.

Currently one of our most important commentators on landscape is Eric Hirsch in his Introduction to *The Anthropology of Landscape* (1995). Here, like Tilly, Hirsch does not wholly reject the representational reading of landscape but argues instead that this makes accessible just one side of the relationship that landscape encompasses. Hirsch, very much like Mitchell from a cultural geography perspective, argues that landscape is a cultural process that brings together the cultural meaning of landscape with 'the concrete actuality of everyday life' (1995: 3).

What appears to have happened to the understanding of landscape in the 1990s, then, is a move away from what some commentators perceive as the static nature of the symbolic reading to an emphasis on the dynamic and constitutive nature of landscape. This, however, need not involve the rejection of the Cosgrove/Daniels thesis, as the most persuasive commentators incorporate the symbolic approach into a multivocal reading of the concept. Bender (1993; 1998) and Bender and Winder (2001), for instance, meld the phenomenological approaches of Bourdieu's 'habitus' and Giddens' 'structuration theory' with the 'structure of feeling' articulated by Raymond Williams, which, as we have already noted, was an important point of departure for the symbolic approach. Far from fading away and being replaced by a more dynamic landscape, the symbolic approach continues to be an important and constituent part of our understanding of the 'scape'. 'Landscape does not simply mirror or distort "underlying" social relations, but needs to be understood as enmeshed within the processes which shape how the world is organized, experienced and understood, rather than read as its end product' (Seymour, 2000: 214).

3   An illustrative example: the crofting landscape

We can illustrate much of the foregoing by reference to the front cover of this book. There you can see what, in many respects, is the archetypal landscape of the Scottish Highlands: a small croft house set in a vast wilderness of bracken, hills, glens and water. It is the landscape celebrated in a multitude of sentimental Scottish songs, in celluloid and in literature. It has a timeless quality that enhances, and is enhanced and suggested by our romantic vision of a Highland wilderness. It would not take a great leap of the imagination to transpose this photograph into one of Landseer's landscapes so elegantly deconstructed by Pringle (1988) in *The Iconography of Landscape*. Pringle identifies in Landseer's representations of the Scottish

Highlands the emergence of a Victorian myth of a tranquil natural order. A myth that hides (taking his inspiration from Barthes, Pringle says 'secreted') the historical processes (the physical, social and cultural transformation of the Highlands) out of which this wilderness landscape has emerged and has been created. If a wilderness is wild, untamed and untouched by human hand then there is no such thing as the Highland wilderness.

This short illustration, however, is not wholly concerned with the Highland wilderness myth. Rather it is concerned with a landscape that emerged alongside the Highland wilderness, is a product of the same forces that produced the wilderness landscape, and exists in a symbiotic, interdependent and intertwined relationship with it. Our concern here is with the Highland crofting landscape, and we can recognise at least two layers of meaning to the Highland crofting landscape as represented by this book's front cover illustration.

At one level this landscape can be seen to symbolise the processes of transformation the landscape underwent as a consequence of the introduction of the capitalist mode of production into the Highlands with the wilderness landscape being created, at first, to facilitate sheep farming and, later, deer forest for sport. Capitalistic change in the Highlands was both physical and social. Over the course of the seventeenth century, the loosening of social ties and obligations from above led to the gradual but inexorable switch from food to cash rents, as clan chiefs increasingly became influenced by 'models of landlord behaviour being transmitted from the lowlands' (Dodgshon, 1989: 193). When combined with demographic pressures within the land-working population, this ultimately impelled the transformation of land-holding, and land-working practices, and led to the dualistic – small crofting and large estate – landscape here outlined.

Over the course of the second half of the eighteenth century, landlords reorganised their estates in order to introduce large-scale sheep farming and to maximise their income from the land. This was a reorganisation that had profound consequences for the land-working tenantry. Where previously the traditional society and economy had been based upon the retention of a large population, sheep production was not. Consequently, the desire to maximise estate income led, in the years around and after 1800, to the displacement of the bulk of the population from the interior to marginal land on the coast. Here, and as a consequence of this first phase of clearance, a new form of agricultural organisation – crofting – began to emerge. In Gaelic, the term for 'croft' means a small piece of arable land and the 'crofter' was recognised as one who held a croft of land and a share in the common grazing. Crofting agriculture is, therefore, a small-scale subsistence agriculture in which arable plots are complemented by shared rough grazing. The crofting landscape, symbolised by the white house and the small, improved arable lot, both surrounded by unimproved waste, emerged as a direct consequence of the desire to create wilderness. In the front-cover picture, the abandoned arable is the greener portion within the fence, with the croft set in a sea of unimproved common land. The croft, in this reading, symbolises the transformation of Highland land-holding and land-working practices consequent upon the introduction of the capitalist mode of production into the region.

However, as Cosgrove and Daniels remind us (1988), there is a further gloss to be put on this particular text. Members of the land-working population did not accept change wholly passively. From at least the 1740s through to the 1950s, there occurred a series of protests aimed at resisting change, the consequences of change and the reinstatement of what the land-working population saw as their lost rights and expropriated land. The croft featured on the front cover, to be found in the township of Cheesebay on the Hebridean island of North Uist, was established by the British government as a direct consequence of the successful land invasion in that area in 1922. Land invasion was the tactic protestors adopted as they attempted to recover 'lost' ancestral land, which they believed was theirs by right of hereditary occupation. The croft house at Cheesebay was built some time in the 1930s on land last occupied in the 1840s. Clearly, whatever the popular image, the crofting landscape is not a timeless and unchanging one.

If we were to follow the Cosgrove (1984) foundational text we may well now proceed to identify the Cheesebay landscape as an 'alternative' landscape. This would be, then, a landscape of disjuncture, present, but less visible than the dominant landscape. We may well go on to say that the crofting landscape has, over time, moved from being an 'excluded' to an 'emergent' landscape, especially given the resurgence in political interest in the land issue in Scotland and the recent purchase of their estates by a number of crofting townships. It is not, however, as straightforward or as reductionist as this. In exactly the same way as relationships between the dominated and the dominant are now seen as considerably more reciprocal and processual than previously imagined, the landscapes that emerge from these relationships need to be 'understood as enmeshed within the processes which shape how the world is organized, experienced and understood' (Seymour, 2000: 214). Landscape, according to Hirsch (1995), amongst others, should be seen as a cultural process. The Cheesebay crofting landscape, then, may well be an alternative landscape that, in its formation, drew on the land-working population's belief in traditional rights regarding land occupation and organisation. But, critically, crofters and cottars were not attempting to reinstate traditional utilisation practices. The land-working population, from at least the 1880s, aspired to crofts and the crofting system of agriculture. Their aspiration, then, was to precisely the system brought into being by the processes of change crofters and cottars were reacting *against*. As an instrument of cultural power, landscape is both embedded in, and a product of dynamic processes of interaction.

These processes of interaction must also include gender. Again, at first glance the crofting landscape can be read off as a typically patriarchally oriented, gendered landscape and our reading of this particular landscape/text may well be seen also as gendered. The latter verdict we leave up to the reader; and, whilst the crofting landscape might well be gendered, we would suggest that it is not gendered in the expected way. The croft was both home and land, and was therefore of central significance to the Highland tenantry. It was the women who did the most to maintain this significance, not least by their labour on the croft, as the following memory of the 1930s testifies.

> The men folk went away to different jobs. Some went sailing on the yachts, quite a number . . . went to them, others away to salmon fishing, others to hotel work . . . before the men went away they cut the peats, planted potatoes, sowed the corn. And of course the women had to do all the work after that. See to the drying and lifting of peats, cleaning the potatoes. Then at harvest time had to see that hay was cut and secured for the winter and . . . see to the cutting and stacking of corn. Look after cattle and sheep as they were all kept tied up and had to be moved every so often in the day. . . . So you can see it was hard work for the women that [*sic*] days and of course look after the family.[2]

In their labour, but more importantly in their permanent, physical presence on the croft, claims to permanent and hereditary occupation of the land were vested in and sustained by women. From this position of strength, women took part both in events of popular resistance to the reorganisation of traditional land-holding arrangements and in the later attempts of the land-working population to reassert their (perceived) customary rights to land, as described here. The conjunction of their role in maintaining a permanent physical presence on the land with that of the maintenance of ideologically based claims to land, weakened patriarchal control, placed women at the centre of crofting society and gave them a central role in the maintenance of the crofting landscape. This is a role, moreover, that has resonance in the contemporary Highlands. According to a recent interviewee:

> 'I think in a community like this your sense of identity, your sense of culture is the only thing that keeps you here.'
> 'And what gives you that sense of identity and culture?'
> 'The ground does, absolutely nothing else I walk down the croft which has been in our family since the sixteenth century and even as a young girl I used to walk down the croft and think if only everybody, I mean it was home, it was always home to me it's still home to me, um, if every single person who ever called this home could come back and stand shoulder to shoulder on this croft how far would they span? – A long way aye – It's the same ground I'm tilling today to plant potatoes and it's the same ground they tilled, same footsteps, same places. [pause] It gives you a very strong sense of yourself and who you are and where you come from. There's nothing worse than having that

vacuum in your life. . . . [Land] is the only thing that keeps us clinging on by our fingernails to these rocks, these windy rocks.'[3]

What our particular reading points towards is an understanding of the crofting landscape as 'always in the making' (Bender and Winder, 2001), always in a state of dynamic tension. In this instance, the tension is between both the crofting and wider sportive landscape and within the crofting land-scape. Pursuing this idea of landscape as cultural process brings us to the notion of taskscape. If we are to accept the centrality of the 'task' to the 'scape', then, at first glance at least, the notion is an attractive one in the crofting context. When we look at acts of protest in the Scottish Highlands these are revealed as clearly motivated by a reaction to agrarian change. But what these acts of protest actually embody is a desire to dwell and a deep sense of rootedness in a particular landscape. Indicative of this is the petition, signed in 1921 by 57 of the 77 families from the township of North Tolsta on the island of Lewis, which contained the claim:

> . . . no one but a Lewisman can understand the Lewisman's love for and pride in, being in possession of a holding in his own island. . . . Our ideal life is that of a crofter fisherman. . . . It is the free and happy life of a contented peasantry living amongst the glens, straths and hills of our ancestors we now look forward to.

But this is a sense of rootedness made meaning *full* by tasks, by the consti-tutive act of dwelling. Again on Lewis, but this time in 1931, six men from Keose went to the Glebe lands and 'as a gesture [of their intention to gain possession of the land] each turned up a sod'.[4]

Taskscape is an attractive notion that, in the Highland context at least, reminds us of the dynamic and constitutive power of work in the making of the 'scape'. It would be wrong, however, to extend this too far. To under-stand landscape as representation does not imply stasis. The constitutive power of the cultural processes involved in the making and meaning of the crofting landscape is only maintained via constant reworking. The latest version of this reworking can be seen in Figure 1. This is but one of a series of public art memorials recently erected to commemorate the land raids and land raiders on the island of Lewis. These memorials are becoming impor-tant markers in contemporary Highlanders' sense of place identity (Withers, 1996). As Cosgrove and Daniels (1988) and the authors in the present volume assert, landscape is a deeply layered text, to which each reading adds new glosses.

4 Approaches to 'reading' the landscape

The essays we have collected for this book have all been commissioned especially for it and represent broadly based cultural responses to 'actual'

Figure 1 Memorial to the Coll and Gress land raiders, the Isle of Lewis (Photo: Iain Robertson)

and 'imagined' landscapes. The authors are drawn from a variety of disciplinary areas. As the foregoing indicates, 'reading' landscapes is an interdisciplinary activity and scholars of literature, art history and media, as well as cultural geographers, contribute to our understanding of the significance of how and why the landscape has been shaped. The essays collected here look at ways in which literary texts have used and developed the symbolic meanings their cultures have found in their surroundings, and the ways in which films create (and distort) our sense of space and place, and their meanings. They look at cityscapes, statues and monuments, at poems, paintings and myths, and, however different their subject matter and approach, they are united by their sense that landscapes are created, and both reflect and inform the way we live and the way we think.

Iain Black's essay, with which this collection opens, argues that buildings are central to the symbolic reading of landscapes in that they frame and embody economic, social and cultural processes. The aesthetic form – the 'look' of the building – is not neutral. Black argues that power is written into the landscape through the medium of design and this is particularly the case for imperial power. Working from case studies of the development, between 1919 and 1939, of the offices of the Hongkong and Shanghai Bank, Black argues that, in their design, western banking practice was successfully implanted in a local and regional culture that had 'little or no indigenous tradition of formal banking'.

One of the principal aims in this book is to provide explicit statements on methods for studying symbolic landscapes. The reader will find that each of our authors engages with methodology in their chapters. To cite Black as an example, he draws upon a range of methodological contexts and concerns. These include 'thick description', a close relationship to archival sources and iconographical analysis, in order to develop and maintain 'a conscious dialogue between "text" and "context"'. Black pays particular attention to private commercial architecture to outline what he feels to be a hitherto neglected but nevertheless key role in the British imperial project and, ultimately, the development of the global economy.

Scott Howard's essay 'Landscapes of memorialisation' describes one of the most ancient and still ongoing western engagements with landscape as a place, space, and means of expressing and transcending grief at death and loss. Moving between Greek, Latin, and nineteenth- and twentieth-century poetry, and between words, images, and memorial architecture and sculpture, Howard shows how landscapes of memorialisation 'enact the work of mourning' and 'manifest the idea of Arcadia'. As a landscape of mourning, Arcadia represents 'an imaginary world at the crossroads between nature and culture where loss may be transformed into gain; the tragic past, into the desired present and/or future'. As he traces his theme across periods, countries and artistic forms, Howard isolates two major paradigms. One seeks to find consolation in nature and one resists such 'closure'; he also points to the ways in which the 'idea of Arcadia' negotiates between public and private experiences of loss. Finally, Howard's analysis of the Vietnam War memorial in Washington posits it as a site that successfully negotiates between these various positions.

Andrew Horton's chapter, 'Reel landscapes: cinematic environments documented and created', offers a survey and discussion of 100 years of cinema's representations of 'reel' landscapes. As he points out, 'cinema has the power to manipulate time and place', as Andrew Charlesworth's succeeding essay also notes with its descriptions of the ways in which *Schindler's List* (1994) altered the placing of Goeth's house in relation to the death camps. Horton demonstrates that landscape is not mere background or even mood in film, rather that, in cinema, we 'experience landscapes as "narrative"', a major part of the way in which the tale is told. Close studies of John Ford's classic western, *Stagecoach* (1939), and Alfred Hitchcock's famous thriller, *Vertigo* (1958), clarify the ways in which the 'story' *is* the 'set/setting'. Landscapes also dictate genre, as Horton shows in his discussion of comic landscape in relation to *Monty Python and the Holy Grail* (1975). If most films want to create the impression that we are seeing a 'real' world, documentaries depend on their ability to create this impression; they are by definition documents of the real world. Yet, as Horton shows, they are also very much documents of the 'reel' world, carefully sculpted, manipulated and created. In all, in taking us through world cinema, Horton projects a strong light on the multiple and integral ways in which the camera and landscape are united and have, for better or worse, shaped many of our perceptions.

Another 'take' on the relationship between landscape and film is offered by Andrew Charlesworth, who discusses the ways in which the horrific landscapes of the Holocaust are mediated through various forms of memorial and, quite specifically, cinema. In his chapter, 'Landscapes of the Holocaust: Schindler, authentic history and the lie of the landscape', he discusses the ways in which Spielberg's film *Schindler's List* (1994) distorts our understanding of these landscapes. Charlesworth describes the ways in which cinematic 'authenticity' is achieved by the director – such as black and white footage for camp scenes, the use of actual buildings surviving from the time and used by the 'real' Schindler – and also the ways that local geographies were transposed and sets reshaped landscapes. The effect of these 'lies' of the landscape, he argues, is to create recognisably 'Hollywood' stereotypes and narrative modes for a tale that 'hangs on contrasts between Schindler and Goeth' – 'the good guy and the bad guy'. The essay goes on to describe the post-*Schindler's List* tourism boom in Krakow, and argues that 'Holocaust history as material for theme park has . . . been brought one step nearer' by the both the film and its subsequent commercial exploitation.

Leah Garrett's chapter, 'Landscape in the Jewish imagination', discusses the 'unique' Jewish sense of land and home as a plural vision encompassing wherever the Jews happen to be living and Eretz Yisrael – the Land of Israel – from which they had been scattered. However, as Garrett also points out, home, as the land in which the Jews found themselves living, was rarely an entirely comfortable or safe place. They were often surrounded by hostile people – their living place in ghettos, parts of a town enclosed by walls; or shtetls, villages in which they were allowed to live and farm – rather than sites chosen by them and voluntarily settled. Home, as permanent living place, in fact, was in many ways unhomely, and home as the Land of Israel was, until the establishment of the State of Israel, unobtainable – a spiritual and mythic rather than 'real' place. Travel, Garrett points out, was experienced differently for Jews than for other 'native' residents of a country. Where the latter could move about freely, always knowing that, however fraught their journeys, they were at home or had a safe home to return to, for Jews a journey was always dangerous, and they were never sure of ultimate safety. Yiddish literature, she argues, often sought to imagine the landscape as safe by remaking it as Jewish in terms of imagery. The Jewish relationship to land and landscape, Garrett suggests, has been altered in the twentieth century by two major events: the Holocaust and the creation of the State of Israel. The Holocaust depopulated the central European lands of the Jews who once lived there, and shrouded that landscape in sorrow and nostalgia for the survivors and their descendants. The establishment of the State of Israel has, for some, made the mythic and the actual homelands into one tangible place. However, this place remains problematic, fraught with border tensions and violence, and the processes of secularisation and assimilation typical of the twentieth and twenty-first centuries have also altered the particularity of Jewish encounters with land and home.

In her chapter, 'Landscape and identity', Catherine Brace discusses the notion of the duplicity of the rural idyll through an exploration of the way in which landscapes help to 'picture' identity. Identity is made and not given, is in flux and not stable. As such, identity is constructed, created and recreated through social and cultural processes, and is constructed through a diverse range of social registers such as gender, disability and age, as well as class and race. Landscape, however, works against these assertions as a vital component in the formulation of the impression that identity 'is fixed, natural and incontrovertible'. However, because identity is made, both socially and culturally, it is also involved in relationships of power. One such, as Keith Halfacree demonstrates in the succeeding chapter, occurs by defining identity via 'what we are not' rather than 'what we are'.

An additional relationship of power can be found in England's landscape of national identity. Working through a number of different case studies, Catherine Brace asserts that landscapes give the abstract concept of the nation material form. In particular, the representation of the rural came to symbolise Englishness in the period between the two world wars. The English rural landscape was appropriated in order to represent England as 'rural, timeless, harmonious and organic'. There is, then, in short, a politics to landscape that embodies issues of power and control.

It is, however, important to realise that the powerful cannot control everything, and that landscape and identity formation are a dialogue constantly in process. Contestation is as much part of a dialogue as is agreement and will therefore equally involve landscape. Brace utilises the example of artistic and poetic representations of the Cornish landscape in order to demonstrate this and to demonstrate further that the relationship between landscape and identity formation can work on a number of different levels. On one level, Cornwall has had (and continues to have), because of its marginal position, 'an ambiguous and at times confrontational relationship with England'. That much is apparent in landscape representations of Cornwall, but the work of Peter Lanyon and Arthur Caddick, in particular, reveals contestation from within over the nature of Cornishness and how the identity of the place may best be represented.

Landscape as representation, as we have indicated, is one of the central facets of the symbolic landscape approach, and central to this has been John Barrell's *The Dark Side of the Landscape* (1980). In his chapter, 'Landscapes of rurality: rural others/other rurals', Keith Halfacree sets out to test the contemporary rural landscape against Barrell's main assertions. Halfacree demonstrates that in exactly the same way that Barrell recognised that the rural poor were confined to the 'dark side of the landscape' (1980: 22), the contemporary landscape also conceals a range of rural others in 'the dark'.

Much of recent work within rural geography has indeed been concerned with bringing these others 'into the light'. Halfacree believes that this endeavour has resulted in a much more fine-grained and richer understanding of the landscape. He illustrates this by working with two contrasting sites: the one obvious (Stonehenge), the other more obscure (the village). Halfacree is, however, also concerned to strike a cautionary note. He believes that it is more appropriate 'to talk of other rurals rather than rural others' as this introduces an element of spatiality and questions of power relationships. He notes that, as in Barrell's landscape, there is a profound 'ambiguity of meaning at the heart of the rural landscape'. As a consequence the duplicity of the rural idyll is that it is 'gendered, racialised and settled'. The English rural landscape, therefore, both historical and contemporary, and unlike some other landscapes, has to sustain a heavy burden of 'work'. This landscape and the symbols attaching to it, both makes and maintains relationships of power and is of significance in identity formation.

These essays aim to demonstrate that whilst we can realise and read all landscapes as dynamic, interacting and polysemic, they are also innately visual. Hence, the 'Afterword' by Gillian Rose offers an elegant consideration of the preceding chapters, together with an indication of how this study can be taken forward. Our culture is deeply saturated with a vast and ever-expanding range of visual imagery. We not only create new images, signs and meanings, but also recycle existing ones, imposing new social, cultural and political meanings through new contexts. The recognition of the power and ubiquity of the visual in articulating culture and experience is inextricably linked with an understanding of the symbolic in landscape and the visuality of culture.

The structure of this book is that each essay has following it both a list of further reading and a list of things to do ('Now do this . . .'), which we hope you will find helpful. As this study is by its nature interdisciplinary, drawing on particular vocabularies, the book is also provided with a 'Landscape glossary', which offers definitions of some of the major terms used by our contributors.

Now do this . . .

Consider the two illustrations this Introduction utilises (the front cover of this book and Figure 1). Both photographs were taken by Iain Robertson, on separate research trips to the Hebridean islands. The croft house was where the author stayed on one trip and the memorial was one of the subjects of the other. The photographs were originally taken for the author's personal collection and only subsequently judged appropriate to stand as illustrative examples. You might like to ask yourself one or two questions about these photographs.

(a) Why choose these?

(b) Why choose a sunny day (when most of the time it was wet and gloomy)?

(c) Why take a viewpoint above the croft house (front cover illustration)?

(d) In what way are the pictures framed?

Think of more questions you might ask yourselves about these visual representations.

Notes to Introduction

1 The following discussion is primarily drawn from the influential work of Denis Cosgrove and Stephen Daniels. See Cosgrove (1982a; 1982b; 1984), Cosgrove and Daniels (1988), Daniels and Cosgrove (1993) and Daniels (1989).

2 Personal letter, Johan M., 1992.

3 Interview, Marissa Macdonald, Lewis, 6 April 1998.

4 Scottish Record Office, AF 83/363, petition from North Tolsta to Board of Agriculture, 8 February 1919; Department of Agriculture for Scotland files, 40917, Keose Glebe, Lewis, Letter to Board of Agriculture.

1

(Re)reading architectural landscapes

Iain S. Black

What messages were buildings, cities, and other works of art expected
to transmit? What meaning did they possess, what ideas did they contain? What can a city, in its capacity as a work of art, accomplish?
What can art do, apart from existing in its own right? It can tell a
story, or many stories. It can establish a mood. It can reinforce selected
virtues. It can surprise and delight by unexpected juxtapositions of
forms, textures, colors, and movements. It can stand for, or *represent*,
ideas, qualities, institutions.

(Olsen, 1986: 283)

1.1 Introduction

Olsen, writing on the city as a work of art, pointed to one of the key
characteristics of architecture: that aesthetic form is not neutral; that
architectural designs are implicated in the construction of meaning and
identity as part of the wider cultural landscape. Indeed, what are termed here
'architectural landscapes' are considered to be one of the principal documents with which to frame our understanding of past and present landscapes, and the economic, social and cultural processes that shape them. This
chapter centres on ways of reading architectural landscapes historically,
reflecting my long-standing research interest in reconstructing the nexus of
relations between money, architecture and social power in cities of finance in
Britain and the British Empire between 1750 and 1950 (Black, 1996; 1999a;
1999b; 2000; 2002). It begins with a review and critique of the use of architecture as a focus for landscape studies in cultural and historical geography,
moving from the study of landscapes as the distribution of material artefacts
as cultural markers, to a consideration of architectural forms as constitutive
of wider socio-economic and cultural processes. Emphasis is also placed
upon the varied ways proposed for reading and decoding the meanings

embedded within the built landscape itself. Following this, a more focused discussion of methodologies proposed to study the historic built environment of modern capitalist cities is undertaken. Finally, a detailed case study is advanced, which seeks to uncover the aesthetic forms and social functions of new commercial spaces, within the context of the development of bank offices by the Hongkong Bank in Hong Kong and Shanghai between 1919 and 1939. The case study is designed to draw upon and extend key principles identified in the earlier methodological section of the chapter, whilst also demonstrating how a detailed discussion of commercial architecture in this period can open windows on the complex relations involved in the long-term development of an imperial and global economy.

1.2 Geographies of architecture and landscape

The origin of modern geography's scholarly concern with architectural form and the cultural landscape is generally traced to the work of North American cultural geographers in the inter-war years. The work of Sauer and his followers in the 'Berkeley School' is frequently cited in papers seeking to locate the roots of traditional cultural landscape studies (Goss, 1988; Harris, 1999; Lees, 2001). In his methodological writings Sauer was concerned to advance a definition of geography as 'a science that finds its entire field in the landscape', and one that gave particular attention not only to its physical morphology but also to 'its cultural expression . . . as the impress of the works of man upon the area' (Sauer, 1925: 318, 326). As Cosgrove and many others have noted, this concern to trace the transformation of 'natural landscapes' into 'cultural landscapes' was set largely within a rural, premodern framework in which relict features extant in the landscape were used as data to reconstruct the historical geographies of past cultures. Though a wide range of particular forms of data were drawn upon, including material structures such as houses and barns, field boundaries, hedgerows and so on, in general terms they were confined within the narrow definition of *visible* elements of material culture. Even accepting this restrictive definition of significant 'cultural objects' for the study of the cultural landscape, the material forms themselves were treated more as data points in defining cultural hearths and subsequent patterns of cultural diffusion, than as worthy of detailed critical analysis in themselves. Indeed, Sauer had relatively little to say on the specifics of architecture *per se*, beyond a generalised concern with various basic architectural forms as markers of the geographical dimensions of cultural groups and their levels of technological development, predominantly in relation to agricultural practice (Leighly, 1963).

A more direct influence in the development of a specific concern with architectural landscapes, albeit as part of a more general concern with the cultural landscape as defined by Sauer, can be traced to the influential work of Kniffen and his co-workers at Louisiana State University between the 1930s and the 1960s (Kniffen, 1936; 1965). Goss, commenting on these early developments in what he terms 'architectural geography', remarks how Kniffen and his colleagues 'produced typologies of primitive (that is, foreign and exotic) and vernacular (that is, traditional and folk) architecture, describing the domain, evolution and diffusion of everyday styles and forms' (Goss, 1988: 393). Kniffen's work, typified as the 'house-as-key-to-diffusion' tradition in American cultural geography, has been subjected to a sustained critical analysis by Holdsworth (1993). The basic assumption underlying such studies was that it was possible to conjoin mental and material geographies in a relatively unproblematic way to delineate the geographical diffusion of 'culture'. As Holdsworth puts it, 'individuals had mental constructs about how dwellings ought to be built and these ideas moved with people as they migrated; thus their folk houses were "sure traces" of culture' (Holdsworth, 1993: 95). Kniffen's 1965 paper, 'Folk housing: key to diffusion', is generally seen as a key programmatic statement of this approach, where he set out a broad research agenda to record the establishment by settlers of European house types on the eastern seaboard of North America and to trace their subsequent westward migration via successive transplants of modified 'folk' housing forms.

Despite opening up some interesting questions, Kniffen's approach can be criticised on a number of fronts: first, the concentration on rural folk housing in a premodern age, continued by Noble and Jakle *et al.* in the 1980s, seemed noticeably adrift from more mainstream concerns in human geography with modern urban landscapes shaped under the forces of industrial capitalism (Noble, 1984; Jakle *et al.*, 1989). As Holdsworth remarks in connection with Noble's two-volume study of the *North American Settlement Landscape*, nowhere:

> . . . is there any sense that industrialization, or class, or economy, might be worth including as a perspective on how and why the built environment was produced in specific ways in different times. In this, as in other accounts, houses are remarkably unconnected to the social and economic fabric of a transforming world.
>
> (Holdsworth, 1993: 99)

Second, such 'artefactual' studies of the distribution of forms and types of housing privilege field observation over other complementary forms of analysis such as archival methods. The lack of a systematic approach linking and comparing a range of different sources to uncover the construction, distribution, meaning and transformation of housing types presents the danger of contemporary interpretations being skewed by the relict features observed extant in the landscape. Third, the treatment of housing as an architectural form is frequently limited to a concern with the materials and practices of their construction (a largely technological perspective), and to the layout and distribution of rooms within such dwellings. Broader concerns with questions of aesthetics and the construction of meaning are left in the background, as are detailed studies of the social production and use of space within houses along class, gender and ethnic lines. The house as a microcosm of the construction and reproduction of social power relations thus receives scant attention.

One writer who addressed such concerns, albeit somewhat idiosyncratically and from a position outside the formal confines of the academy was, of course, J.B. Jackson. Founder and editor of the magazine *Landscape*, Jackson frequently asserted that the house was the elementary and most important unit of the landscape, which would repay careful study as a microcosm of past and present social relations. Interestingly, in a sharply observed portrait written at the end of the 1970s, Meinig drew attention to the nature of Jackson's contacts with the Berkeley School to which, 'despite close affinities at the outset and a long fruitful relationship, Jackson's approach was different ... and as he began to give much greater attention to urban topics and the contemporary American scene, this became more apparent' (Meinig, 1979: 227). That said, Jackson's concern to eschew what he saw as a dry and formal academic style, unencumbered with structured modes of argument and detailed references, meant that he said little directly on methodology. The power of his work is perhaps best summed up by Cosgrove, who remarks upon 'the influence of his consistent demonstration that landscapes emerge from specific geographical, social and cultural circumstances ... embedded in the practical uses of the physical world as nature and territory' (Cosgrove, 1998: xi).

The appeal of the 'house-as-key-to-diffusion' approach in analysing what could be called 'geographies of architecture' faded in the 1970s. Never a mainstream concern even among historical geographers, its perceived theoretical naivety sat uncomfortably with geographers' increasing engagement with a philosophical and methodological critique of the positivist tradition in post-war Anglo-American geography (Holdsworth, 1997). As new approaches to the study of landscape emerged in the 1970s and 1980s, concern with the historical interpretation of architecture and the built environment within human geography was deepened through the efforts of leading critics such as Cosgrove, Daniels and Duncan (Cosgrove, 1984; Daniels, 1989; Cosgrove and Daniels, 1988; Duncan, 1990). In an important summary of the state and status of cultural geography in the later 1980s, Cosgrove and Jackson identified two principal strands within this general critique of traditional approaches to studying landscape (Cosgrove and Jackson, 1987). The first of these they termed 'landscape as text'. Within this approach, rooted in a critique of work in cultural anthropology, a predominant concern was the conception of landscape as constituted through 'configurations of symbols and signs', whereby explanation rested more on decoding interpretative structures than with the morphology-driven interests of Sauer and his followers. The metaphor of seeing the landscape as a text, which drew upon the influential work of the cultural anthropologist Clifford Geertz, suggested that landscapes could be read as a social document, using the techniques and methodologies of literary theory (Barnes and Duncan, 1992).

The contours of this approach were outlined further by Duncan and Duncan (1988) in a significant paper entitled '(Re)reading the landscape'. Drawing upon the work of Barthes, they argued for a greater sensitivity to notions of textuality, intertextuality and theories of reader reception in the interpretation of landscape, whilst cautioning against idealising the textual metaphor by privileging it over the broader contexts of those social processes involved in the creation, maintenance and transformation of particular landscapes. Thus, textual metaphors can and should be pursued to illuminate the crucial relationships between landscape and ideology, by helping to identify how landscapes can transform ideologies into a concrete, visible form. Landscapes can, therefore, serve to naturalise asymmetrical power relations and cultural codes, thus serving to stabilise various hegemonic practices, and the role of the critical reader of landscapes should be, in part, to penetrate what Barthes called their layers of ideological sediment (Duncan and Duncan, 1988).

The importance of explicitly acknowledging the role that landscape plays in the articulation of ideology was also signalled in a thoughtful essay by Baker (1992) introducing a collection entitled *Ideology and Landscape in Historical Perspective* (Baker and Biger, 1992). Indicating that ideology involves systems and structures of signification and domination, Baker acknowledged that 'any landscape is likely to contain all manner of ideological representations so that a description of its appearance must also logically be "thickened" into an interpretation of its meaning' (Baker, 1992: 4). In particular, Baker argued for three key characteristics of ideology that have a special relevance for landscape: first, a quest for order, whereby a simplified, ordered view of the world can be translated into an ordered landscape; second, the assertion of authority, whereby landscapes can be seen as part of a wider struggle for power between conflicting interest groups, signalling in their organisation a non-verbal communication of hegemonic power relations; third, a project of totalisation, whereby ideologies offer an overall representation of society and, in consequence, that the reorganisation of a landscape (via utopian planning projects, for example) can signify a reconstruction of existing power relations. In all these ways, it is clear that there exists a vital politics to the reading, representation and reconstruction of landscape (see Harvey, 1979; Cosgrove, 1982a; Daniels, 1993).

The second approach highlighted by Cosgrove and Jackson's survey they called 'the iconography of landscape'. Within this umbrella phrase, particular attention was given to the development of the study of landscape as a way of seeing or representing the world. Cosgrove, in particular, has done much to illuminate the ways in which the *idea* of landscape evolved in a European context from the Renaissance, bringing together new techniques of visualisation and representation such as perspective drawing, with the changing material context of land use (Cosgrove, 1985). Indeed, some of his most effective detailed studies of architecture are those that see the development of a villa landscape in the Veneto as part and parcel of the changing nature of agrarian capitalism in the region (Cosgrove, 1993). That said, it is important to recognise that Cosgrove's arguments here are culturally and historically specific. Augustin Berque (1995) has shown that an aesthetic view of landscape, as a way of conceptualising and representing the world, emerged in China some 1500 years before the European Renaissance. Subsequently, this sophisticated 'idea' of landscape was diffused to other parts of East Asia, embracing not only an aesthetics of vision, but also making reference to the role of landscape in place-bound imaginations and memories. Thus the idea of landscape in Europe developed relatively late in this comparative context and was intimately connected to the project of modernity and a scientific conception of space rooted in the ideas of Bacon, Galileo, Descartes and Newton (Baker, forthcoming).

The term 'iconography' has become well established in the lexicon of historical and cultural studies of landscape. In their introduction to *The Iconography of Landscape*, a seminal collection of essays pioneering the iconographical approach to landscape, Cosgrove and Daniels define iconography as, broadly 'the theoretical and historical study of symbolic imagery' (Cosgrove and Daniels, 1988: 1). Although the use of a formal iconographical approach to interpreting images reaches back to the Renaissance, in its modern form the concept was deployed by the discipline of art history to:

> ... probe meaning in a work of art by setting it in its historical context and, in particular, to analyse the ideas implicated in its imagery ... consciously [seeking] to conceptualise pictures as encoded texts to be deciphered by those cognisant of the culture as a whole in which they were produced.
>
> (Cosgrove and Daniels, 1988: 2)

This broad conceptualisation of iconography was refined and codified into a systematic approach to the study of art by Erwin Panofsky, whereby iconography in its narrower sense 'was the identification of conventional, consciously inscribed symbols', whilst a more interpretative conception of iconography (termed iconology) sought a deeper level of meaning in art by reconstructing the cultural, political and ideological context(s) surrounding its production, and which the art communicated consciously or unconsciously (Cosgrove and Daniels, 1988: 2; Mitchell, 1986).

These principles of iconographical study have become widely used in a variety of attempts by geographers and others to interpret symbolic landscapes in a range of different settings. It is important to note that, whilst concentrating on the work of cultural and historical geographers, the study of landscapes in general, and architectural landscapes in particular, is very much an interdisciplinary field. In a recent review essay, Harris (1999: 434) notes that, in addition to geographers, 'landscape analysis has started to appear with increasing frequency in the works of scholars who define themselves as art, architectural, and environmental historians, or as literary critics, anthropologists, archaeologists, and scholars of material culture'. A comprehensive survey reinforcing this point can be found in Pregill and Volkman's recent volume, *Landscapes in History* (Pregill and Volkman, 1999; see also Boyer, 1994; Groth, 1999).

The two approaches grouped here as 'landscape as text' and 'iconographical landscapes' are not mutually exclusive, of course. Interestingly, in a retrospective essay introducing the republished volume *Social Formation and Symbolic Landscape*, Cosgrove remarks how he finds 'particularly stimulating the idea of combining the text metaphor for landscape with the visual and iconographic emphasis' of his earlier study, an idea developed in his treatment, with Daniels, of landscape as theatre (Cosgrove, 1998: xxvi; Daniels and Cosgrove, 1993). Nonetheless, he continues to remind us of the need, when dealing with issues of representation, to ensure that the landscape is not disconnected from 'productive social relations with the material earth' (Cosgrove, 1998: xxvi). The concern with combining specific methodologies in the study of architectural landscapes in particular is now developed.

1.3 Methods for studying architectural landscapes

Explicit statements on methods for studying landscapes, let alone architectural landscapes in particular, are relatively rare. One exception is Domosh's essay setting out a methodological framework for landscape interpretation, illustrated via a case study of the New York World Building. The methodological problem is stated as follows: 'How can one determine the links between a particular landscape artifact, its socio-economic and aesthetic contexts, and the actors who directly produced and/or created that artifact?' (Domosh, 1989: 347). The focus on one historical landscape artefact – the New York World Building – is helpful in allowing a deep description of the critical context surrounding the design and production of the building; an approach, moreover, that demonstrates the value of taking Geertz's invocation to 'thick description' seriously. Domosh begins by outlining the particular social and economic context of New York in the later nineteenth century, including its changing spatial structure. The location of the New York World Building, between City Hall and Wall Street, indicated its primary function as the house of Pulitzer's newspaper *The World*. The building was 16 storeys high once constructed, the tallest in the city, marking it out as a leading example of the general wave of early skyscraper construction. But the building had particular meanings too, related to the individual motivations of its owner, who explicitly sought to express his growing cultural power within a competitive corporate context, coupled with a sense of public duty to help beautify New York City. These conventional readings of the building are then pushed further by Domosh, asking why did Pulitzer feel impelled to construct a building that embodied this particular combination of signs communicating status, power and legitimacy? Answers can only be found in reconstructing the broader context of the highly competitive business community of New York, the unstable nature of the city's elite and the need for the *nouveaux riches*, such as Pulitzer, to find a material expression of their role. Set alongside this was the changing technology of building, whereby steel frame construction and the development of the elevator allowed the skyscraper to become the logical building type to maximise returns at peak land value locations in the city. These technical and social imperatives are then grounded in the changing nature of industrial capitalism as it affected New York at the end of the nineteenth century: the capital of capitalism, housing a growing number of corporate head office functions controlling capital enterprises across the United States and beyond. Thus, beginning with a single, albeit special, building, the methodological argument constructed by Domosh has spiralled out to encompass a series of interrelated 'layers' of explanation: functional, symbolic, personal and ideological. The building itself informs the entire process of interpretation, through a continuous dialogue between 'text' and 'context'. In later work, Domosh goes on to apply this methodological framework, broadly conceived, in more detailed studies of New York's skyscrapers, and in a more fully developed historical and comparative analysis of the landscapes of New York and Boston in the nineteenth century (Domosh, 1988; 1992; 1996).

These arguments are extended in a broad critique by Holdsworth, arguing for a commitment to move beyond the visible evidence traditionally accorded priority in landscape studies, to interrogate the archival records that can provide a firmer basis for analysing the social and economic production of different landscape features (Holdsworth, 1997). Usefully, he has much of interest to say about architectural landscapes in particular. He begins by indicating that whereas the visible evidence of past landscapes extant in the field can often provide the initial stimulus to pose interesting research questions, it 'can rarely stand alone in providing convincing explanations about questions of human geography' (Holdsworth, 1997: 44). Taking the long-established tradition of analysing house forms as cultural markers, therefore, it is clear that the physical evidence extant is often ephemeral, ambiguous or misleading in representing a window on to the culture of the society that produced it. To place such visible evidence in context, Holdsworth argues that varying built forms of housing need to be critically related to a whole series of parallel documentary sources, such as censuses, tax records and mortgage deeds to situate the architectural evidence within land and property markets, planning systems and, ultimately, the broader structural shifts within industrial capitalism. Taking Ford's work on reading American city skylines as an exemplar, he argues that the apparent separation, or non-communication, between reading the 'landscape as text' and relating the landscape 'text' to its 'context' via archival research, is evident in the work of many cultural geographers who are 'preoccupied with height and style of buildings, and who project some phallocratic importance to height alone'; indeed, they 'do not try to go beyond the skyline and behind the façade to probe the forces that produced the need and the demand for office space at certain sites at certain times' (Holdsworth, 1997: 48; Ford, 1992).

On the surface, Holdsworth's position seems close to that of Domosh outlined earlier. However, there is an important distinction pinpointed by Dennis in a recent, perceptive, essay on the methodologies of historical geography and their application to the modern urban landscape (Dennis, 2001). Referring to Domosh's study of the New York World Building as an illustration of a 'multi-layered approach to landscape interpretation', Dennis indicates that 'while she referred to the need to situate her primarily symbolic interpretation in the context of economic and technological change, her own evidence was drawn principally from newspaper and magazine reports and illustrations, and she relied on existing accounts of, for example, land values and skyscraper technology that were not specific to the building'. In other words, her approach was multi-scale and sensitive to context, 'but it was not really multi-method' (Dennis, 2001: 24). Holdsworth's approach, while acknowledging the importance of cultural interpretations such as that by Domosh, offers, according to Dennis, a deeper analysis of particular built environments by drawing on 'corporate archives, fire insurance plans, assessment records, property transfer records, mortgage records, and the manuscript census to try to make visible, to bring out of concealment, what is not visible in today's landscape' (Dennis, 2001: 24). In short, to provide a fuller analysis of the forces behind the production of particular built environments, and to try to establish the way they were perceived and used, a range of methods and sources needs to be brought to bear upon the particular architectural landscape that caught the imagination in the first place. This involves using multiple methods to interrogate multiple sources, not simply to try and confirm consistencies between different types of data, but also to identify inconsistencies that might throw new light on why particular architectural landscapes were built, where they were built, for whom, and how they were represented and used. Dennis supports his case by drawing upon recent methodological debates by contemporary social geographers – such as McKendrick, and Baxter and Eyles – arguing that historical geographers too should be encouraged to adopt the principle of 'triangulation' where different methods can be brought to bear on a particular research question. In the case of architecture and landscape, such methods might include oral history, iconography, textual analysis and techniques for the study of visual sources of evidence. Indeed, in his essay Dennis provides an insightful multiple reading of one particular aspect of the landscape of modern London – French flats – by drawing upon data from novels, mappings, census returns, building histories and the architectural press, and combining these through a range of methodological approaches (Dennis, 2001).

This review of methods for studying architectural landscapes has empha-sised a number of key features to take into account when researching and writing on architecture as a vital component of the cultural landscape: first, the importance of maintaining a close relationship with archival and histor-ical sources, taking Geertz's notion of 'thick description' seriously to outline the detailed historical and geographical contexts surrounding an interpreta-tion of particular architectural forms; second, to give due weight to the importance of politics and ideology embedded within architecture by pro-viding a close reading of the signs and symbols encoded within particular landscapes; third, to ensure a rigorous study of architectural aesthetics by drawing upon the methods and techniques of iconographical analysis; fourth, recognising the importance of linking the 'deep descriptions' of particular architectural projects to wider social, cultural and economic processes, maintaining a conscious dialogue between 'text' and 'context' in the social production of specific architectural landscapes. These themes are now developed in the case study that follows.

1.4 Money, architecture and empire: the Hongkong Bank in Hong Kong and Shanghai, 1919–1939

The Hongkong Bank was established in the British Colony of Hong Kong in March 1865 to meet the needs of the business communities of the China coast, in particular through the provision of efficient and secure means of financing trade within the region and beyond. Prior to its formation most trade finance had been organised by the hongs, or European merchant trad-ing houses (Jones, 2000). Following its establishment, the bank proceeded to develop a network of branches and agencies around the world, though remaining firmly focused on the Pacific-Asia region, with new branches in Japan (1866), Thailand (1888), India (1867), the Philippines (1875) and Singapore (1877). In addition to commercial banking activities, it was closely involved in government finance too, by the 1880s 'acting as banker to the Hong Kong government and as sole or joint banker for British gov-ernment accounts in China, Japan, Penang and Singapore' (HSBC, 2000: 7). It also issued bank notes throughout its spheres of operation. In many of its new branches the bank played a key role in the diffusion of modern western banking practices to the Far East, becoming the leading bank in the region by the early twentieth century.

Though much research has emphasised the economic imperatives for such business expansion overseas, relatively little attention has been paid to the detailed cultural practices deployed by emerging international com-panies to establish, consolidate and transact their business abroad (Jones, 1993; 2000). One key strategy used by such institutions has been to repre-sent themselves through the design, production and use of distinctive office spaces. The focus here on private commercial architecture is significant. Formal colonial architectural projects, such as the building of imperial Delhi by Edwin Lutyens and Herbert Baker, have received detailed attention, of course (Irving, 1981). In Crinson's recent study, *Empire Building*, too, the role of architecture in the establishment and maintenance of British power overseas provides a central focus, with particular attention paid to civil government and religious building in the Near East during the nineteenth century (Crinson, 1996). However, the wider consequences of such empire building, especially by commercial and financial companies that were ostensibly private, though dependent upon the wider imperial project, have been remarkably little studied (see Black, 2002). This case study will take a detailed look at the design and building of bank offices by the Hongkong Bank in Hong Kong and Shanghai between 1919 and 1939, assessing the significance of their construction, in both formal and informal imperial spaces, to the diffusion and negotiation of western business practices in the Far East. Methodologically, it will also serve to demonstrate the value of developing deep descriptive analyses of key architectural projects to inform an understanding of larger-scale processes such as globalisation, by taking seriously the social practices embedded in the production of architecture as an important dimension of the long-term development of the global economy (see King, 1984; 1990; Alsayyad, 1992).

Shanghai, 1923

Shanghai, following the Nanjing Treaty of 1842, quickly developed into the most important of the treaty ports on the China coast. Its position at the mouth of the Yangtze River encouraged the establishment of European trading houses articulating the entrepôt trade between China and the wider world (Bergère, 1996). The Hongkong Bank established a branch in Shanghai in April 1865, which from the outset was seen as a crucial site for the bank's business. By the 1870s business had flourished to such an extent that the bank commissioned a new, purpose-built office on the Bund, to be designed by the Scottish architect William Kidner (1841–1900). Little is known about Kidner, though Izumida has pieced together a few details about his career in the Far East, which appears to have begun in 1866 in Shanghai (Izumida, 1991). The new bank building (see Figure 1.1) was, however, the subject of a brief notice in the *Architect* on 6 October 1877. Remarking upon the façade, the correspondent noted that:

> ... apart from its architectural merit it is of considerable interest as showing in its way the importance of our settlement in the Far East, and also of the manner in which Chinese workmen can adapt themselves to the carrying out of European requirements.
>
> (*Architect*, 1877)

Figure 1.1 Hongkong Bank, Shanghai, 1877: new office designed by William Kidner (Source: HSBC Group Collection)

Behind the imposing classical façade was a complex division of internal space. The *Architect*'s correspondent indicated that 'the ground storey, 24 feet high, is devoted to business purposes ... [with] the Compradore's offices, treasurers, &c., being provided for in an attached building in the rear' (*Architect*, 1877). Marking off the Compradore's space from that of the European bank was significant, pointing to the ways in which the internal divisions of architectural space both reflected and reinforced a special set of business practices drawn upon by the Hongkong Bank to establish and transact a western form of banking business in the radically different social and cultural context of the Far East. The term 'compradores' derived from the Portuguese *comprar* and originated after the founding of Macau as a trading port in the sixteenth century (King, 1987). The compradores were required because of the difficulties foreign merchants had in understanding the Chinese language, customs and business practices. Far from the Hongkong Bank ending the compradore system, by taking over their role as middlemen, compradores played a vital role in the banking system, assuming responsibilities for all the bank's business with its Chinese customers. Their continuing role in the performance of the bank's business continued to exercise a strong influence upon bank office design well into the inter-war years.

By the early twentieth century, the original office on the Bund was becoming cramped and in need of repair, and in 1919 the bank's directors chose the colonial architectural firm of Palmer and Turner, then based in

Hong Kong, to design a new building. The driving force behind the Shanghai project was the bank's then chief manager A.G. Stephen, and its conception and grand design reflected Stephen's own vision of the bank and its role in the emerging financial metropolis of the East. When the architects requested a further one million dollars to enhance the building, Stephen replied 'spare no expense, but dominate the Bund' (King, 1988: 132). George Wilson, chief architect on the project, designed the Shanghai branch in the Grand Manner (see Figure 1.2), representing a translocation to the Far East of contemporary architectural fashion in England where imperial Baroque styles, drawing upon Wren and Vanbrugh, were often favoured for major public building projects (Yip, 1983). That the bank, clearly a private company albeit with a number of quasi-public functions, preferred such a style, indicated its desire to underscore in architectural form its vision as the dominant institution in eastern banking. A critic writing on the occasion of the bank's opening noted:

> The building is of the type known as Neo-Grec, and to achieve the dignity with simplicity which that name implies the Architects have eschewed the use of carving or sculpture almost entirely and relied upon proportion and line. The frontage of approximately three hundred feet to the Bund and two hundred feet to Foochow Road formed the ideal site for this memorial to the commerce and prosperity

Figure 1.2 Hongkong Bank, Shanghai, 1923: façade facing the Bund (Source: HSBC Group Collection)

of the world. Rising one hundred feet to the long line of the roof and a further eighty feet to the finial of the massive dome, the whole building stands out clear to the view of the merchant ships of all nations sailing up and down the Huang Pu, a recognition of their courageous industry which has made possible all that this memorial stands for.

(HSBCa, 49)

The interior of the new bank was of a scale and richness far beyond most financial headquarters in the City of London at the time (see Black, 1999a; 1999b). The interior not only gave further clues to the bank's vision, but also to how it negotiated the practical problems of translating western business practices into a radically different socio-cultural context. Passing through the arched entrances one entered a large octagonal hall with a central dome supported by eight Sienna marble columns (Figure 1.3). Above these, eight panels showed decorative motifs of the principal banking centres of East and West: London, New York and Tokyo, together with Paris, Hong Kong, Shanghai, Bangkok and Calcutta. Figure 1.4 shows one-half of the banking hall running parallel to the façade facing the Bund. The critic continued his description:

... the first impression of the Banking Hall is of the grandeur of sheer space and proportion and light. This Hall, which occupies practically

Figure 1.3 Hongkong Bank, Shanghai, 1923: octagonal entrance hall (Source: HSBC Group Collection)

Figure 1.4 Hongkong Bank, Shanghai, 1923: principal banking hall (Source: HSBC Group Collection)

the whole length of the building, has an area of twenty-one thousand five hundred feet. The walls and columns faced with soft-toned grey Italian marble.

(HSBCa, 63)

The composition and organisation of the bank staff at Shanghai clearly influenced the design and disposition of internal spaces within the new bank. The main distinction was that between the British Eastern staff and the Chinese, though Portuguese, too, staffed the banking hall. The manager, Mr G.H. Stitt, was accommodated in a richly decorated private office (Figure 1.5) with elaborately coffered ceilings and teak panels with fluted pilasters. This office provided considerable difficulties for the architect as it functioned as a room forming the hub of the entire bank, where 'the walls had to be so broken with doors and windows . . . [the architect] might well despair of achieving the dignified aspect which the Manager's Office should present'. However 'the difficulty has been overcome by a combination of large proportions and richness of detail which has a most happy effect' (HSBCa, 68). The conduct of business with Chinese customers relied, as stated, upon the compradore system. Figure 1.6 shows the Chinese Bank, accessed through the marble archways at the south-west corner of the main banking hall. The cultural significance of this hybrid architecture was clear to contemporaries, the bank's official opening brochure remarking how:

Figure 1.5 Hongkong Bank, Shanghai, 1923: manager's office (Source: HSBC Group Collection)

Figure 1.6 Hongkong Bank, Shanghai, 1923: the Chinese Bank (Source: HSBC Group Collection)

... one is arrested on the threshold ... [of the banking hall] by the totally unexpected sight of a blaze of Chinese decoration. This is the Chinese Bank. The Architect has attempted here the boldest scheme of decoration ever tried in a modern building ... [whilst] the design, both in the mass and in its details, is entirely new, one feels the influence of the best traditions of fourteenth century Chinese art in this gorgeous Oriental decoration of a Hall of twentieth century Western construction.

(HSBCa, 72)

Passing through the Chinese Bank, the Compradore's outer office was reached where:

... one's joy sobers to smiles of appreciation of the intricacy of the gilded ornament of the beams, the gold, and red and black ... thence to the Compradore's private room. The brightness is dimmed. The reds and greens and yellows have gone. Here the splendour curbs all smiles. Black and the dark blue of calm; the fit setting for the dignified office of Compradore of the Hongkong and Shanghai Bank.

(HSBCa, 76)

Hong Kong, 1935

From the establishment of the bank in 1865, Hong Kong had been the administrative hub and emotional heart of the organisation and by the 1880s the bank was playing a dominant role in the colony's economic and business life. This status was clearly reflected in its first purpose-built headquarters, designed by Clement Palmer of the architectural firm of Wilson and Bird (Lambot and Chambers, 1986). The project's inception and spirit, however, owed much to the bank's then chief manager, Sir Thomas Jackson. Opened in 1886, the building effectively merged two distinct structures to form a hybrid architecture known as 'compradoric', which was common along the China coast in the nineteenth century and drew its inspiration from earlier Anglo-Indian building projects (Yip, 1983).

The façade facing the waterfront (Figure 1.7) clearly indicated the adaptation of western classical style to the climatic conditions of the Far East, in an era before the advent of air conditioning, with windows opening on to a series of loggias to gain shade and the best of passing breezes. Further details were provided by a notice in the *China Mail* of 9 August 1886:

... the main door which is about 14 feet above the level of the Praya is gained by a flight of steps, over which is a handsome portico. The building from this side appears as a solid three-storeyed structure, the ground floor of Doric architecture, the first floor Corinthian, and the upper floor, Composite, forming all together an imposing and beautiful classical design.

(*China Mail*, 1886)

Figure 1.7 Hongkong Bank, Hong Kong, 1886: façade facing the waterfront (Source: HSBC Group Collection)

Meanwhile, the main entrance in Queen's Road (Figure 1.8) was a more orthodox affair, with grand columns and portico announcing the home of Hong Kong's premier financial institution. Here, though, the *China Mail* noted how:

Figure 1.8 Hongkong Bank, Hong Kong, 1886: façade facing to Queen's Road (Source: HSBC Group Collection)

... the beauty and full effect of its appearance from the Queen's Road side, are somewhat obscured by the closeness of the surrounding buildings, and it is only when one approaches near that the massive granite Corinthian columns and the imposing dome are seen ... [however] on the Praya side, the building naturally shows to greater advantage, and to visitors coming into the harbour it will doubtless form, when completed, one of the most interesting landmarks.

(*China Mail*, 1886)

Figure 1.9 shows an early photograph of the grand domed banking hall, the inspiration for which clearly stems from British bank design tradition, particularly the work of Sir John Soane at the Bank of England between the 1780s and the 1820s (Schumann-Bacia, 1991). Such parallels in architectural form can be misleading, though, when seeking to interpret the social organisation of such spaces as places of business. In the case of 1880s' Hong Kong, the layout of the ground floor was sharply influenced by the need to accommodate two banks, the Western and the Chinese, within the same overall ground plan. Such complexities were captured in the *China Mail*'s contemporary commentary on the building:

The bank building is cut into two equal halves by a corridor which run [*sic*] the whole length of the structure from Queen's Road to the Praya. On the right hand side is the general office for Europeans, while on the other side is the compradores' office, where the Chinese will do business. These offices have each broad counters in front of them,

Figure 1.9 Hongkong Bank, Hong Kong, 1886: principal banking hall (Source: HSBC Group Collection)

bending inwards at the centre of the passage so as to give more space for moving out and in to the Bank. They have doors opening on the verandah, and on the left or Chinese side the verandah will be utilised for the money-counting stalls.

(*China Mail*, 1886)

The Hong Kong head office was, therefore, a complex architectural and social space. Its design drew upon hybrid notions of architectural style to present a broadly western classical image within the tropical climate of the colony, whilst its internal spaces were shaped by the need to incorporate both western and Chinese banking traditions within the same building.

By the later 1920s, the head office of 1886 was becoming too small to house the head office functions of a rapidly growing organisation. A leader in the *South China Morning Post*, discussing the rebuilding project, commented that:

... the old building was by common consent one of the Colony's most pleasing examples of the architecture of the period. In its day moreover, it was an imposing structure, not dominating its neighbours but offering itself with quiet confidence as an artistic contribution to the appearance of the district. It is significant of Hong Kong's rapid growth that, in a short fifty years from its erection, the old building became inadequate for the Bank's needs.

(*South China Morning Post*, 1934)

Significantly, too, it was felt that the new Shanghai office was beginning to overshadow the group's headquarters. As the *Post*'s leader continued, 'for some time now the Colony's pride in the Bank has been reduced to the fact that Hong Kong is the Head Office, the magnificent Shanghai Branch having usurped the primary claim to structural grandeur' (*South China Morning Post*, 1934). For these two reasons, space and status, Sir Vandeleur Grayburn, then chief manager, decided that the bank needed a new head office building in Hong Kong. The decision to rebuild was made shortly after the Wall Street Crash and was also intended to provide a stimulus to the local economy of the colony at a time of increasing economic depression. Employing George Wilson, who had designed the new Shanghai branch in 1923, Grayburn instructed him simply 'please build us the best Bank in the world' (King, 1988: 250).

The structure designed by Wilson showed an obvious debt to the stylistic innovations of the Modern Movement (Figure 1.10). Crucially, though, it was not England but North America, and specifically the high-rise commercial architecture of Chicago and New York, that Wilson turned to for inspiration. There were no comparable projects in England to draw upon, London remaining a relatively low-rise city until after the Second World War. Such observations challenge the conventionally accepted notions of colonial dependence, where colonial architectural styles are often read as

Figure 1.10 Hongkong Bank, Hong Kong, 1935: head office designed by George Wilson (Source: HSBC Group Collection)

simple transplants from the metropolitan core. The Hongkong Bank's new headquarters, whilst clearly a product of western architectural practice, was a considerable stylistic innovation seen in the context of, for example, the City of London in the 1930s (see Black, 1999a; 1999b). The 'Moderne' style used by Wilson allowed motifs to be applied to the basic geometrical forms that cloaked the building, as appliqué rather than structural elements. Sculptured heads of Men of Vision surmounted the buttresses of the tower, flanked by lions' heads, symbolic of strength and also a traditional reference to the guardians of British commerce (Lambot and Chambers, 1986). Each was carved from a five-ton granite block. A contemporary critic wrote how:

> ... following the modern trend in architecture ... the design is simple and dignified with practically no ornamentation. It is built of the wonderful local granite with the result that it stimulates the imagination and satisfies the eye. The strong vertical treatment above the horizontal base gives the impression of great strength and stability, which has always been associated with this Banking Corporation.
>
> (HSBCb, 19)

The question of symbolism was also referred to by Mr N.L. Smith, the colonial government's presiding officer at the opening ceremony:

> I wonder if it is too fanciful to suppose that buildings do in some degree reflect the characteristics of their occupants; perhaps I have got this the wrong way round. But look at the Law Courts across the

way; do they not embody the dignity and solidity of Sir Atholl
MacGregor and Mr. Justice Lindsell? Look a few yards further at the
Club, typically superior and uncomfortable and die-hard. Now the
building which I have to-day had the very great honour of opening
seems to me to be in the first place completely efficient; it is up-to-
date, not to say quite a few minutes ahead of the clock; it has imagination and above all else it is honest. I do not think that I could
discover a better epitome of the characteristics of Mr. Grayburn and
his wonderful staff.

(HSBCb, 14–15)

Like Shanghai, the Hong Kong Head Office was staffed by a predominantly British Eastern staff and Chinese compradores. To accommodate their
differing social and business requirements the building's modern shell
cloaked an interior of considerable complexity (Figure 1.11). This plan,
though not in fact the final version, nonetheless indicates the challenges faced
by the architect as he attempted to incorporate the European and Chinese
banks within one general ground-floor space. In the absence of wider documentary sources it also demonstrates the valuable nature of such architectural evidence in reconstructing the detailed micro-spatial practices and
social relations involved in the organisation of this major head office building, which needed to respond to a distinctive interplay between different
ethnic groups in the prosecution of a wide range of banking business. The
central area of the floorplan was divided into departments dealing with bills
(inward and outward) on the left-hand side and those dealing with cash and
current accounts to the right. In the top right corner was the savings bank.
The far right-hand side of the building, adjoining the Chartered Bank, was to
be devoted to the Chinese bank, with the Compradore's office placed in the
centre, flanked by rooms for the chit coolies and a Chinese staff lavatory.
Further spaces were used for messengers, servants' stairs and lifts. The space
behind the frontage to Des Voeux Road was to be reserved for the principal
managers' offices, including those of the chief manager, manager and chief
accountant. These functions were to be supported by brokers and secretaries,
together with rooms for telephones and telegrams. Finally, besides a private
lift for Grayburn to reach his flat, separate lavatories were to be provided for
British and Portuguese staff respectively.

The banking hall itself captured the imagination (Figure 1.12). A contemporary reaction on the bank's opening noted how:

. . . on entering this fine spacious hall, one is immediately impressed by
its vast and simple grandeur. The walls are lined with highly polished
Botticino marble which contrasts pleasingly with the dark rich
Ashburton marble of the columns in the Public Space. Looking up into
the barrel vaulted ceiling over the Public Space one sees that it is
finished in Venetian glass mosaics.

(HSBCb, 21)

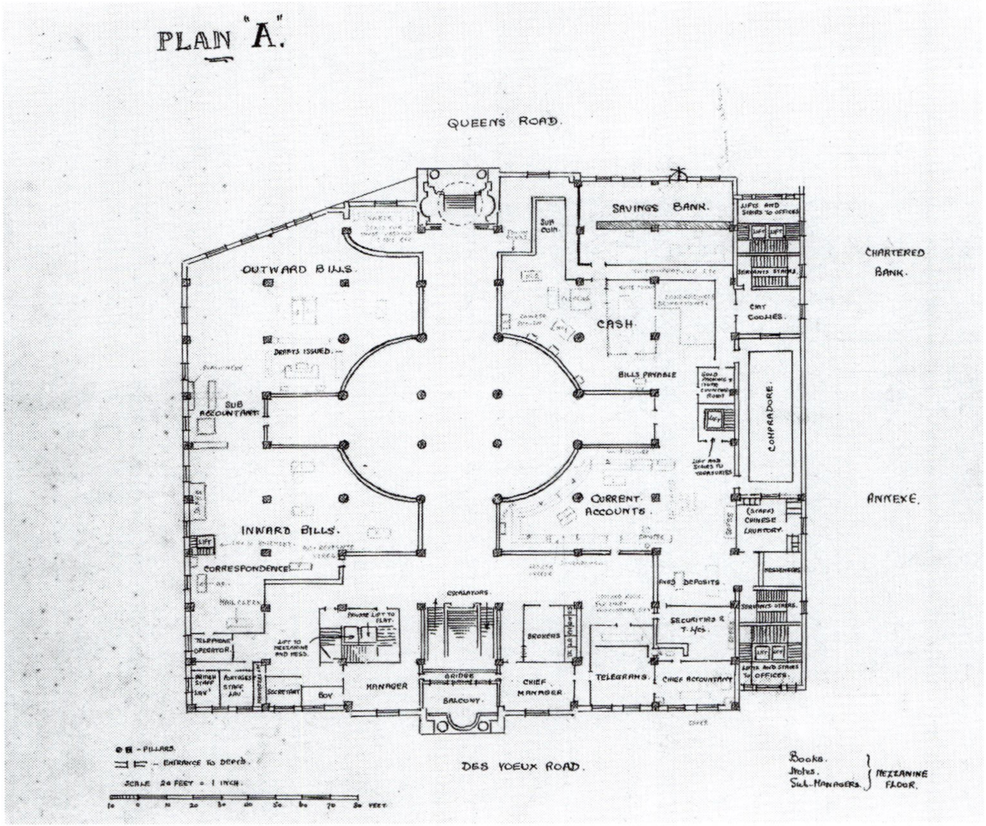

Figure 1.11 Hongkong Bank, Hong Kong, 1935: preliminary ground floor plan (Source: HSBC Group Collection)

Figure 1.12 Hongkong Bank, Hong Kong, 1935: principal banking hall (Source: HSBC Group Collection)

The mosaic was designed by Podgoursky, a Russian émigré artist from Shanghai, and contained approximately four million pieces, which were made in Italy, pasted on to paper by Italian craftsmen and shipped in sections to Hong Kong for fixing. In contrast, the management rooms, including the chief manager's office shown in Figure 1.13, reflected the restrained and unadorned style of the bank generally, and were finished with unpolished marble on the walls, travertine floors and simple plaster ceilings, with all the doors and the furniture of metal, designed by the English company Roneo with an Art Deco quality. Upper floors were designed as offices for rent, with the exception of the ninth floor, which contained a flat for the chief manager. The new head office was clearly an exceptional building, towering above the predominantly Victorian 'compradoric' architecture in Hong Kong's harbour setting (Figure 1.10). When finished it was the tallest building between Cairo and San Francisco, and incorporated the latest in building technology, including the use of a special high-tensile steel known as Chromador and an advanced air-conditioning system. Symbolic of the bank's position not only in eastern banking, but also worldwide, the building was officially opened on 10 October 1935.

The Hongkong Bank's two major rebuilding projects of the inter-war

Figure 1.13 Hongkong Bank, Hong Kong, 1935: chief manager's office (Source: HSBC Group Collection)

years, in Shanghai and Hong Kong, posed a common design problem: they were the pre-eminent branches in the group and needed to establish a clear identity within their local setting to impress their customers, shareholders and competitors; they both also occupied waterfront sites, the Praya in Hong Kong and the Bund in Shanghai. Yet they seemed to offer quite different architectural solutions. This judgement rests more upon the aesthetics of the two schemes than their overall plan. Yip notes how 'the Head Office that Palmer & Turner designed cloaked a very traditional plan and massing in a contemporary veneer'. Comparing the design to Wilson's Shanghai branch, he suggests that 'both elevations show a medium rise block with a high focal element . . . whereas the Shanghai Branch had a dome, the Hong Kong Head Office used a tower block' (Yip, 1983: 129–30). Though both schemes were based on neo-classical principles, they articulated quite distinct symbolic qualities. The Shanghai branch drew upon established modes of authority, echoing the imperial Baroque styles popular in Edwardian England for important public buildings, such as Edward Mountford's Central Criminal Court (the Old Bailey). The new head office in Hong Kong, by contrast, eschewed British architectural tradition by drawing upon the new wave of corporate styles produced in Chicago and New York in the early decades of the twentieth century (see Willis, 1995). With their modern constructional techniques and appeal to modernity, tempered by the familiar neo-classical lines dressed in Art Deco style, the North American skyscraper model fitted the requirements set by Grayburn to build the best bank in the world.

1.5 Conclusion

This case study of two of the key branches built by the Hongkong Bank in the Far East between 1919 and 1939 indicates the value of taking a deep descriptive approach to understanding architectural landscapes. British overseas banks have played a prominent role in the long-term development of the global economy, not least because of their close relationships with British imperial power. This imperial context, especially between the 1830s and the 1930s, provided an important political-economic structure for the extension of British banking practices and techniques to large parts of the world, many of which had little or no indigenous tradition of formal banking. However, viewing this diffusion of British banking culture from the perspective of localised transformations of the built environment in particular regional contexts can help illuminate the process of putting in place the physical infrastructure of international banking business. The process was complex. Before the advent of air conditioning the challenge of a subtropical climatic context was a vital controlling factor for architectural design. Both internally and externally, the bank's architects made significant modifications to traditional design solutions to provide extended areas of shade and to increase the circulation of air. The case study also emphasises the considerable extent to which western architectural principles were (re)negotiated in the radically different social and cultural contexts in which the bank operated, in particular, the need to design complex divisions of internal space to facilitate the operation and interaction between the western bank staffed by Europeans and the Chinese bank controlled by the compradores. In these examples, the design and building of the physical infrastructure for international banking were central to the successful negotiation of western business practices in a distinctive and different cultural environment. Interpreting these distinctive buildings involves (re)reading such architectural landscapes, not only by drawing upon a range of methods and sources, but setting these within a critical reading of often separate academic discourses. By combining perspectives from architectural history, cultural geography, economic and business history the detailed architectural studies that provide the principal research focus can be made to carry a greater interpretative weight, including a more conscious appreciation of how the built form itself structures, as well as is structured by, wider social, cultural and economic change.

Now do this . . .

1. Visit Bank Junction in the City of London
    Bank Junction was a key site of British imperial power in the nineteenth and early twentieth centuries. A visit to this area today, concentrating on the public space between the Bank of England, the Royal

Exchange and the Mansion House, provides an excellent opportunity to read and decode one of Britain's most valuable architectural ensembles.

Prior to your visit, read the following two essays.

Black, I.S. 1999: Rebuilding *The Heart of the Empire*: bank headquarters in the City of London, 1919–1939. *Art History* **22**, 593–618.

Jacobs, J.M. 1996: Negotiating the heart: place and identity in the postimperial city. In Jacobs, J.M., *Edge of Empire: Postcolonialism and the City*. London: Routledge, 38–69.

The first deals with the late-imperial rebuilding of the area of Bank Junction, known also by the title of Niels Lund's painting *The Heart of the Empire*. The latter deals with the controversy over plans for demolition and rebuilding in the area since the 1960s.

(a) Identify the following key buildings at the site: Bank of England, Royal Exchange, Mansion House. When were they built? Which architectural styles have been used and how do they differ? What materials were used in their construction? How do they use sculpture or decoration to encode their purpose? Are there common design elements in each of the buildings? How do they 'work' together to define the public space between them?

(b) Now consider the series of monumental bank headquarters surrounding the site, including Lloyds Bank in Cornhill, the former Westminster Bank in Lothbury, the National Westminster in Princes Street and the former Midland Bank (now HSBC) in Poultry. When were these built? Think about the architectural styles of these buildings. What symbolic qualities do they embody? How do they use sculpture or decoration to encode their purpose? How do they relate to each other and to other buildings nearby?

(c) Standing with your back to the entrance portico of the Royal Exchange, look across Bank Junction to the new building at No. 1 Poultry. How would you describe its style? What does it symbolise? What impact does it have on the visual qualities of Bank Junction as a whole? How does the style, and the materials used in its construction, contrast with other buildings in the immediate vicinity?

2. To explore the building of the Bank of England further . . .
    Visit the Bank of England Museum (see www.bankofengland.co.uk). To help you recreate historically the use of Bank Junction as a place of work, ceremony and spectacle, visit the Guildhall Art Gallery (see www.cityoflondon.gov.uk).

3. Read *The River at the Centre of the World* by Simon Winchester (Penguin Books, 1996)

This is travel writing at its best and recounts Winchester's journey up the Yangtze River from Shanghai to Tibet. How different is your appreciation of the book once you have applied the principles of textual analysis to it?

Further reading

Baker, A.R.H. and Biger, G. (eds) 1992: *Ideology and Landscape in Historical Perspective*. Cambridge: Cambridge University Press.

Cosgrove, D.E. 1998: *Social Formation and Symbolic Landscape* (2nd edn). Madison: University of Wisconsin Press.

Crinson, M. 1996: *Empire Building: Orientalism and Victorian Architecture*. London: Routledge.

Domosh, M. 1996: *Invented Cities: The Creation of Landscape in Nineteenth-century New York and Boston*. New Haven and London: Yale University Press.

Irving, R. 1981: *Indian Summer: Lutyens, Baker and Imperial Delhi*. New Haven and London: Yale University Press.

2

Landscapes of memorialisation

W. Scott Howard

O what shall I hang on the chamber walls?
And what shall the pictures be that I hang on the walls,
To adorn the burial-house of him I love?
> Walt Whitman, *When Lilacs Last in the Dooryard Bloom'd* (in Whitman, 1973)

Nature repeats herself, or almost does:
repeat, repeat, repeat; revise, revise, revise.
> Elizabeth Bishop, *North Haven* (in Bishop, 1994)

This chapter examines relationships between works of art, mourning and memory.[1] Our primary concerns here, to be more specific, address the pivotal role of landscape in artistic creations that strive to transform loss (either personal or public in magnitude) into gain, sorrow into consolation and the tragic past into redemptive visions of the present and/or future. Such imaginative reconfigurations of the natural world thus may serve as vehicles for the expression of grief, the construction of memory and the writing of historical narratives either subjective or cultural in scope.[2] Land is transfigured into landscape by the artist's shaping intention to create an ideal world of harmonious interaction between nature and culture wherein mortality and human corruptibility may be mitigated by the vitality of life forms that change and regenerate. Landscapes of memorialisation are therefore, by virtue of these factors, idealised other places – visions (and versions) of Arcadia – that exist apart from this place of human suffering, yet which, precisely because of their experiential and ontological differences, provide regions that we may visit (if only briefly) and where we may place our sorrow in order to return with renewed strength to the known, imperfect world. Just as our journey, within such a work of art, to that other place enacts a mourning process, our path back from that devised utopian space involves a corresponding reflection upon how the landscape has received and responded to our expression of grief.

The poems quoted at the start of this chapter each illustrate the pivotal role that nature may play in that work of mourning and memorialising across a spectrum of artistic compositions, including the Vietnam Veterans Memorial in Washington DC (Figure 2.1). Walt Whitman's *When Lilacs*

Figure 2.1 Vietnam Veterans Memorial (Photo: Katharyn C. Howard)

Last in the Dooryard Bloom'd (1881) and Elizabeth Bishop's *North Haven* (1978) are both, in terms of literary genre, pastoral elegies – that is, poems that craft relationships, within an idealised natural landscape, between three fundamental human modes of expression: lamentation, praise and consolation (Lambert, 1976; Ramazani, 1994; Sacks, 1985; Zeiger, 1997). In this equation, lamentation (sorrow) and consolation (solace) are diametrically opposed, contrary in their emotional tenors; a direct experience of both together would result in strong ambivalence for the individual who suffers from a loss. Praise (love) balances the scale, providing a vehicle for the transformation of loss into gain, absence into presence, sorrow into solace and also – by logical extension – forgetting (the tragic past) into envisioning and remembering (the wished-for present and/or future). An imagined, natural setting in both of these pastoral elegies mediates the tensions between those conflicting desires and motives. Whitman's and Bishop's landscapes, however, respond quite differently to that work of mourning and memorialising, and thereby offer two interpretative models, which could also be called paradigms of loss, which will illuminate our comparative, interdisciplinary study in this chapter on pastoral elegies, Greek mythology and commemorative sculpture.

Whitman's poem mourns the death of Abraham Lincoln and was composed during the weeks immediately following the former US President's assassination on 14 April 1865. Bishop's elegy laments the loss of her personal friend, the poet Robert Lowell. Both poems offer subjective expressions of grief for cultural figures, and accordingly combine personal and public contexts of meaning. However, while Whitman uses landscape to memorialise Lincoln's spirit and achieve an unqualified consolation, Bishop undercuts the sympathetic bond between nature and human suffering, playfully resists the hopeful project of preserving the essence of Lowell and thereby shapes an ironic consolation. Whitman's text, in this regard, may be considered a classic elegy – that is, a poem that achieves positive consolation; Bishop's, a modern elegy, or a work that resists or at least strongly qualifies consolation (Ramazani, 1994). These two variations upon the work of mourning – i.e. the tendency toward remembrance and achieving consolation on the one hand, and toward forgetting and resisting consolation on the other – complement two similar paths for the work of memorialising in landscapes fashioned by artists working in other media, as we shall see.

The Vietnam Veterans Memorial (or VVM) designed by Maya Lin not only commemorates the lives of the nearly 60 000 American men and women killed in the Vietnam War, but also acknowledges the personal and social, traumatic consequences of that conflict between 1959 and 1975 that continue to signify points of cultural and political tension in the United States. Since the VVM's construction in 1982, 'The Wall' (as it is popularly known) has gained an international reputation as an unprecedented memorial that paradoxically facilitates personal mourning and consolation while also resisting conventional social codes for grieving, remembering and transfiguring the past. The Vietnam Veterans Memorial therefore functions within both paradigms of loss suggested by Whitman's and Bishop's poems. Although not a pastoral elegy in the same sense as either of those texts, The Wall is a pastoral, elegiac work of art, one that, as Lin herself remarks, combines the aesthetics of poetry and sculpture within an idealised landscape (Sturken, 1997). In this regard, the Vietnam Veterans Memorial participates in a long-standing and interdisciplinary artistic tradition of works that refashion land into a landscape of memorialisation – a tradition that begins, in the western literary canon, with the pastoral elegy (the second oldest poetic genre after the epic) where the idea of Arcadia first takes shape (Rosenmeyer, 1969; Ramazani, 1994; Sturken, 1997).

Through comparative studies in poetry, Greek mythology and commemorative architecture, this chapter investigates the central theme of landscape and memorialisation. Works to be examined include, respectively, Whitman's *When Lilacs Last in the Dooryard Bloom'd*, Bishop's *North Haven* and Virgil's 'Eclogue 10'; retellings of the Orpheus myth by Ovid (in Ovid, 1958) and Gaiman, as well as the Vietnam Veterans Memorial together with its accompanying memorial-objects. The chapter's individual sections progressively establish an interdisciplinary context for the study of relationships between works of art, private and public expressions of grief, and the role of landscape as mediator in the linked processes of mourning and memorialising. The chapter's 'Conclusion' and 'Further reading' sections provide web links to digital reproductions of each of those poems, myths and commemorative sculptures as resources for further study. In keeping with the guiding principle for this volume on cultural landscapes, this chapter thus constitutes a palimpsest that offers several layers of comparative analysis, each linked to a cluster of key terms, principles and themes:

- the work of mourning
- the work of memorialising
- the idea of Arcadia
- the principles of dialectical temporality and sympathetic nature, and
- the motif of the backward glance.

All of these are addressed in this chapter's following sections and are also defined in the 'Landscape glossary' towards the end of this book.

My central argument will be that landscapes of memorialisation both enact the work of mourning and manifest (in some way) the idea of Arcadia – that is, an imaginary world at the crossroads between nature and culture where loss may be transformed into gain; the tragic past, into the desired present and/or future. Whereas monuments offer a tribute to the departed and strive toward historical closure, memorials concern the ongoing struggles of the living who confront losses that have yet to reach points of resolution. Landscapes of memorialisation therefore reveal continuing negotiations between personal and public narratives that both affirm and resist consolation and remembrance. Imaginative transformations of land into landscape that engage with those dynamic tensions thus may perform the writing of cultural history.

2.1 Whitman and Bishop: two visions/versions of pastoral

In reply to the questions he asks, in the lines quoted above, Whitman states his choice to adorn President Lincoln's coffin with pictures of an Arcadian world – that is, an idealised landscape in which nature's regenerative bounty sympathetically sustains those who live in both country and city: 'Pictures of growing spring and farms and homes,/With the Fourth-month eve at sundown, and the gray smoke lucid and bright' (81–2). Within that imagined landscape Whitman then places this pastoral elegy's pivotal figure of the thrush, the 'shy and hidden bird' (19) that sings a dirge, 'Death's outlet song of life' (24), which the poet later translates in lines 135–62. The thrush's aria unfolds within the poem's picture of the ideal landscape bestowed upon the coffin's interior wall; the poet's translation of that song of praise for both life and death moves the elegy toward consolation and memorialisation:

> Yet each to keep and all, retrievements out of the night,
> The song, the wondrous chant of the gray-brown bird,
> And the tallying chant, the echo arous'd in my soul,
> With the lustrous and drooping star with the countenance full of woe,
> With the holders holding my hand nearing the call of the bird,
> Comrades mine and I in the midst, and their memory ever to keep, for
> the dead I loved so well . . .
>
>   (198–203)

The song of the thrush, the shooting star, the sprig of lilac, all of the elegy's key images and symbols converge in this imagined portrait of these three figures – 'the knowledge of death', the poet and 'the thought of death' (120–1) – walking together within a sympathetic landscape that will receive Abraham Lincoln's body and preserve his spirit. Through the gift of that ideal world, Whitman creates a landscape of memorialisation, which enfolds the departed President within nature's cycles of diurnal and seasonal change, thereby investing his spirit with principles of regeneration and transformation. Whitman's consummate pastoral elegy, as a work of mourning and memorialising, concludes with a vision of redemptive time poised within the present on the cusp of the future – 'There in the fragrant pines and the cedars dusk and dim' (206) – that signals the poem's engagement with both personal and public historical discourses.

In *North Haven*, Bishop imaginatively returns, one year later, to a place she often visited with Lowell and describes the setting, noting in particular the subtle differences in the landscape between the time of her last visit with her friend and her present excursion without him. In the fourth stanza, Bishop introduces a key theme that will return in this pastoral elegy's final stanza to undercut the work's prospect of memorialising Lowell's spirit:

> The Goldfinches are back, or others like them,
> and the White-throated Sparrow's five-note song,
> pleading and pleading, brings tears to the eyes.
> Nature repeats herself, or almost does:
> *repeat, repeat, repeat; revise, revise, revise.*
>
> (188)

Here Bishop implies a sympathetic bond between landscape and memory, but gently questions that link between the past (as shared by two friends) and the present (as observed by one): 'The Goldfinches are back, *or others like them*' (188; my emphasis). Nature gives signs of repetition, renewal and change just as the poet's memory and imagination negotiate differences between past and present. Through this rhythm of return and departure, disappearance and emergence Bishop alludes early in the elegy to an affinity between the process of writing poetry – '*repeat, repeat, repeat; revise, revise, revise*' (188) – and the landscape's forces of change and renewal, thereby suggesting that Lowell's spirit, like Lincoln's in Whitman's elegy, might be invested with those regenerative principles. The text's final stanza undercuts that possibility, however, and draws a sharp distinction between past and present:

> You left North Haven, anchored in its rock,
> afloat in mystic blue . . . And now – you've left
> for good. You can't derange, or re-arrange,
> your poems again. (But the Sparrows can their song.)
> The words won't change again. Sad friend, you cannot change.
>
> (189)

The dynamics of change – repetition and revision – establish a sympathetic bond between language and nature that is irrevocably broken by mortality. Lowell's death removes him from Bishop's idea of the regenerative potential in both poetry and landscape. Her elegy concludes ironically, qualifying the work of mourning and memorialising by resisting consolation and emphasising not remembrance, but forgetting.

Although Lowell now occupies a realm of relative stasis, Bishop's picture of the landscape bristles with evidence of his departure, suggesting that her friend may now be remembered best through his present absence from both his poetry and this shared, idealised natural setting. *North Haven* thereby raises a difficult question in our examination of relationships between grief expression and landscape: can the resistance to consolation and the forgetting of the past paradoxically strengthen the work of mourning and memorialising (Howard, 2002)? The Vietnam Veterans Memorial, as noted earlier, accomplishes exactly that – consolations both positive and resistant – thereby participating in both paradigms of loss set forth by Whitman's and Bishop's pastoral elegies. All three of these works of mourning and memorialising also significantly construct notions of Arcadia as a nexus of those conflicting psychological drives, artistic themes and cultural codes. In fact, since at least the ninth century BCE, representations of Arcadia have not only realised the premise that an ideal landscape may serve as a place of memorialisation, but have also always involved discrete negotiations between accepting and resisting consolation, and remembering and forgetting the past in order to envision the present and future.

2.2 Arcadia: landscape of loss and gain

Arcadia is both a real and an ideal place, at once geographic and symbolic, that signifies not only a mountainous and somewhat inhospitable region in the centre of the Peloponnese peninsula, but also a utopian landscape in which the human and natural worlds are imagined to co-exist harmoniously.[3] For Homer and generations of artists and philosophers since his time, Arcadia represents a vision of perfection – existing in a realm parallel to but separate from our own world – where an idealised rural landscape shelters and provides for the individual who has grown weary of human conflict and corruptibility. The notion of Arcadia therefore pertains not to the terrain of rugged nature, but to a realm of cultivated rusticity that the experience of art makes possible through the work of imagination. In representing Arcadia, though, the artist cannot avoid a fundamental paradox: we only know about that perfect other place from the perspective of our world of human imperfection. Arcadia thus signifies more than just an idealised portrait of the individual existing peaceably in nature, but importantly highlights a veil of worldly complications that we may wish to lose, even if only temporarily, in order to gain experience in a territory that sympathises with our wishes to be elsewhere and other than what we are. More than merely a pleasant or lovely place (i.e. *locus amoenus*) Arcadia is a landscape of and for the mind.[4]

Dialectical temporality

Two principles just mentioned warrant further reflection because they are essential for understanding with greater depth and subtlety the idea of Arcadia. The first is that of contradistinction, or what may also more properly be called dialectical temporality. Because Arcadia exists primarily in an imaginary realm distinct from the everyday world of human activity, artists tend to portray that idealised landscape in terms of contrasts with our own place in civilisation. Such contradistinctions become dialectical, however, when the artist who wishes to portray Arcadia – the other place – first realises that any utopian vision necessarily embodies some traces of an imperfect world – the 'this place' – and then permits those touches of human complication and conflict to be present and active in the idealised landscape. The contradistinctions of Arcadia are thus not exclusionary and do not deny our entrance into that other world, but they are constructive and relational – that is, dialectical – because they both permit and limit our ability to imagine a more harmonious balance between the human and natural realms. The idea of Arcadia, therefore, involves a deliberately nimble and self-conscious negotiation of that balance and those points of contrast in a work of art concerned not only with a vision of a utopian landscape, but also (and perhaps more importantly) with the various ways in which such a fictive, perfect world both engages with and disengages from the imperfect sphere of human community. Our limitations paradoxically condition the possibilities for Arcadia and also guarantee our return from that other place back to the civilised world. Arcadia exists by virtue of the fact that we simply cannot stay there, but may often visit. Representations of landscape in that more perfect realm therefore reveal much about not only our wishes to live in a more harmonious balance with nature, but also our eventual need to depart from that utopian space and return to a place for human time. Arcadia is a region of many entrances and exits, each bearing the marks of our appearances and disappearances, which together underscore a fundamentally experiential component to this imaginary land. More than a place, Arcadia is an idea; but more than a notion, Arcadia embodies a dialectical experience of our own temporality and necessary erasure from an imagined community where we may wish to remain, but cannot. Indeed, perhaps the most enduring characteristic of the Arcadian landscape – realised either through poetry, sculpture or painting – is a visible sign of some confrontation with mortality as a token of our imminent departure.

Sympathetic nature

The second principle, related to the first, is that of sympathetic nature, or the idea that nature sympathises with the spectrum of human passions, offering gifts that correspond to our emotional and psychological needs (Ruskin, 1971). Because the notion of Arcadia, as addressed above, is dialectical our experience of that perfected, imaginary landscape underscores the human imperfections we may wish to change or lose entirely by way of our journey away from and back to civilisation. However, since we cannot stay in Arcadia the predominant emotion associated with a visit to that ideal place is an ambivalent combination of anxiety, elation and sorrow, which can be described more precisely as tragic joy. Just as the perfection of the Arcadian landscape inspires in us feelings of exuberance, that same beauty serves as a bracing reminder that we must eventually depart. Nature in Arcadia often replies accordingly to such ambivalence with gifts and seasons both generous and cruel. The principle of sympathetic nature in Arcadia, like the conflicting emotions and dialectical relationships to which it corresponds, hence turns upon a precarious balance between loss and gain. On the one hand, the individual who visits Arcadia wishes to lose the world of human conflict and corruptibility in order to gain the perfection of a utopian place. On the other hand, gaining entrance into Arcadia also means confronting the fact of our necessary departure from and loss of that idealised landscape. Both the dialectical temporality and sympathetic nature particular to Arcadia are thus fundamentally elegiac principles – each suffused with the individual's struggle to find consolation for the loss of a sustainable vision of perfection; each equally involved with the work of either positive or resistant mourning and memorialising.

2.3 Virgil's Arcadia

We owe most of our contemporary notions about Arcadia to the Roman poet, Publius Vergilius Maro – otherwise known simply as Virgil (70–19 BCE). In 37 BCE Virgil completed a collection of pastoral poems, *The Eclogues*, that has (perhaps more than any single literary work in the western canon) directly shaped our keenest perceptions about the Arcadian landscape. In fact, many scholars argue that the artistic idea of Arcadia begins with Virgil's *Eclogues* (Lee, 1989). Virgil is the first writer explicitly to set a poem, 'Eclogue 10', in a place called Arcadia. In that pastoral elegy, Gallus (Virgil's close friend in life and also a poet) suffers from unrequited love so much that he is near death. Three unsympathetic gods visit him, of which two offer advice. In reply, Gallus first asks the Arcadians to sing about his love, then confesses his desire to live in the woods where he will carve the name of his beloved, Lycoris, on the trees. As soon as he declares those intentions, however, Gallus confronts their impossibility, reflecting that nothing will satisfy Love, the power that indiscriminately rules all. 'Eclogue 10' thus not only enacts the popular Arcadian theme of love melancholy, but intertwines the principles of dialectical temporality and sympathetic nature. Gallus's near-fatal love predicament therefore marks his possible entrance into and necessary exit from the utopian landscape wherein nature both echoes and silences the singer's desires.

The elegy's eight-line introduction accordingly links the contradistinctions of Arcadia to the landscape's indiscriminate power either to mend or mar. The poet begins by requesting permission from Arethusa – a nymph, one of the Nereids, who was changed into a fountain by Artemis – to sing of Gallus's dilemma with love:

> Permit me, Arethusa, this last desperate task.
> For Gallus mine (but may Lycoris read it too)
> A brief song must be told; who'd deny Gallus song?
> So, when you slide along below Sicanian waves,
> May bitter Doris never taint you with her brine.
> Begin then: let us tell of Gallus' troubled love,
> While snub-nosed she-goats nibble at the tender shoots.
> Not to the deaf we sing; the forests answer all.
>
> (1–8)

Virgil describes his task as 'desperate' (1) because Gallus's insatiable desire necessitates his eventual return from Arcadia to the world of human imperfection and strife. Without hesitation nature 'answers all' (8), offering consolations that ultimately fail to satisfy Gallus because, as Pan chastises, 'Love cares not for such things;/You'll never glut cruel love with tears, nor grass with streams,/Nor worker-bees with clover, nor she-goats with leaves' (28–30). Gallus replies to this rebuke by announcing his wish to remain in Arcadia, proclaiming his love melancholy to nature: 'The choice is made – to suffer in the woods among/The wild beasts' dens, and carve my love into the bark/Of tender trees: as they grow, so my love will grow' (52–4).

Here in particular, dialectical temporality works in tandem with the idea of sympathetic nature to create a landscape of memorialisation. Gallus states his intention to carve his 'love into the bark/Of tender trees' (53–4) – that is, to inscribe not merely the name of his love, Lycoris, upon the living surface of the Arcadian trees, but his elegiac song of longing for and loss of love. In other words, Gallus desires to create a written record, a testimony, of his melancholy predicament in Arcadia where he feels love for Lycoris who loves him not. The landscape may receive his story sympathetically, faithfully representing his sweet agony, but may also indiscriminately pervert Gallus's lamentations, transfiguring his writing upon the tree bark into indecipherable scrawl as the tree grows and matures in this land of altered time. Through this plan to engrave upon the Arcadian landscape a record (i.e. memorial) of his unrequited love, Gallus therefore confronts a paradox: he may only remain in Arcadia through the vehicle of writing, but the record of his love melancholy demands his departure:

> Now, once again, we take no joy in Hamadryads,
> Nor even in song – again wish even the woods away.
> No alteration can our labours make in him,
> Not if we drank of Hebrus in the middle frosts
> Of watery winter and endured Sithonian snows,
> Nor if, when dying bark shrivels on the lofty elm,
> Beneath the Crab we herded Ethiopian sheep.
> Love conquers all: we also must submit to Love.
>
> (62–9)

Just as dialectical contradistinctions condition the possibility of both Gallus's entrance into and departure from this ideal land, the principle of sympathetic nature works antithetically, marking his presence in Arcadia through a narrative of his eventual absence, thereby creating a living memorial to his unrequited love and emotional ambivalence.

2.4 The backward glance: Ovid to Gaiman

Our contemporary understanding of an Arcadian landscape also owes much to another Roman poet, Publius Ovidius Naso (43 BCE–18 CE) – otherwise known as Ovid – who, in the year 8 CE, completed a major work in the western literary canon, *The Metamorphoses or Transformations*, that gives us one of the earliest written records of many of the Greek myths, including an extensive treatment of the elegiac Orpheus and Eurydice story, which also follows the paradigms of loss previously addressed by way of Whitman's and Bishop's pastoral elegies. Ovid creates an elaborate narrative about Orpheus, which contributes a significant motif to the working relationships between the principles of dialectical temporality and sympathetic nature within a landscape of memorialisation: the backward glance. As with any of the Greek myths, there are many versions of the Orpheus story; each retelling offers new twists in plot and character development. The following summary primarily follows Ovid's rendition in *Metamorphoses*, Books 10 and 11.

A son of Calliope and either Oeagrus or Apollo, Orpheus was reputedly the greatest musician and poet of Greek legend. His songs were so magical that they could conjure wild beasts – even rocks and trees – into actions sympathetic with his desires. On his wedding day, just before the marriage ceremony, his bride, Eurydice, was killed by the bite of a serpent. Orpheus 'sang loud his loss/To everyone on earth' (273) before journeying down to the underworld to retrieve his lost love. During his negotiations with King Hades and Queen Persephone, Orpheus sang a beautiful song about his love for his lost bride that moved even the Furies to tears. Hades and Persephone then granted Orpheus's request, but under one condition: that he not look back while making the ascent to the world of mortals. As Orpheus and Eurydice approached the surface of the earth, Orpheus, 'fearful that she'd lost her way,/Glanced backward with a look that spoke his love –/Then saw her gliding into deeper darkness' (275). After this redoubled loss of his true love – 'her second death' (275) – Orpheus goes 'melancholy-mad', as Ovid puts it (275), and grows inconsolable despite his supernatural powers (which seem to become proportionately strengthened by each tragic turn in the story) to charm the landscape into gestures of great sympathy with his plight.

At the height of that sympathetic magic, when he has conjured an idyllic landscape replete with the signs of consolation for his grief – 'All beasts, all birds, all stones held in their spell' (299) – Orpheus meets his tragic end at the hands of a group of Ciconian Maenads (female devotees of Dionysus) who attack him with rocks and tree branches. For a time, Orpheus defends himself by singing – his music deflecting the crude weapons they hurl at him. The Maenads, however, drown out his magical voice with their screams and eventually overwhelm Orpheus, tearing him limb from limb. As luck would have it, though, the river Hebrus then carries Orpheus's head to the open sea where it journeys to the shores of Lesbos, near Methymna, inspired melodies murmuring all the while from the mutilated poet's lips. Orpheus's spirit finally descends to the underworld to be reunited with Eurydice, but again only on the condition that, 'as they move, however they may go,/Orpheus may not turn a backward look at her' (301).

The theme of the backward glance, in this particular text's work of mourning and memorialising, signifies Orpheus's heightened self-consciousness of dialectical temporality. Ovid's language tells us that the poet, 'fearful that she'd lost her way,/Glanced backward with a look that spoke his love' (275) – in other words, that Orpheus was moved to look back not only by his love for Eurydice, but also by his fear that she might not be there following his steps. Orpheus's motivation, during the ascent back to earth, is thus complicated by a tangle of contradicting emotions and existential characteristics, all of which augment the contradistinctions of the ideal landscape where he wishes to (but may not) remain either with or without his true love. Orpheus may only regain an Arcadian landscape – one in which nature will hear his lament and reply sympathetically with signs of consolation – on the paradoxical condition that he return alone only to depart soon again. Upon his second farewell from that utopian place, in Ovid's version of the story, nature offers the most elaborate show of sympathy for his tragic life:

> The saddened birds sobbed loud for Orpheus;
> All wept: the multitude of beasts,
> Stones, and trees, all those who came to hear
> The songs he sang, yes, even the charmed trees
> Dropped all their leaves as if they shaved their hair.
> Then it was said the rivers swelled with tears,
> That dryads, naiads draped their nakedness
> In black and shook their hair wild for the world to see.
>
> (300)

Here the bond of sympathetic nature works most powerfully as a sign of Orpheus's final exit, turning the landscape into a habitat of memorialisation. Nature in this state of perfection bears the mark of the inspired poet's presence through his absence, the landscape thus mirroring contradistinctions intrinsic to Arcadian dialectical temporality.

Neil Gaiman's adaptation of the Orpheus and Eurydice story in his comic series, *The Sandman* (1993), emphasises Orpheus's psychological struggle with powerful male figures – especially Hades and Apollo – consequently imparting to the backward glance theme a more internalised role in shaping the landscape. Hades and Persephone grant Orpheus's request to return with Eurydice, but they mock him during their bargaining. Thus as Orpheus departs from Gaiman's vision of the underworld 'the dark laughter of Hades [follows] him for many leagues' (Gaiman, 1993: 186). As he progresses on his journey, Gaiman's Orpheus becomes increasingly self-conscious about this humiliation to the extent that, during the key moment of the first backward glance, his internalised anxieties cloud his perceptions and create the impression that Eurydice has abandoned him (Figure 2.2). Orpheus's backward glance in this retelling, as an index of dialectical temporality, therefore signifies a contradiction between his desire to return with Eurydice and his shame for making such an immoderate request from the king and queen of the underworld. On the following page Gaiman accordingly depicts the image of Eurydice fading from sight as Orpheus stumbles along a snow-covered path near the edge of a precipice in a landscape that sympathetically mirrors his anguish and humiliation, yet offers no gesture of recompense.

Gaiman's conclusion to the story is far less optimistic than Ovid's but also employs the backward glance motif to underscore not only Orpheus's ultimate exclusion from an Arcadian landscape, but also his utter alienation from his father, Apollo. In the final scenes on the shore of Lesbos, Apollo appears just in time to prevent a viper from biting Orpheus's head. Ovid tells us that Apollo 'glazed the creature into polished stone,/And there it stayed, smiling wide-opened-jawed' (Ovid, 1958: 301). In other retellings of the myth Apollo turns the viper into stone and then erects a modest temple dedicated to Orpheus. Gaiman's Apollo alludes to that possibility, reassuring Orpheus that he has 'visited certain priests on [the] island, in their dreams [who] will find [him] soon, and care for [him]' (1993: 198). Gaiman's version, though, stresses the inter-personal struggle between father and son and uses the backward glance theme to underscore Orpheus's emotional, physical and psychological isolation (Figure 2.3).

Here the backward glance motif delivers a fatalistic reversal. Just as Eurydice was abandoned, so now is Orpheus left behind as Apollo turns his head to speak, over his right shoulder, his last words to his son: 'We shall not meet again' (Gaiman, 1993: 198). Gaiman's sardonic treatment of the theme, especially in these last three frames, emphasises Orpheus's ultimate exclusion from the Arcadian landscape so commonly associated with his magical gift of inspired poetry and song. This reversal of the backward glance motif importantly recreates for the reader the inner experience of Orpheus. We literally see through his eyes three images of Apollo walking away to the horizon – 'His father never even tried to look back' (Gaiman, 1993: 198) – and thereby experience the impossibility of Orpheus's effort to reconcile his former existence with his present tragic state. Here he suffers, following Eurydice, a second death. The backward glance has thrust upon Orpheus in this instance a staggering self-consciousness of the contradistinctions of

Figure 2.2 'The Song of Orpheus' (Source: Neil Gaiman, *The Sandman*, Vol. 6, Chapter 3, 187)

Figure 2.3 'The Song of Orpheus' (Source: Neil Gaiman, *The Sandman*, Vol. 6, Epilogue, 198)

Arcadia to the extent that he may now only see an interminable gap between that ideal landscape of memorialisation and his present relegation to oblivion.

For both Ovid and Gaiman the theme of the backward glance thus signifies not only emotional and psychological ambivalence, but, most importantly, a greater self-consciousness of the Arcadian dialectic of temporality and accompanying principle of sympathetic nature. As a visible, externalised sign of that internal effort to comprehend the contradistinctions between utopian and dystopian realms, the backward glance articulates, in a single human gesture, the intersections of an array of contrasting relationships (e.g. presence/absence, life/death, gain/loss, pleasure/pain, etc.) that determine an individual's conditions for embarking upon and struggling through the work of mourning and memorialising. Ovid and Gaiman each significantly place the moment of that recognition within a fallen territory – that is, outside of the idealised landscape – thereby suggesting that such heightened self-consciousness (i.e. the work of memorialising) displaces the individual from either positive consolation or a utopian vision of sympathetic nature. That human gesture of recognition and concomitant displacement, though, complements the tragic history of Orpheus, a character who gains the epitome of the Arcadian landscape only to lose forever his ideal vision of harmony. If, however, a sign of the backward glance were to be placed explicitly within the idealised landscape, then the work of mourning and memorialising would become inextricably bound together with the principles of dialectical temporality and sympathetic nature. As we shall see, this is precisely the case with the Vietnam Veterans Memorial in which the dominant and tangible role of the backward glance motif informs both positive and resistant paradigms of loss.

2.5 The Wall as modern Arcadia

The Vietnam Veterans Memorial (The Wall) is a modern vision of the Arcadian landscape open to all who wish to confront one of the most painful chapters in late twentieth-century US history: the legacy of the Vietnam War (Figure 2.4). More than just a landscape, the memorial site is also a park managed by the National Park Service and located in the northwestern corner of the Constitutional Gardens within the western section of the National Mall in Washington DC. Framed by the Lincoln Memorial to the west, the Washington Monument to the east and the Korean War Veterans Memorial to the south, The Wall was dedicated on 13 November 1982. The VVM consists of two triangular walls of black granite from Bangalore, India – each 246 feet 9 inches (75.21 metres) in length – placed together in the shape of a V set into the earth. The total length of the entire structure is 493 feet 6 inches (150.42 metres). The end tip of the west wall points to the Lincoln Memorial; that of the east, to the Washington

Figure 2.4 Vietnam Veterans Memorial (Photo: Katharyn C. Howard)

Monument. At the central hinge, where the two granite walls meet, the angle is 125 degrees and the height, 10 feet 3 inches (3.12 metres). The memorial sits in a pastoral landscape, surrounded by a grassy field bordered by trees to the north. A pedestrian path parallels the southern edge of the two walls, allowing visitors gradually to descend into and emerge from the memorial's V-shape cut into the earth, which reaches its lowest point at the central hinge. Visitors may also walk around the VVM to the north side of the slope where The Wall virtually disappears from view.

Each main section of the VVM contains 74 separate panels on which are engraved the names of the 58 196 American men and women killed in the war. These names are listed chronologically by date of death,[5] beginning at the top of the panel on the right-hand side of the central hinge with that of the first US soldier who perished in the Vietnam conflict in 1959. The names progress from there to the low point of the east wall, then continue from the low point of the west wall back to the bottom of the panel on the left-hand side of the central hinge where the chronological listing concludes with the name of the last US soldier killed in the war in 1975. The dates of 1959 and 1975 are the only ones to appear on the panels and frame the progression of names, which are presented both chronologically according to each casualty day and alphabetically within each day's tally. A diamond shape precedes the name of each soldier whose death is positively known; a small cross, of each of the approximate 1300 MIAs – those missing in action. (Upon the positive identification of a soldier's remains, a cross is changed to a diamond.) At an entrance point to the south of the lawn a podium holds, in a case protected from the elements but open to access, a directory of all of the names included in the memorial, indicating their placement in The Wall according to each specific panel and casualty day.

Since 1993 the Vietnam Veterans Memorial has been accompanied by one other memorial-object and two other commemorative sculptures, each located south of The Wall. A bronze flagpole 60 feet (or 18.3 metres) tall was installed in 1983 and bears, around its base, emblems of the Army, Navy, Air Force, Marines and Coast Guard. The second addition, the Three Servicemen Statue – a bronze sculpture 7 feet (2.13 metres) in height – was dedicated on Veterans Day, 11 November 1984. Designed by Frederick Hart, this commemorative work presents a realistic portrait of three soldiers (one black, one Hispanic and one white) who appear to gaze toward The Wall to the north. A second sculpture, the Vietnam Women's Memorial, designed by Glenna Goodacre, was dedicated on Veterans Day, 1993. This work realistically depicts three uniformed women beside a wounded soldier. These three additional commemorative pieces construct a landscape of memorialisation rich in cultural and political complexity.

Maya Lin's winning design for the memorial met fierce criticism long before construction began (Sturken, 1997). A minority of war veterans and an elite group of conservative political insiders perceived her plan as a morbid glorification of defeat emphasising the nation's collective guilt over the controversial war. Lin's model was derided as a 'black gash of shame and sorrow', 'a boomerang' and 'a black flagless pit' that was 'intentionally not meaningful' (Sturken, 1997: 51–2). Defenders argued that Lin's proposed memorial upheld the original conditions set forth for the design contest by the Vietnam Veterans Memorial Fund (VVMF): 'The memorial will make no political statement regarding the war or its conduct. It will transcend those issues. The hope is that the creation of the memorial will begin a healing process' (Scruggs and Swerdlow, 1985: 53). Debate raged in Washington DC and in the national media with detractors arguing that Lin's plan be thrown out and the contest re-opened. At one crisis point, James Watt, Secretary of the Interior during the Reagan administration, refused to issue a building permit to the VVMF for Lin's design. In order to save The Wall, members of the VVMF struck a compromise with their opponents: the inclusion, within the landscape site, of both the flagpole and Hart's sculpture, which would together emphasise the heroism and patriotism felt to be lacking in Lin's proposal. Glenna Goodacre's design for the Vietnam Women's Memorial was originally rejected from the same competition that Hart won because – according to J. Carter Brown, director of the National Gallery of Art and Chair of the selection commission – the addition of a statue honouring the estimated 11 500 women who served in Vietnam would inappropriately encourage other special interest groups to seek representation within the memorial's widening context of cultural signification (Sturken, 1997).

As this outline of events suggests, the Vietnam Veterans Memorial provoked remarkable controversy, and continues to generate new avenues for debate about private and public practices of mourning and memorialising in the USA.[6] Maya Lin's design has since become world famous as a hallmark of modernist, commemorative architecture, the memorial site in the Constitutional Gardens being the single most heavily visited installation on the Washington Mall as well as one of the most frequented and written about of America's National Parks. The VVM's unprecedented success underscores the dynamic and paradoxical ways in which the site as a whole facilitates a diversity of private expressions of grief within a public context of mourning. The Vietnam Veterans Memorial is a highly self-conscious work of art in which each of the five themes central to this chapter's investigation (i.e. the work of mourning and memorialising, the principles of dialectical temporality and sympathetic nature, and the motif of the backward glance) are made explicitly tangible by the landscape. Consequently the two paradigms of loss initially suggested by Whitman's and Bishop's pastoral elegies – either working toward or against consolation – converge here on the subjective and cultural levels. At the same time that The Wall invites the individual visitor to achieve positive consolation and remembrance, the memorial also counters conventional social discourses of grief expression and the commemoration of loss, resists narrative closure and thereby performs oppositional cultural work – that is, the work of mourning and memorialising that actively questions traditional customs, thereby engendering new social practices to emerge and contribute to a collective writing and rewriting of cultural history (Ramazani, 1994).

The memorial's explicit manipulation of chronology confronts the visitor with a dialectical experience of the difference between the temporality of official historical discourse and the unusual way time works in this Arcadian landscape. Although the names of the dead, as noted above, are arranged chronologically according to historical record, their alphabetical presentation within each casualty day as well as their continuous unfolding within the context of the whole site articulate a non-linear, fluid and expansive experience of time for the individual mourner. This strategy was important to Lin, who explains that she intended The Wall to read 'like an epic Greek poem' in order to 'return the vets to the time frame of the war' (quoted in Sturken, 1997: 61). The names begin and end at the central hinge, simultaneously radiating outward to the open landscape as well as inward to the memorial's origin. The Wall's dialectical temporality thus simultaneously guides the visitor upwards, into the surrounding landscape as well as downwards, toward the central hinge and into the earth, underscoring the memorial's evocation of sympathetic nature. A walk to The Wall's origin (where the framing dates of 1959 and 1975 converge) literally involves a descent into the ground where the black granite panels and the names of the dead overwhelm one's sensibilities, as if the earth itself were grieving. Reflections upon the black granite enact, at every step along the path, the motif of the backward glance for each visitor who gazes into the names to recognise their own participation in a collective work of mourning. (The other commemorative objects – i.e. the flagpole and two statues – in this landscape also dramatise the theme of the backward glance, each signifying the changing cultural politics of remembrance associated with the legacy of the Vietnam War as engendered by the VVM.) A journey up and outward

Figure 2.5 Vietnam Veterans Memorial (Photo: Katharyn C. Howard)

Figure 2.6 Vietnam Veterans Memorial (Photo: Katharyn C. Howard)

from the origin takes one back into the light and on to a path toward positive consolation.

On the level of public discourse, however, The Wall resists the conventional work of mourning and memorialising established by other prominent commemorative structures installed on the National Mall, especially the Washington Monument (to the east) and the Lincoln Memorial (to the west) toward which the VVM gestures. Traditional western monuments emulate great achievements in the history of classical architecture. Just as the obelisk of the Washington Monument gains authority from Roman and Egyptian symbols of imperial power, the Lincoln Memorial imitates the form and stature of a Greek temple. The Wall, however, departs from those motifs and strategies. Whereas the Washington Monument and Lincoln Memorial are constructed from white stone and are designed to rise triumphantly from the ground in order to be seen from great distances, the Vietnam Veterans Memorial is fashioned from black stone and sinks defiantly into the earth. Whereas traditional war memorials strive toward narrative closure sanctioned by official historical discourse, The Wall, on the level of public discourse, resists a conclusion to the cultural work of mourning.

Through such oppositional work, the VVM achieves a living vision of the Arcadian landscape wherein the individual may encounter their active participation in the construction of collective memory and the writing of cultural history. According to the National Park Service, an estimated 30 million people have visited the Vietnam Veterans Memorial. As a testament to those individual acts of devotion, expressions of grief and contributions to that cultural work of mourning and memorialising, visitors have placed scores of offerings beside the wall: e.g. motorcycles, flowers, combat boots, photographs and letters (Allen, 1995). The memorial and its accompanying commemorative works (i.e. the flagpole and two sculptures) have also sparked many virtual communities on the web, including *The Virtual Wall, a Digital Legacy Project for Remembrance* (at http://www.thevirtualwall.org/) and *The Vietnam Women's Memorial Project* (at http://www.vietnamwomensmemorial.org/pages/index2.html). A travelling, half-size replica of the memorial, *The Moving Wall* (also to be found on the web at http://www.vietvet.org/movwall.htm), visits as many as 50 US cities and towns each year. All of these interactive media underscore the ongoing cultural work of mourning and memorialising integral to The Wall's provocation of the historical imagination on both personal and public levels of discourse.

Now do this . . .

1. For digital copies of Whitman's, Bishop's and Virgil's pastoral elegies as well as of Ovid's elegiac retelling of the Orpheus myth, see respectively:

- http://www.geocities.com/~spanoudi/poems/whitm01.html
- http://www.shadowpoetry.com/famous/bishop/elizabeth2.html#3
- http://classics.mit.edu/Virgil/eclogue.10.x.html, and both
- http://classics.mit.edu/Ovid/metam.10.tenth.html and
- http://classics.mit.edu/Ovid/metam.11.eleventh.html.

2. For digital images of the Vietnam Veterans Memorial, the Lincoln Memorial, the Washington Monument and the Korean War Veterans Memorial, see respectively:

- http://www.nps.gov/vive/
- http://www.nps.gov/linc/
- http://www.nps.gov/wamo/, and
- http://www.nps.gov/kwvm/.

3. For a digital map of the National Mall, see:

- http://sc94.ameslab.gov/TOUR/tour.html.

4. For digital images of the flagpole, the Three Servicemen Statue and the Vietnam Women's Memorial, see respectively:

- http://www.nps.gov/vive/memorial/servicemen.htm, and
- http://www.nps.gov/vive/memorial/women.htm>.

5. Having explored the various websites noted above that concern the Vietnam Veterans Memorial and other commemorative works at the VVM site, compare and contrast the ways in which The Wall and the AIDS Memorial Quilt (see http://www.aidsquilt.org/Newsite/) – as represented by and reconfigured through digital media – perform the work of mourning and memorialising on both personal and public levels. Does landscape still play an important role in these virtual communities and, if so: how and why? How and why do these websites refashion the idea of Arcadia to work with as well as against the principles and motifs central to this chapter?

6. Compare and contrast the visions and versions of Arcadia discussed in this chapter with the representations of nature in three landscape paintings: the first, *Et in Arcadia Ego* (*c*.1621–23) by Giovanni Francesco Guercino (1591–1666); the other two – both of which respond directly to Guercino's earlier work – *Les Bergers d'Arcadie I (Et in Arcadia Ego I)* (*c*.1626–28) and *Les Bergers d'Arcadie II (Et in Arcadia Ego II)* (*c*.1638–39) by Nicolas Poussin (1594–1665). Digital reproductions of these paintings may be located, respectively, at the following websites:

- http://www.galleriaborghese.it/barberini/it/arcadia.htm
- http://www.abcgallery.com/P/poussin/poussin4.html, and
- http://www.abcgallery.com/P/poussin/poussin42.html.

(a) How and why do these landscape paintings embody the theme of *et in Arcadia ego* – 'even in Arcadia, there (am) I' – as part of their work of mourning and memorialising?

(b) Do the paintings engage with the principles and motifs central to this chapter? If so, how so and why? If not, why not and how so?

Further reading

Caruth, C. (ed.) 1995: *Trauma: Explorations in Memory*. Baltimore: Hopkins.

Freud, S. 1953: Mourning and Melancholia, in Rickman, J. (ed.) *A General Selection from the Works of Sigmund Freud*. London: Hogarth, 142–61.

Mitford, J. 2000: *The American Way of Death Revisited*. New York: Random House.

Ramazani, J. 1994: *Poetry of Mourning*. Chicago: University of Chicago.

Sturken, M. 1997: *Tangled Memories: The Vietnam War, the AIDS Epidemic, and the Politics of Remembering*. Berkeley: University of California.

Notes to Chapter 2

1   I wish to express my gratitude to my colleagues at the University of Denver – Jan Gorak, Jessica Munns, Alexandra Olsen and Catherine O'Neil – for their comments on early drafts of this essay.

2   This relationship between grief, memory and historiography complements current psychoanalytic and sociological theories of the mourning process that posit grief as an internalised, private experience and mourning as an externalised, public manifestation of forces that remain largely hidden within the individual. Just as the mourning process makes visible a struggle with, for and against the remembrance of things lost and gained, landscapes of memorialisation may also serve as physical and public records of continuities and gaps between notions of the past, present and future. See Freud, 1953: 142–61; Scarry, 1985: 3–23; Houlbrooke, 1989: 1–24; Caruth, 1995: 3–12 and 151–7.

3   In one of the earliest recorded references to Arcadia, the Homeric Hymn 'To Hermes' (*c*.800 BCE) describes the landscape as 'rich in sheep' (see Lang, 1899: 134). For architectural, literary and sociological studies of the idea of Arcadia, see respectively Ritvo, 1992; Haber, 1994; and Hugill, 1995. On the related literary themes of Arcadia and the pastoral mode, see Empson, 1950; Loughrey, 1984; and especially Toliver, 1984. For studies of interrelationships between poetry, painting and landscape architecture, see Spencer, 1973; Hunt, 1976; Janowitz, 1990; and Fitter, 1995.

4   See Curtius, 1973: 195–200. According to the *Oxford English Dictionary*, 'Arcadia' entered the English language in 1590 by way of Thomas Watson's elegy on the death of Sir Francis Walsingham, *Meliboeus*: 'And let *Arcadians* altogether sing/a woeful song against heaven's tyranny' (see Watson, 1895: 139–75, line 49).

5   The name of an American killed in 1957 that was discovered after the memorial's
    completion was added to the panels out of order (see Allen, 1995: 242).
6   For a provocative critique of both the funeral industry and customs of mourning
    in the USA, see Mitford, 2000. For a trans-historical and cross-cultural study of
    funerary architecture, see Ragon, 1983.

|3|

Reel landscapes: cinematic environments documented and created

Andrew Horton

3.1 All landscapes in cinema are 'reel'

That is to say, both landscapes that look like we could touch them, walk
through them and smell them, as well as those that look entirely fanciful or
theatrical, are presented to us through the medium of film. And film traditionally has been a piece of plastic running through a machine with a strong
light that throws a two-dimensional image on a screen. Modern digital
technology has somewhat altered this formula, but the fact remains: to
speak of landscapes and cinema is to speak of the representation of landscapes through another medium.

We begin with two primary characteristics of film: cinema has the power
to manipulate time and place and thus 'take' us anywhere or into any time
period. We can be in outer space in George Lucas's *Star Wars* films, or in
eighteenth-century England in Tony Richardson's *Tom Jones* (1963), the
American West in John Ford's *Stagecoach* (1939) or even Ridley Scott's
Thelma and Louise (1991), ancient Rome in *Gladiator* (2000) or crossing
the endless deserts in David Lean's *Lawrence of Arabia* (1962). Film has such
a power to transform landscapes for its viewers. Landscapes in film, therefore, may be used in 'open' (documentary/representational as in *Lawrence
of Arabia*) or 'closed' (expressionist such as *Star Wars*) modes. Part of the
focus of this chapter will be to distinguish the dimensions and the differences
of each, for as critic Leo Braudy has noted, 'Too often we accept a film as a
window on reality without noticing that the window has been opened in a
particular way, to exclude as well as include' (Braudy, 1977: 22).

Yet cinema possesses another important aspect: film presents images that
move, both through time and space. We thus experience landscapes as
'narrative' – that is, as elements of storytelling. And we can even come to

think of landscapes as *characters* who change, disappear, and reappear in the lives of human characters. Landscapes in film therefore exhibit that power of film to capture the 'flow of life'.

According to theoretician Siegfried Kracauer:

> The concept 'flow of life', then, covers the stream of material situations and happenings with all that they intimate in terms of emotions, values, thoughts. The implication is that the flow of life is predominantly a material rather than a mental continuum, even though, by definition, it extends into the mental dimension.
>
> (Kracauer, 1978: 71)

We will explore the fascinating intertwining of landscapes and cinema over the past 100 years as a new century with new possibilities for the intertwining of these two worlds begins. In all cases, our goal is to understand better how no landscape or film exists apart from human perception. The act of 'seeing' is socially (and psychologically) constructed. Thus in 'understanding how viewers interact with film', we will necessarily also be coming up with a 'theory of subjectivity' (Bordwell, 1996: 14).

Four cinematic landscape shots to start us off

1. On a misty and rugged coastline a group of Maori natives await the arrival of a boat, bringing a young woman in nineteenth-century dress, thus setting the time, her 8–10-year-old daughter and a grand piano inside a large crate along with other boxes and suitcases. As the boat and natives depart, the woman opens one section of the crate so she is able to play the piano there on the misty beach in a foreign country she has yet to discover: New Zealand.

2. In our next scene, two men – one in his late fifties and the other a young man – hug on a seashore with a rugged coast that suggests where they are: Greece. They then begin to dance a Greek dance as the bouzouki music picks up in tempo and as the camera rises into the air, framing the joyously dancing men against the landscape and, increasingly, dwarfing them against that landscape as the camera rises higher and higher.

3. Our third image is of a rusty gate with a sign saying 'NO TRESSPASS-ING' [*sic*]. Vaguely through the iron gate we can see what looks like a castle through the dark distance as the camera moves through the spaces in the gate, thus beginning to trespass and approach the castle, which looks more imaginary than real.

4. Lastly, we have a young man in an old movie theatre, which has a small orchestra up front (clueing us that this is the silent film era), walking up to the screen and actually walking into the film that is playing! As each scene and landscape changes, however, our young hero is in trouble.

When the landscape appears to be an ocean and our protagonist is standing on a large rock in the sea, he dives into what he believes to be water only to find out the scene has changed and he has actually fallen into deep snow in the mountains with his feet sticking out of the snowdrift.

Since the beginning of film, landscapes have helped to define the nature and potential of this most popular of storytelling mediums in the twentieth century, which is continuing to be a major form of entertainment in this new century as well. That said, I will in this chapter explore some of the most significant ways in which landscapes are used and created in films around the world.

The most basic observation to be made is this: in film, real landscapes can be filmed and thus incorporated into a narrative or documentary, or they can be created and presented as 'real' even though we understand they are actually imaginary. The early history of cinema gives us the double nature of cinematic landscapes quite clearly.

The Lumière brothers amazed the world by filming a real train arriving at a real train station in 1895. Film historians report that audiences for such early work often ducked to avoid a train coming at them from the screen (Mast and Kawin, 2000). And Georges Méliès in his short, *Trip to the Moon* (1902), created a moonscape in his studio, which delighted audiences everywhere. No one for a moment believed it was an actual moonscape, for it was clearly a stage production complete with chorus girls and props representing stars and snow, and other 'special effects'. But such a playful creation of an imaginary landscape was the whole point. It was the artifice itself that made the landscape enjoyable for those early audiences in Paris.

Likewise, the images mentioned above help limn significant dimensions of cinematic space.

1. Our first image (Figure 3.1), taken from Jane Campion's *The Piano* (1993), suggests that real landscapes can become a powerful presence that functions in a visual way to help define a particular narrative. In this scene, the striking incongruity of a dignified-looking nineteenth-century woman and her daughter with a piano on a beautiful but strikingly isolated beach, surrounded by mist and rugged cliffs, embodies and foreshadows the conflicts the young woman will have to confront and overcome. The famous Russian director Sergei Eisenstein often spoke not only of conflict emerging between two different shots in a film, but *within* the frame we are watching as well. 'Conflict is the basis of every art,' he noted, adding that, as in this early scene from *The Piano*, the conflict may be between character and the surroundings, but that it is also between light and shadow and, since the use of colour, between colours as well (Eisenstein, 1999: 21).

2. The two men dancing on the seashore (as mentioned above) is the final scene of Michael Cacoyannis's *Zorba the Greek* (1964), based on Nikos Kazantzakis's novel of the same title. The dance represents a joyful expression of friendship between the young 'academic' man (Alan

Figure 3.1 Jane Campion's *The Piano* (1993): Holly Hunter and Anna Paquin on an isolated New Zealand beach in the nineteenth century (Source: Museum of Modern Art, New York City)

Bates), who is the older man Zorba's (Anthony Quinn) boss. It is also a triumphant gesture in the face of a number of personal and financial disasters that occur in the young man's life. In terms of landscape and cinema, the camera movement from up close on our two protagonists to a bird's eye shot of them against a sea-coast landscape exemplifies how cinema can shift between the intensity of human experience – the two men dancing – to the 'larger picture' of an ageless environment of land, sea and sky, in which this individual tale has unfolded. Bill Nichols summarises in general the importance of composition and framing within a film when he comments, 'composition plays two important roles, both common to film and melodrama: developing characters and developing relationships between characters' (1981: 113).

3. Orson Welles' *Citizen Kane* (1941) is our third example, and one in which we experience a studio-constructed landscape, carefully assembled to create a sense of mystery and foreboding with lighting and

shadows, a distant castle and the 'NO TRESSPASSING' sign, of course. I shall go on to say more about the history of constructing landscapes and how, in some sense, these constructions represent a bridge between theatre and 'real' landscapes, for the studio allows for the complete control of what is made and seen, whereas actual locations, as represented in our first two examples, depend on 'finding' locations that actually exist in New Zealand and Greece, and using them for a film-maker's particular narrative purposes. Lastly, in the Orson Welles' opening, we should also note that since the whole film is one about trying to discover who Citizen Kane really was, this sense of going beyond the safe and allowed is established from the first scene *by a violation of space and landscape*. Welles is thus cueing us to acknowledge how important landscape can be to the actual narration and even the theme of a film.

4.   Buster Keaton's *Sherlock Jr* (1925) is the final sequence mentioned above. Keaton was one of the screen's greatest silent comedians and *Sherlock Jr* has remained one of the most memorable of film comedies (Horton, 1996). The basic plot concerns a small-town projectionist in the local cinema who falls in love with the 'girl' down the street. Keaton is the projectionist who is thrown out of the girl's home by her father, falsely accused of stealing. Keaton, dejected and rejected, returns to the cinema to start up the evening's film and then falls asleep next to the projector. But his 'dream self' comes out of his body and proceeds to enter the film screen, becoming part of the film on the screen but transformed through dreaming to be the projectionist's own life. The confusion of landscapes mentioned earlier represents Keaton's descent deeper into dreams, and thus cinema, as he is at first a victim of the editing within the film. The changing landscapes from sea to desert to forest to snowscape thus represent the Keaton figure's inability to comprehend the 'landscape' of film language. But as he dreams even more 'deeply' in the projection booth, we see Keaton finally become part of the film's landscape on-screen. Comedy, cinema and landscape intertwine imaginatively and to the delight of audiences everywhere, and beyond the laughter is yet another truth about cinema and landscapes, as Stephen Heath (1981) observes: in any film shot, there is both a presence – what we see – and an absence – what has been left out 'off camera'. Thus even the space or landscape beyond the frame is 'there in its absence and given back, as it were, in the editing of shot with shot or in camera movement with its reframings' (1981: 33). In fact, let us turn next to absent landscapes as potent presences in viewers' minds.

3.2 Absence as landscape

Before we discuss landscapes *seen* on film, we should consider landscapes that are suggested or implied, but not seen within the frame.

There is a scene near the end of Greek director Theo Angelopoulos's

Ulysses' Gaze (1995) when the main character, played by Harvey Keitel, reaches Sarajevo during the Bosnian War. He is on a personal mission to find the first film ever made in the Balkans; and, in that war-torn city, he does manage to locate it. While it is developing, he goes for a walk in the mist with the film archivist of Sarajevo and his family.

The archivist explains that only during the mist can the people of Sarajevo come out and forget the war for a few moments, either simply strolling or by listening to music or even theatre in the park (Figure 3.2). At a certain point, the mist becomes a total white shield, and we the audience see no landscape at all. The white on the screen is the white of the mist in Sarajevo, yet the effect is that of a 'blank' screen.

But the scene cannot be described as 'blank' for we hear more than we wish to hear. The soundtrack carries the noise of a Serbian truck pulling up, grabbing the family of the film archivist and shooting them, in the mist, one by one, tossing their bodies into the nearby stream and then driving off. For part of this sequence we see Harvey Keitel staring into the mist, but for the rest of it, we too see nothing.

What we *feel* is something else. Many viewers comment on how much more powerful such a scene is because we do not see the violence with all the graphic power that cinema, especially Hollywood films, can muster these days, with special effects and computer graphics. In fact, it is not by accident that Theo Angelopoulos chooses to present the war in such a way: on the one hand we have all seen too many landscapes of war on television news, in short but horrifying clips; yet on the other hand, Angelopoulos as a Greek

Figure 3.2 Theo Angelopoulos's *Ulysses' Gaze* (1995): an orchestra of young Serbs, Muslims and Croats playing in the mist of Sarajevo during a break in the bombing while the Bosnian war rages (Source: Museum of Modern Art, New York City)

is echoing the ancient Greek tradition of tragedy in which violence happened off-stage while the dramatic tragedy dealt with the results of the violence.

Such a use of landscape implied rather than shown suggests a powerful tool of cinema that is far too rarely used and that thus appears all the more meaningful when we have a chance to be reminded. It is no surprise, therefore, that Angelopoulos has frequently made imaginative use of landscapes to create such emotions. In fact, one of his Oscar-nominated films, *Landscape in the Mist* (1988), announces the power of landscapes in the title. In this film a young Greek girl and her even younger brother take to the open road as voyagers searching for their father whom they have never met but who is rumoured to be working in Germany.

The journey in this film, as in *Ulysses' Gaze*, mirrors Homer's *Odyssey* in a landscape that is both modern and yet ageless. Angelopoulos has thus consciously shot his films suggesting that landscapes can be both real and mythical (Horton, 1999b). The mist helps to blur the boundaries between history and myth, real time and archetypal time.

Absence can also be used to describe landscapes seen but lacking humans. The well-known Japanese director Ozu Yasujiro incorporates landscapes in *Tokyo Story* (1953) in a way that is clearly influenced by the Japanese tradition of minimalist landscape painting, in which simple scenes of nature evoke emotional feelings. The 'story' of the film traces an older couple from a small rural town visiting their grown-up children in Tokyo. But the use of exterior shots of nature throughout the film suggests what Kathe Geist (1997) identifies as a spirit of Buddhism. Geist speaks of several scenes in which the protagonists are absent but the shots of nature represent their feelings, especially a sense of loss as the mother figure, Tomi, lies dying: 'As Tomi lies dying, Ozu inserts shots of Onomichi (their town) at dawn, which include an empty pier, an empty sidewalk ... and empty train tracks where a train ran in the opening sequence' (Geist, 1997: 111). Landscape in such a film and in such a Japanese tradition evokes therefore, in Geist's terms, 'Buddhist eschatology of transience' (1997: 104).

The final shot of the film clearly brings together all of these themes. The husband whose wife has just died returns home and is now completely alone. He sits silently in his living room where we saw him and his wife at the opening of the film. Ozu then cuts to the landscape of the town, the river, the hills beyond and a ship moving along the river.

We the audience feel that the 'emptiness' of the landscape represents our character's loneliness as well. Landscape and human feeling are one and the same, as Geist would propose, thus suggesting a Buddhist view of life.

3.3 Landscape as genre and genre as landscape

Landscape and genre are totally interwoven elements in cinema. We can't think of a western without conjuring up wide-open spaces, mountains and rugged rock formations, cattle roaming on open prairies and cactus plants scattered all around. Whether it is Henry Fonda riding off alone into the landscape, leaving the attractive school teacher waiting behind in John Ford's *My Darling Clementine* (1946) or John Wayne riding hell bent for leather through the wide-open spaces in Henry Hathaway's *True Grit* (1969), westerns by definition call up not just a specific landscape, but a precise time in American history – roughly 1870–90 – when horses, rather than cars and trucks, were the means of transportation through the landscape.

Similarly, gangster movies and *film noir* stories evoke an urban landscape of dark city streets, dangerous neighbourhoods, crowded centres of glass, steel and concrete, in classical crime flicks from Howard Hawks' *Scarface* (1932) and John Huston's *The Maltese Falcon* (1941) to contemporary revisions of the genre such as Quentin Tarantino's *Pulp Fiction* (1994) and Mike Hodges' *Croupier* (2000). And how can we imagine action-adventure movies without flashing to exotic and overpowering landscapes, be they in Steven Spielberg's *Raiders of the Lost Ark* (1981) or Michael Anderson's *Around the World in Eighty Days* (1956)? Lastly, purely fictitious landscapes abound in genres such as science fiction and space-related films, be they scenes of monoliths in lunar landscapes as in Stanley Kubrick's *2001: A Space Odyssey* (1968) and the landscapes of strange planets in the *Star Trek* film series (1982; 1994; 1996; 1998), or even the final lunar shot in Clint Eastwood's *Space Cowboys* (2000).

Simply put, a single shot of a landscape often clues us into the genre and thus the *kind* of film we are about to view. Stated another way, landscapes evoke story or narrative expectations within us. We do not, for instance, expect to meet space aliens if we see buffalo roaming an open prairie, just as we would be surprised to see a Maori warrior with a tattooed face walking down the dark streets of Chicago during a 1930s period film.

Consider briefly the role of landscape in determining genre as well as location, narrative context and even a sense of character in the following three films.

John Ford's Stagecoach *(1939): mythologising the American west*

It is impossible to separate John Ford's westerns from his use of one particular area of the American West: Monument Valley, Utah. Tag Gallagher comments about Monument Valley that, 'the valley is not simply a valley, but a valley melodramatized' (1986: 146). That rugged vista with rock formations filling the horizon with canyons as well as flat spaces in between has come to symbolise 'the West' for generations of movie-goers around the world. And while *Stagecoach* (Figure 3.3) opens with a sequence 'in town', it is important that we first meet John Wayne in this, his first major film role,

Figure 3.3 John Ford's *Stagecoach* (1939): John Wayne and fellow stagecoach travellers in the American West of Monument Valley, Utah (Source: Museum of Modern Art, New York City)

standing in the open spaces of the landscape, gun in hand as the Ringo Kid. John Wayne is the landscape and the landscape is John Wayne. He is an outlaw and not one to live comfortably in town. The ending of the film as he and Claire Trevor head off to Mexico represents this theme quite clearly as we hear a character say 'They're safe from the blessings of civilisation.'

The landscape for Ford represents freedom from 'civilisation'. It is a natural state where an individual can live 'naturally'. Of course we immediately recognise how much this is a product of the Romantic movement in Europe and America. Western art historian Peter H. Hassrick underlines this point (1989) in that many of the artists of the American West, including Charles M. Russell wanted to detail both the realities and 'myth' of the West. Ford loved Monument Valley and beginning with *Stagecoach* worked to preserve his myth of the American West through his films. Finally, John Wayne's character throughout the John Ford westerns, including *Fort Apache* (1948), *She Wore a Yellow Ribbon* (1949), *Rio Grande* (1950) and *The Searchers* (1956), aged in Ford's ageless western landscape. What one can trace, more specifically, is a changing attitude or implication of the meaning of that landscape as Wayne ages. The ending of *The Searchers* is particularly poignant, for Wayne is standing in the doorway of the woman he had loved but someone else married, looking out at Monument Valley. That landscape is his life but the 'freedom' it represents is also the absence of a life spent 'inside' with the only woman he ever truly loved.

Note that while John Ford's reputation remains very solid in film history, not all critics praise his westerns or his use of Monument Valley. British film historian David Thomson, for instance, notes that Ford's 'lust for epic' and 'clichéd panoramas' blurs the real beauty and meanings of the landscapes (Thomson, 1995). Such an observation should invite us all, as movie-goers, to be critical viewers of both landscapes and cinema.

Alfred Hitchcock's Vertigo (1958): falling into landscapes – the art of cinematic suspense

Hitchcock was almost a genre unto himself. This British director, coming of age during silent cinema's heyday and receiving training at the famous UFA studios in Germany, but moving to Hollywood during the sound period, loved to mix landscapes real with landscapes fabricated in the studio. The urban landscape of an apartment complex in *Rear Window* (1954) was completely created as a set, while the remake of *The Man Who Knew Too Much* (1956) used locations in Africa and England as well as interiors shot in Hollywood. *Vertigo* remains, however, as one of his most accomplished works, and it too mixed location and sets for a seamless interweaving of elements.

A set designer himself originally, Hitchcock specialised in the crime or suspense genre and thus came to know how to work in an 'expressionist' mode: that is, one in which studio sets and a careful use of light and shadow control the mood, tone, theme and character of each scene for the total effect of a given film. *Vertigo* announces its overriding impact in its title, and as David Sterritt comments, 'If there is one element that crystallises the impact, ingenuity, and sheer strangeness of *Vertigo*, it is the repeated shot representing Scottie/James Stewart's troubled gaze into an abyss far below' (1993: 82).

Heights and the sense of falling – or vertigo to be exact – characterise the sense of suspense Hitchcock orchestrates for this memorable film. And while a number of exterior landscape shots were done in the San Francisco area, production designer for the film, Henry Bumstead, makes it clear (Bumstead, 2000) that the tower was the set he designed for Hitchcock.

In terms of our interest in landscape and genre, Hitchcock is thus a classical example of how 'reel landscapes' can be created using all of the artifice of Hollywood including rear projection (projecting a film or single shot of a real landscape behind the actors in the foreground) and, more recently, digitally added details or landscapes, specially constructed sets, ingenious lighting and, lastly, real landscapes.

Simply stated, Hitchcock scares us in *Vertigo* and many of his other films because the locations *seem* so real even when they are not. On a final note, however, when Hitchcock does use an actual natural location, it stands out and apart from the rest of the film. In *Vertigo* this most clearly occurs when Stewart stops in a California redwood forest with Kim Novak. The giant trees and shadows with streaks of sunlight create an immediate contrast to the San Francisco and also the Mission sets. But most important is the scene as they look at a cross-section of a giant redwood, which is historically marked to show over 1000 years of human history. Novak traces with her finger 1000 years and more of history and then becomes depressed, explaining to Stewart how her life would not even be a line in this tree's life or the world's memory. A natural landscape thus becomes a moment of truth in this film about obsession.

Monty Python and the Holy Grail *(1975): comedy and landscape considered*

The genre of comedy suggests, overall, that anything goes; and, it often does! Certainly the Monty Python team has for over 25 years proved that the carnivalesque spirit of play in cinema can be great fun and produce waves of laughter. The 'real' landscape of *The Holy Grail*, their first feature, was Scotland, and clearly a lot of the pleasure of the film is to see these characters dressed as medieval knights clowning through a recognisable Scottish landscape.

The landscape thus becomes a counterbalance to their comic performances. The scene in which they pretend to gallop off on their make-believe horses, knocking together coconut shells to make the sound of hoof beats is all the more hilarious because the landscape is real even if the horses aren't. In short, the gap between the landscape and their behaviour accounts for a lot of the laughter. Similarly, camera operator Howard Atherton noted that a lot of the humour of the special effects was because they were so crude and obviously fake (Morgan, 1999). Python member Terry Gilliam agreed: 'I want it [the film] to be both great looking *and* funny' (Morgan, 1999: 168).

I could continue going through, genre by genre, but I think I have made the point by now. Landscapes are some of the major 'cues' or 'clues' to cinematic genres. Perhaps for this reason, some of the 'spaghetti westerns' of the 1960s and 1970s evoked laughter when audiences saw olive trees appearing in these 'western' landscapes in several films!

3.4 Revisionist genres and landscape

As a new century begins, we are very aware how many genres and narrative forms in film and fiction either fall by the wayside or become revitalised in revisionist or 'postmodern' forms. In this section, I will briefly consider the role landscapes can play in revisionist takes on old film genres.

George Roy Hill's *Butch Cassidy and the Sundance Kid* (1969) is and is not a western. With a script by William Goldman, who researched the original historical figures behind the 'myths' of these two outlaws, Hill's film becomes revisionist by clearly showing how the 'Old West' was being invaded by a new corporate mentality as well as by such modern inventions as bicycles and cars. But what most emphatically makes this an unusual western is the last half-hour of the film, which takes place not in the 'Wild West' or in John Ford's Monument Valley, but in Bolivia, South America, where Butch and Sundance actually went.

As the train leaves them in an isolated Bolivian landscape, we sense how much their lives have changed and how different this story then becomes for these two 'western' outlaws (for starters they have to learn Spanish to enable them to rob banks in Bolivia!). William Goldman has said he was trying to show two fellows who simply no longer fit in either in America or elsewhere (Horton, 1981). The landscape and the Bolivian towns they pass through announce this fact strongly and visually (the actual location shooting took place in Mexico).

Similarly, Ridley Scott's *Thelma and Louise* plays off contemporary crime road films as well as westerns with a specific nod to *Butch Cassidy and the Sundance Kid*. Screenwriter Callie Kouri has often commented (Horton, 1999a) that she was playing with the male buddy film, both the road film and *Butch and Sundance*, but casting her narrative through the eyes of two women, Thelma and Louise. Unlike *Butch and Sundance*, however, she has kept her film in the American West, and, more specifically, brings the film directly into Monument Valley towards the end of the narrative at the point that the two women have bonded as soulmate friends. To see them driving through John Ford country as 'liberated' women in an open convertible is a powerful scene indeed. For the landscape echoes with memories of past westerns, yet we 'get' that this is a retake rather than a remake of this landscape. It is both director Ridley Scott and writer Kouri inviting us to 'replay' in our own memories the old western male-centred stories seen through the eyes of these women on the run who have no place to hide and who, finally, let the landscape be their end: they drive off the cliff plunging, literally, into the landscape. The Bolivian army killed Butch and Sundance, and John Ford's Ringo Kid escapes to Mexico. But Thelma and Louise in this 'revisionist' or mixed-genre film fatally become part of the landscape.

Finally, I will consider Emir Kusturica's *Time of the Gypsies* (1985), an award-winning film that was shot in Kusturica's homeland of Yugoslavia and northern Italy, especially the areas surrounding Venice. This Balkan tale, based on the actual case of thousands of Gypsy children sold into slavery each year, is also a 'revisionist' take on the Hollywood gangster/crime film. Even more specifically, Kusturica has consciously constructed his narrative as a remake, or makeover, of Francis Ford Coppola's *The Godfather* and *Godfather II* (Horton, 1998).

We recognise, of course, that part of the power and popularity of Coppola's films is that the *Godfather* films, based on Mario Puzo's novel, 'revise' the gangster genre themselves in important ways: the use, for instance, of Italy and the Sicilian landscapes as well as the use of real Italian (complete with English subtitles) and an emphasis on 'family', complete with wives, grandchildren and cousins, in a way that classical Hollywood crime films never articulated or mentioned.

Coppola thus shows us the 'original landscapes' – Sicily – from which the Americanised Italian family came, and we as viewers carry that physical and cultural landscape with us in our viewing of this three-part epic of crime (note that *Godfather III* (1990) returns to Italy, completing the circle). Kusturica does an ironic switch of landscapes and cultures as his tale tracks Yugoslav Gypsies living in their very Balkan landscape of rivers, hills and mountains, moving to the urban edges of Italian cities for the second half of the film. Just as the Sicilian sections of Coppola's films imprint a specific landscape on the viewer's memory, Kusturica presents several important scenes involving the Serbian landscape, which we remember long after the film ends. The most memorable, according to critics and audiences, is a Gypsy celebration of St George's Day in a large river. The combination of the river, the surrounding lush countryside, the Gypsy hymns being sung, and the acting out of a kind of baptismal ceremony in the river, creates a magical mood in which we feel 'anything can happen'. Kusturica goes on to trace a crime story with a main character who comes to look more and more like Al Pacino in Coppola's films; but the Serbian landscape we carry with us in our memories throughout the film becomes a significant part of what we the audience come to feel is a 'revisionist' take on an old American genre: the crime film.

3.5 Actual locations vs substituted landscapes

Beyond the issue of 'are we watching a "real" landscape or a digitally added or animated landscape', lies another question worth considering. What difference, if any, does it make whether a film is shot in the actual location of the story it is telling? Yes, we expect documentaries to take us to actual places (see the documentary discussion below), however, for feature/narrative films, Hollywood and the film-makers of most countries around the world have conditioned us to accept a 'real' location for an 'actual' one.[1] Thus audiences do not protest or, probably, think about the 'switch' of artificial snow in Spain for the blizzards of Siberia (David Lean's *Dr Zhivago*, 1965), or the smouldering remains of a real village in the Czech Republic for the firebombed city of Dresden during the Second World War in George Roy Hill's adaptation of Kurt Vonnegut's *Slaughterhouse Five* (1972). Nor do they focus on the hills of southern California substituted for the oil fields of Oklahoma (in Stanley Kramer's *Oklahoma Crude*, 1973), or the New Zealand bush for a television image of ancient Greece (*Hercules*).

Budget and practical logistics, of course, have been the order of the day for most film-makers in choosing locations. Sergio Leone didn't have the budget in 1968 to shoot *Once Upon a Time in the West* in the American West, thus his creation of a sub-western genre we affectionately call 'spaghetti westerns' shot on location in ... Italy. Clearly, for a myriad of practical reasons, shooting in the distant or obscure landscapes that stories may evoke seldom happens.

Yet we should pay momentary tribute to those who do go out of their way to shoot in the landscapes conjured up by the stories the films they are shooting tell. In this small group we have such devoted souls as the Coen brothers who shot *Fargo* (1996) in the frozen landscapes of North Dakota and surrounding areas that they knew from their childhood. David Lynch's *The Straight Story* (1999) also went to great lengths to shoot this tale based on a true story of an old Iowa farmer going to visit his estranged brother in Wisconsin by driving the only vehicle he owned, a tractor lawn mower, 'on the road' in those states. And German director Werner Herzog has gone to extreme lengths to shoot 'on location' in difficult landscapes including the jungles of the Amazon for *Aguirre: Wrath of God* (1972) and *Fitzcarraldo* (1982). Similarly, Theo Angelopoulos, the Greek director mentioned earlier, feels strongly that shooting on location adds something significant to his films, even if he is the only one to feel that way (Horton, 1999b). Thus *Ulysses' Gaze* was shot, in part, in Bosnia and Belgrade during the Bosnian War. One can argue that such action needlessly endangered the lives of the cast and crew, and yet all those I have interviewed (Horton, 1999b) who worked on the film felt that 'the real landscape' did add to the depth and emotion of the film as a document of our times. Finally, take Gabriele Salvatore's Best Foreign Film Oscar-winning production *Mediterraneo* (1991). A large part of the pleasure of the film is that it was shot on an Aegean island. Here we enjoy what happens to six hapless Italian soldiers during the Second World War, stranded on an isolated Greek island that has nothing but beautiful women, good food and the beauty of land, sea and sky in the blissful Mediterranean.

In this small but dedicated category, we must finally pay tribute to John Huston for his insistence in shooting *The African Queen* (1951) in Africa. The swamps and rivers of Louisiana would have done fine by Hollywood's standards; however, Huston wanted true authenticity for this tale of a Canadian alcoholic gun runner (Humphrey Bogart) and a British straight-laced sister of a man of God (Katharine Hepburn) who join forces and hearts as they work to foil a German plot in deepest Africa during the Second World War. The film has an excellent cast, script and direction, but the actual Belgian Congo landscape does make a real difference. How else, for instance, could Huston capture, in a single take, Bogart clowning with giant hippos as his boat sails past them? Huston apparently really did tell Bogart at the Oscars that year, when Bogart won Best Actor, that 'real leeches would make a difference'!

3.6 Adaptation and landscape

A large percentage – perhaps more than 40 per cent – of feature films derive from other narrative sources. Traditionally, adaptation in cinema has meant plays or short stories or novels made into films; and if we are speaking of Hollywood, we especially mean popular works of the stage or in print that will automatically provide a following for 'the movie' when it is released. Thus Anne Rice's *Interview with the Vampire* had already sold millions of copies in paperback before Neil Jordan signed up Brad Pitt and Tom Cruise to attempt to bring the book to life on-screen (1994). That the film was downright boring, even though the actual landscapes and riverscapes (the Mississippi River) of New Orleans were brought to silver screens around the world (Maltin, 2000), suggests an important issue regarding landscapes imagined (through reading or stage representations) and landscapes depicted through film. We all have our own 'vision' of landscapes we read about, just as we have our view of characters too in novels and short stories, and thus we do become 'critics' when we go to see a film, for part of the pleasure and frustration of seeing a film 'based on' another source is making that comparison: is the film better or less successful than the book, play or story?

Kurt Vonnegut Jr once told me something that perhaps few novelists have ever said in watching films based on their works: he said that, flat out, George Roy Hill's film *Slaughterhouse Five* (1972) was much better than his book (Horton, 1981). With locations and landscapes chosen by Hill's art director, Henry Bumstead, the film was able to make creative use of Prague to substitute for Dresden, Germany, before it was firebombed by the Allies (Figure 3.4) and, as we have mentioned, a burning village in the countryside outside of Prague for Dresden after the bombing. Vonnegut and millions of viewers clearly felt that this 'before and after' power of cinema to show us the beauty and the destruction left an even stronger impression of the horror of this incident than did the original novel.

Not all adaptation, however, occurs between literature and drama and the screen. Think of the cinematic versions of comic books from the *Batman* (1989) and *Superman* (1978) films to Warren Beaty's *Dick Tracy* (1990), as well as films made from television shows such as the *Star Trek* films (1982; 1994; 1996; 1998). In these cases, landscapes taken from comic books and old television shows have, as in the examples above, wound up as highly elaborate sets that suggest their sources while adding dimensions of detail and perspective that the original sources could not provide.

Figure 3.4 A village in the Czech Republic became the 'landscape' for the city of Dresden after it had been firebombed in the Second World War in George Roy Hill's *Slaughterhouse Five* (1972) (Source: Museum of Modern Art, New York City)

3.7 From animation to computer graphics and on to Disneyworld: landscapes painted, programmed and planted

Animation and cartoons have existed since the early days of cinema. But it was with Walt Disney's exploration of full animation as opposed to line drawings, and of feature-length narratives as opposed to the five-minute or less cartoons, and of colour instead of black and white that put him on the cutting edge of animated film. Thus in terms of landscapes and cinema, part of the glory of an early feature such as *Snow White and the Seven Dwarfs* (1937) is that we see forests and other landscapes in full colour and in full detail.

Cinema met both stage and landscape gardening, as well as merchandising and big business, however, as the Disney film organisation became the Walt Disney Company, the huge international conglomerate creating first Disneyland then Disneyworld in Orlando, Florida, with EuroDisney following later. As Janet Wasko pinpoints, 'Disney represents the ultimate example of synergism in action' (1995: 210). How do we describe the landscapes of Disneyland, but particularly of Disneyworld? On one level the Disney Corporation has turned a real environment into an animated one, which became known on film but which now allows viewers to become participants and players. 'Landscape gardening' and design thus take on completely different meanings in this new era of corporate playgrounds for kids from two to ninety-two than was meant throughout the history of landscape control. I personally, for instance, have met a number of young couples who became either engaged or married at Disneyworld. Cinema, landscape and an individual's real life intersect and, I suggest, become blurred or tangled, or both, in such a crossing of mediums and domains. When you and your bride or groom can have your photo taken with Mickey Mouse while waiting to get into the Little Mermaid area, what meaning do landscapes come to have?

The digital world of computer graphics, Internet access and websites with amazing digital landscapes is part of the future that is already here. Digital computer graphics have already transformed landscapes in films ranging from the purely 'expressionistic' worlds captured in films such as the Wachowski brothers' *The Matrix* (1999) to the 'digitally enhanced' work in James Cameron's *Titanic* (1997), which helped create a 'landscape of disaster' that mere sets or actual shooting could not. Film-makers have always been able to enhance or subdue landscapes with lens filters, special films sensitive to particular colours, or through the control of colours and shading in the lab. But the computer, and the work of digital cameras and graphics, can completely blur the line between actual and altered landscapes. The future for landscapes on screens and in cyberspace? Technology is changing so swiftly that no simple answer written today will hold up for long. We are already in an age of interactive media in which we can 'walk through' landscapes familiar and strange on computers and television screens equipped with joysticks. Can the delivery of any landscape to us anywhere be far behind?

3.8 Televised landscapes

My focus in this chapter is primarily on cinema, but I should at least acknowledge the large world of television landscapes. On a satirical level, let us nod to Peter Weir's *The Truman Show* (1998) in which a scheming producer (played with sly malice by Ed Harris) creates a show that follows one man, Truman (Jim Carrey), from birth in a completely manufactured landscape that is shown instantly around the world.

As with our question about the blurring of boundaries between Disney films and Disneyworld, so with *The Truman Show*: at what point is real life becoming more like a televised show than anything of real substance? This goes for landscapes as well.

If we had a double feature of television satirical films, the second entry would have to be Hal Ashby's *Being There* (1979). Based on Jerzy Kosinski's novel and script, Peter Sellers gives a memorable performance as a simple man raised in a wealthy man's estate so that he only understands two things: gardening and television. Even more so than *The Truman Show*, therefore, *Being There* combines *the* machine of the twentieth century in many ways with the garden, that civilised version of nature controlled by man. That the film ends with Sellers leaving all behind and walking into a lake, which is neither a garden nor a television show but an eternal body that has religious connotations as well, closes out this tale with a landscape that man cannot control.

Before leaving the broadcasted landscapes behind, however, we should note the ironic movement of television from its early days in the 1950s when live broadcasting meant that 'landscapes' were kept simple, through some 40 years of taped programming – both drama and comedy – almost always staged on sets rather than in nature, with rare exceptions such as the *Northern Exposure* series. Finally, we have come to a period of live 'on location' improvised 'reality' shows including the surprise US hit of 2000, *Survivor* (also shown for the first time in the UK in 2001 with a second series in 2002), and its imitators. Suddenly real landscapes (filtered through television and thus, once more, mediated or 'representational' rather than actual) have returned with a vengeance.

3.9 Landscape and documentary film

Ever since the Lumière brothers amazed audiences by showing them workers leaving a factory or a train arriving in a station, the documentary power of cinema to show real landscapes captured on film has been an important part of what films can, have and will do. Whether we are talking about a family's home movies or home videos, or documentary series for the BBC in Britain or PBS in the United States, or even those rare feature documentaries that make it into the cinemas such as Steve James's *Hoop Dreams* (1994) or Michael Moore's *Roger and Me* (1989), documentary film attracts us because of the promise (not always fulfilled) of being 'true'.

Thus travel or exotic location documentaries, and nature and wild animal films have, since the silent period, fulfilled our curiosities and spurred on our appetites for more. *Kon-Tiki* won the Oscar in 1951 as best documentary, for instance, capturing the excitement and hardship of Thor Heyerdahl's solo raft trip from Peru to Tahiti, thrilling millions around the world with a sense of 'being there', on a seascape that was all the more interesting because we could 'see' and 'hear' it. Even Disney jumped into the animal/nature film business early on, taking the 1953 Oscar for *The Living Desert*, which brought the American western desert to life in a way that westerns never could or would.

Film-makers and students of film have always been aware, even when audiences have not, that no documentary is totally objective: someone always chooses what to shoot and how, and such a process implants to one degree or another, a perspective on the material, the characters, the landscapes shot. Furthermore, documentaries have often been faked for one reason or another. This is true even of classics like Robert Flaherty's

Nanook of the North (1922), which tracks the life of Eskimos (Inuits) in the frozen Arctic. Flaherty is rightfully praised for documenting an Eskimo family's life. But as William T. Murphy observes, 'Flaherty carefully selected his "cast" and directed them to "play" their roles' (1997: 681), even when those roles – such as hunting for polar bears – had not been carried out for more than 30 to 50 years. Be that as it may, the Arctic as landscape and locale was real and that was a large part of the selling point for this and so many documentaries: we respect that the film-maker 'went there'.

3.10 Landscaping cinematic realities

Few films have had a landscaping credit to them, but this chapter would not be complete if I did not mention several films that do have such a credit. I am speaking of Victor Fleming's *Gone with the Wind* (1939), Sidney A. Franklin's *The Good Earth* (1937), George Cukor's *Romeo and Juliet* (1936) and Richard Boleslawski's *The Garden of Allah* (1936), which all had landscapes and gardens designed by Florence Yoch. Yoch was a natural, it turned out, for such a job for she had designed the gardens for the homes of many of the studio executives and actors in Hollywood. A list of her projects includes the homes of William S. Hart, Cecil B. DeMille, Howard Hawks, David Selznick, Jack Warner and George Cukor (Yoch, 1989).

It's hard to imagine a more perfect match between landscape gardening and cinema than this inspirational individual, Florence Yoch, who was able to move freely between both worlds, influencing each. Yoch (1890–1972) was simply 'one of the most original and versatile landscape architects of the twentieth century' (Yoch, 1989: 1).

For *Gone with the Wind*, producer Selznick wanted to capture Scarlett's return to her ruined plantation, Tara, as a return to a 'lost Eden' (Yoch, 1989: 104). To carry this out, Yoch did research in Georgia to study the kinds of plants and trees that are typical of the area, and then figured out how to use Californian greenery to help recreate this atmosphere and landscape. According to James J. Yoch:

> The finished product became photogenic through landscaping devices that Yoch had used throughout her work to dramatize the facades of houses. Huge trees frame Tara's porch. As she had arranged similar in Selznick's own garden, she did not make them simply symmetrical but balanced masses against each other. Continuing this informal poise in other parts of the composition, a crape myrtle on the right side of the porch answers the large vine clambering up a pillar on the left. Trees seem to flourish behind the house and shade the roof. The rough edged drive rolls lazily up to the side of the house, and a low hill rather than the smoother lawns of suburbia, lies in front. These relaxed shapes and plantings give Tara the grace of refined country life.
>
> (1989: 107)

What a pleasure to imagine Yoch at work 'on the set', and her example highlights one reason for writing this chapter: the full history of landscaping and cinema has yet to be written!

3.11 Fade out in a landscape

Japanese master film-maker Akira Kurosawa's eight-part 1990 film made late in his life, *Akira Kurosawa's Dreams*, presents a multitude of different landscapes ranging from a breathtaking shot of cherry orchards in bloom to dark mountains full of the dark smoke of an ongoing war. Two landscapes in particular are worth mentioning in more detail.

In one episode, a young Japanese student (male), looks at Van Gogh's original late painting, *Wheat Field With Crows* (1890) in a museum. As he studies the landscape in Van Gogh's painting, the camera tracks forward to the painting so that Van Gogh fills the frame. At that moment, the painting 'comes to life' and we are in a 'real' wheat field in southern France (captured, of course, on film!). But that is not the end: our Japanese student now enters the frame and walks along a country road until he actually meets Van Gogh (played with playful amusement by American director Martin Scorsese). A conversation about art begins.

What has Kurosawa done to and with us as viewers? He has playfully and cleverly acknowledged the 'sliding' influence between the art of painting and cinema, as well as between Europe and Japan. For Van Gogh himself was greatly influenced by Japanese art and so it is only fitting that Kurosawa reverse the homage in his own film with the young Japanese student. But even more simply, Kurosawa pays tribute to the power of film to 'enter' any landscape it wishes, and to find characters and stories we as audiences will follow.

At the end of his *Dreams*, Kurosawa returns to a natural landscape: a waterwheel spinning by a river as a funeral goes by. The young Japanese student watches as an old villager joins the funeral, which has become a joyful celebration of liberation rather than of grief – much like a New Orleans jazz funeral – and then goes on his way following his path beyond the river. The final shot, however, is of the river. That landscape that goes on and on as the human parade comes by, lingers and passes on. As in Ozu's *Tokyo Story*, Kurosawa reminds us that, beyond cinema and art and even human life, landscapes endure. FADE OUT.

Now do this . . .

1. Watch Buster Keaton's *Sherlock Jr* and list the different shots, saying what landscapes are depicted, in the scene described at the start of this chapter. Discuss more fully the humour 'editing landscapes' in Keaton's

comedy. Then, using a video camera, make your own 'montage of changing landscapes', aiming similarly for humour. Choose whatever 'inappropriate' behaviour winds up being enacted in each shot. Do you have someone jump on a skateboard only to land in a river, or sitting down on a lawn chair only to collapse on to a highway? Your choice! For best effect, do this exercise with a partner and present all videos during an agreed-upon presentation class.

2. Watch one of Theo Angelopoulos's films, such as *Eternity and a Day* (1998) or *Landscape in the Mist* (1988), and write about the use of landscape in each to depict both a 'real' and a 'mythical' landscape. Make your own video in which either characters from clearly different historical periods enter the same frame or in which a 'blank screen' is set up to evoke a powerful landscape and action off-camera.

3. Watch at least three of John Wayne's westerns, made with both John Ford and Howard Hawks, and write a short paper comparing the relationship between the western landscape and Wayne's character in each film.

4. Study *Monty Python and the Holy Grail* carefully for its mixture of zany humour but 'real' Scottish landscape. Make your own short video comedy using the landscape of your own area to good advantage. Like the Pythons, recreate a 'historical' period in this short comedy. A western shot in Wales? A Napoleonic battle carried out in Louisiana? Above all else, have fun, and then, of course, have a screening!

5. To a large degree, the kind of landscape represented in a film depends on the genre of the film, as described in this chapter. Choose a film you wish to write about and explain in a written essay or an oral report what genre that film belongs to and thus in what ways landscape is used and, in fact, what kinds of landscapes are depicted. What genre, for instance would you say *The Full Monty* (1997) belongs to and how important is it to show the Sheffield steel mill landscapes and surrounding communities?

6. Documentary film-maker Les Blank made a feature documentary, called *Burden of Dreams* (1982), about the making of Werner Herzog's *Fitzcarraldo*. View both films, and discuss or write about the use of and significance of the landscape in relation to film-making and the film-makers in each. To what degree do Blank's and Herzog's films bring out similar themes and perspectives, and how do they differ in their views of the landscape?

7. View Alain Resnais's documentary about the Holocaust, *Night and Fog* (*Nuit et Bouillard*, 1956), and discuss or write about the effect of seeing the actual landscapes of the concentration camps then and 'now' (1956). Mention how seeing them differs from simply reading an essay or book on the same subject.

8. Adaptation: take a novel in which the landscape is an important element and compare/contrast it with the film version in writing or in

your discussion group. Henry Fielding's *Tom Jones*, for instance, would be a strong candidate as it captures, on paper, much of the English countryside of the eighteenth century. To what degree does Tony Richardson's 1963 film enhance or reduce the role of the landscape in Fielding's work? Put together an oral presentation using clips from at least four films to discuss what you see as various uses of landscapes in feature films. Choose either films from the same director, so you can talk about her/his style, or from the same genre to suggest comparisons and contrasts, or even four films from one geographical area to discuss how that location becomes represented in film and why. How, for instance, is New Orleans seen in four different films, or the British countryside?

9. Do a study (oral report or paper) on *one film* from beginning to end in terms of how landscape is used throughout the film.

Further reading

Arnheim, R. 1958: *Film as Art*. London: Faber & Faber.
Bordwell, D. 1985: *Narration in the Fiction Film*. Madison: University of Wisconsin Press.
Braudy, L. 1977: *The World in a Frame*. Garden City, New York: Anchor Books.
Gombrich, E.H. 1972: *Art and Illusion*. Princeton: Princeton University Press.

Note to Chapter 3

1 This is a point also discussed in Andrew Charlesworth's essay in Chapter 4 of this volume.

4

Landscapes of the Holocaust: Schindler, authentic history and the lie of the landscape

Andrew Charlesworth

> We did our research to guarantee authenticity
> . . . but all we found was dust.

Think of a Nazi death camp, and images from grainy black and white footage or black and white newspaper photographs will almost certainly jump into your head. The footage will be from a distant past; the photos may be contemporary shots. The imagery will, however, be common: barbed wire and electrified fences, watchtowers, a gateway into the camp and possibly a railway line but always black and white images. From the start, our imagery of the Holocaust has been shaped by the newsreel footage of the discovery and liberation of the concentration camps by the Western Allies and the death camps by the Red Army in 1945. The landscapes of the Holocaust that those different troops encountered, and the way they were represented were not the same. The camps in the West seem to present landscapes of hell: tormented and tortured souls wandering through compounds of barbed wire dotted with huge mounds and pits of emaciated dead bodies. This was Dante's Inferno made flesh, an abstract evil embodied. It was only later that it became clear that what was being caught on the newsreel was a landscape of chaos when the terror system had broken down.

In the East a different re-presentation occurred. From the start, what was shown to the public here was deliberately staged. The Soviet troops were shown being welcomed by the prisoners. The liberation was done at an interior gate in Birkenau, the slave labour and death camp in what is now Poland, not at the two infamous gates: the main arch gateway at Birkenau or the 'Arbeit Macht Frei' gate at Auschwitz main camp. In the film more emphasis is put on the nature of the barbaric system. Birkenau is seen from the air with its endless ranks of barracks. The victims of medical experiments are shown posed sometimes in the very laboratories where the experiments took place. Masses of goods confiscated by the Germans are shown. Here the emphasis is not on unreconstructed evil but on the causes of that evil. The footage is edited to show a landscape of modernity and rationality under capitalism's rules gone inevitably wrong, almost seeming to pervert the very name of progress.

When it was still costly to get to Europe from Britain, USA and Israel, and when it was also politically difficult to get behind the Iron Curtain, it was the replaying and reproduction of those images that gave us any sense of the landscapes of the concentration and death camp systems. Those early films had such an impact because they were shown in cinema houses all over the nations of the victorious Allies. In terms of the Holocaust nothing comparable happened until the release in 1993 of Steven Spielberg's *Schindler's List*.

It is important to reiterate that film has been so crucial in the way Holocaust landscapes have been represented. That is why this chapter looks at the most widely known and seen of all Holocaust films, *Schindler's List*. Certainly more people will encounter Holocaust landscapes through that film than will ever travel to Holocaust sites in Germany and eastern Europe.

But why is landscape important to our understanding of the Holocaust? Part of the answer is to be found in another film, Lanzmann's *Shoah* (1985). In one section of the film, Lanzmann interviews Raul Hilberg, the historian, concerning a document recording the transport of Jews to Treblinka death camp. Lanzmann questions Hilberg concerning what is special about this document. Lanzmann says 'Because I was in Treblinka, and to have the two things together, Treblinka and the document . . .'. In other words, I have been to the place of extermination. I have stood in that landscape of farms and fields just as it was when they killed thousands in a day and burnt the bodies. And here is this document, which I can touch. Hilberg as the representative of History says what is special is that this is an authentic document produced by the Germans. Once the survivors are dead it is the only evidence that the Holocaust ever happened. But Hilberg is wrong, and this is Lanzmann's point. The landscape still survives. To make his point he cuts to the bucolic landscape in which the site of the former death camp sits. The landscape is almost in denial as 'the imperviousness of place' dominates (Edholm, 1988: 204). What these sometimes idyllic, bucolic landscapes do is to provide the antidote to the landscapes of the liberated camps: here is colour in both landscape and skyscape, ordinariness, life going on. The image works against our attempts to grasp that genocide on such a scale happened in such places. And yet they did and those ordinary landscapes should reaffirm that the deeds were done primarily by ordinary men. By their enigmatic quality those landscapes can make us wary of explanations of what happened that are cut and dried. It may be significant that Spielberg has always said that he can only see the landscape of Auschwitz in black and white, and eschews colour for all of the Holocaust scenes in *Schindler's List* (Shandler, 1997: 156).

4.1 Spielberg's list

In *Schindler's List* Spielberg seeks to make the Holocaust accessible in a serious form to a mass audience for the first time. That Spielberg succeeds at one level we can perhaps all testify to, with scenes inside cinemas of unprecedented reactions to a film: silences, crying, audiences not wanting to leave the theatre long after the film ended. But I would argue that a price has had to be paid. We need to examine the film critically, particularly as Loshitzky (1997a; 1997b) has asked to what extent has the film's global popularity begun to define the shape and dominant imagery of the historical memory of the Holocaust. My particular purposes in this chapter are to look at how Spielberg strove for authenticity in his use of landscape and how this search for authenticity has added a twist to the recreation and reconstruction mores of representation that hold sway in Holocaust museums and sites. Spielberg's approach raises questions about how the Holocaust is to be re-presented particularly in relation to popular culture, and I attempt to suggest a counter-approach to his.

Dancing on the pages of history

From the film's promotional literature through the film-maker's comments, to the reception by the critics, the dominant theme, as Zelizer (1997: 22) has noted, was one stressing the historical accuracy of the film. Zelizer found one critic who 'proclaimed it to be "more real then reality"'. One of Spielberg's claims to authenticity is in the very act of locating the events in the landscapes where they occurred. In an interview during the filming of *Schindler's List* he stated that:

> I am looking at that town (Krakow) as if it were a stage. A stage that we didn't have to build. We are filming in <u>authentic places</u> where the events depicted in *Schindler's List* really happened. Krakow has presented us with its history and opened its history books for us so that we could dance on their pages.
>
> (Palowski, 1994: 12)

Though there is a certain self-conscious innocence in what Spielberg purports to have happened in selecting the locations for filming, this is a contrivance that Spielberg uses to try to distance his making of *Schindler's List* from all his other films and perhaps from all other films. As Koch (quoted in Loshitzky, 1997b: 104) has argued, Spielberg is not innocent; he knows exactly what he is doing, what he is quoting and what style of film-making he is using. As Loshitzky (1997b: 109) explains, *Schindler's List*, like most Hollywood narratives, is a realistic film but in this case 'the realistic code of the film is recreated in documentary style'. As Shandler (1997) notes, Spielberg consciously strove for a more 'realistic' approach by his use of the black and white newsreel imagery noted above.

What has not been looked at in detail in relation to Spielberg's quoted claim on authenticity and the film's realistic code is the three types of set Spielberg employed whilst filming in Poland. Critics have seemed to take Spielberg and the pre-publicity for the film at its word. Cheyette (1997) talks of Spielberg foregoing the Hollywood studio for the actual landscape of suffering. Even Horowitz (1997: 122), a forthright critic of the film, writes of 'the painstakingly accurate reconstructions of the Krakow ghetto, of the camps at Plaszow and Auschwitz-Birkenau ... [which] invite the viewer to imagine that one is looking at the Holocaust itself'. She further makes the point that the 'close resemblance to the topographies represented helps assert the claim that the scenes depicting Oskar Schindler, Amon Goeth, and others also closely resemble reality'. If that is so, then it is important to read critically the landscapes and topographies of *Schindler's List*.

Putting oneself in the characters' places

The first type of location are the ones where the events actually happened at those places. This is what Andrew Horton in Chapter 3 of this volume describes as 'real landscapes'. The front of the Schindler factory as seen in the film is a slightly modified version of the factory in Lipowa Street as it is today. At one point in the film, the Schindler 'character' is shown outside the apartment the real Schindler occupied, with the Wawel Castle, one of the landmarks of historic and present-day Krakow, clearly visible at the end of the street. This search for the actual places where the events depicted took place leads Spielberg to film Schindler and his mistress at their vantage point on Lasota Hill watching the clearing of the ghetto below, and then to film from that location into the area that was the actual ghetto.

At first it is unclear what Spielberg is striving for. The explanation may have to do with Spielberg's attempt to understand Schindler. A significant number of the scenes at real locations do involve Schindler. One gets the sense that in going to these locations and filming there, Spielberg wanted to get into Schindler's mind. All the real locations where Spielberg films Schindler are non-Jewish locations (the Catholic cathedral, the expropriated factory, the street where his apartment is and the hillside overlooking the ghetto) so here is the Jewish Spielberg attempting to understand the Aryan Schindler through being at these real places in the real Schindler's life. This directorial approach tells us about Spielberg as a Jew wrestling with the enigmatic German Oskar Schindler. Moreover, as we shall see, it is an approach that Spielberg cannot be consistent with against the demands of the Hollywood good guy/bad guy trope that will assert itself even through the very set itself. The enigma of Schindler cannot be allowed to stand; we need to see which side he is on and what motivates him. As we watch the film we are not immediately conscious of why Schindler is being placed in these real locations, but these real places do become a benchmark for Spielberg's construction of other places. They alert us to the malleability of history for purposes of telling a tale, just as in the script and Thomas Keneally's novel real people are synthesised to make characters.

Through the looking glass

Despite what he claimed, Spielberg must have recognised early on in the film's production that he could not always be both truthful to history and give the film the feeling of authenticity. He would have to use what Andrew Horton calls 'substituted landscapes'. These were actual places but not ones where the historical events took place. Spielberg justified his use of these locations in terms of the inauthenticity of the sites where the real events occurred. Such places had been so changed over the preceding 50 years they would have looked anachronistic in the film. For example, the ghetto square in Podgorze has, besides its small-scale commercial development, a large postmodern building dominating it (Palowski, 1994). Spielberg then sought more authentic-looking sites in Krakow. This is a well-tried production device: for 1950s Paris read 1990s Prague in the 1990s television series of Simenon's *Maigret*; for the film version of the musical *Oklahoma!* (1955) the filming was done in Arizona because the former state was regarded as too developed with oil wells. However, in such cases the places and landscapes chosen are not location-specific, they are merely 'sets' that give a period landscape feel. For *Schindler's List* Spielberg chose, in a number of cases, easily recognised locations in the Jewish quarter of Krakow, Kazimierz. Perhaps these are not as easily recognisable as the Wawel Castle but they have become well known from tourist brochures, tourist and professional photographs since at least the early twentieth century. The ghetto square in the film is in fact Szeroka Street in Kazimierz. The registration scene in the ghetto is played out against the background of the well-known profile of the Old Synagogue in Kazimierz. Two of the scenes in the Aktion are done in the courtyard of 12 Jozefa Street, a courtyard that has been photographed on many occasions since the last century. Doneson (1997) is wrong, then, to say there are no visual signs of a Jewish presence in the landscapes of Krakow in the film. They serve, however, to disorientate us rather than remind us of a Jewish presence in Krakow.

So for a number of key scenes in the film, Kazimierz, the old Jewish quarter of Krakow, became the ghetto, when in fact the ghetto was located in the Podgorze district of Krakow on the other side of the river. Spielberg has created a through-the-looking-glass world. This is most strikingly shown in the scene where the Jews of Krakow are moved into the ghetto. Here Spielberg's demand for authenticity of appearance has the extras move from Podgorze over the river bridge into Kazimierz, a reversal of the real direction taken. This is clearly a very different kind of 'dancing on the pages of history' than the reading Spielberg would have us take from his interview quoted above. The events of the Holocaust in Krakow are being re-presented at historically inaccurate sites. For example, some of the ghetto scenes in the film could give the impression that the built environment was much better than it was and hence conditions in the ghetto were better than they were, whereas in fact Podgorze was one of the poorest and most run-down parts of the city, which is one reason why the Germans selected it to be the ghetto.

The landscape never lies

To the third type of sets belong those that Spielberg built at locations in Krakow and at Auschwitz-Birkenau. These are principally the two sets for the camps of Plaszow and Birkenau. Spielberg had wanted to film inside the Auschwitz-Birkenau death camp but the museum authorities refused to allow this. Their experience with previous film and television companies (such as the makers of the film *Triumph of the Spirit* (1989) and the television mini-series of Herman Wouk's *Winds of War* (1983)), they claimed, had not been good, with parts of sets and equipment being left behind long after filming had been completed. Spielberg therefore constructed a film set of the inside of the camp in front of the gatehouse entrance directly outside the camp.

The same problem of obtaining permission to film on the actual site of the Plaszow camp would not have occurred. The site is now an open, unmanaged urban parkland. The camp was dismantled by the Germans in late 1944. Many people who first encounter the site think that it is a 'green lung' near the centre of Krakow; it is 15 minutes by tram from the Rynek, the main square in Krakow, and is surrounded on two sides by high-density social housing. But if gaining permission to use this virtually abandoned site was not a problem why did Spielberg build his set of the camp in the adjacent quarry? McBride (1997) wrongly suggests that it is because of post-war changes at the site. A more likely explanation at first sight is the topography of the site. It is an undulating basin. The choice of the adjacent flat-bottomed quarry could have been made for very practical film-making reasons particularly if one is using all the modern technology associated with a high-cost Hollywood film. Yet, early on, Spielberg had decided to favour hand-held camera techniques to give a documentary feel to a number of scenes. The cost of constructing such a large set at the actual site may have been a factor in choosing the quarry because building huts on steep slopes would have been neither easy nor cheap.

Be that as it may, choosing the adjacent quarry was to mean that Spielberg could invert the topography of the set crucially for one building in the story: Amon Goeth's house, the camp commandant's villa. The actual house is there to this day but Goeth's house sits below the camp. On the film set the house sits above the camp and in a number of scenes Spielberg frames his shot so Goeth's house dominates the scene. The presence of the house is even felt in the closing credits where we see it reflected in a pool of water on the road of broken Jewish tombstones, a road that hardly figures in the finished cut of the film. The brooding presence of the house becomes a metaphor for the apparently total domination of the Jews by the Germans.

But it is more than that. The mansion on the hill is surely a reference back to the Bates mansion, that other house of murderous intent, in Hitchcock's *Psycho* (1960). In the set he built for the Plaszow concentration and slave labour camp we find that Spielberg's flair for referencing back in cinematic terms has not left him despite what he says to the contrary. Again in his interview he claims:

> My problem is I have too much of a command of the visual language ... And certainly not until *Schindler* was I really able to *not* reference other film-makers. I'm always referencing everybody. I didn't do any of that in this movie.
>
> (Brode, 1995: 236)

Goeth looks down from his first-floor balcony on to the camp and contemplates shooting one of the innocent victims below. Mother/Norman Bates watches from the first-floor window waiting for an innocent victim to come in view. In reality Goeth shot from his balcony up into the camp, but for the audience that would not have the same effect; it would not underline Goeth's overbearing power and evil, and the helplessness of his victims. Spielberg has a tale to tell in Hollywood fashion and that tale hangs on the contrasts between Schindler and Goeth. The power of Goeth's evil has to be manifested on the set. *Schindler's List*, much more than Keneally's novel, is a black and white morality tale. Bartov (1997: 49) has similarly commented on this 'heroic, epic struggle between the good guy and the bad guy, cast in true Hollywood fashion' where these two characters tower over all others. What I am arguing is that the sense of the epic struggle and the scale of Schindler's heroic deed is heightened by this house of evil standing above Schindler, the victims and us. At the end of the film, Goeth's house returns in the closing credits to make sure we remember who was the villain of the piece.

Spielberg's flattening of the terrain in his re-presentation of the Plaszow camp itself leads to closed minds in the audience just as much as his staging of a Hollywood morality play does. A concentration camp built on undulating topography with steep slopes is not what we expect. If it would have cost Spielberg a lot of money to construct his set on such terrain, it equally cost the Germans a lot of time and resources to build barracks on such terrain. The question is why they chose to do so. Our imagination then starts to engage with that of the camp's creators. Spielberg misses that opportunity with his audience and reinforces the stereotypical landscape of a concentration camp, rows of aligned barracks on a flat plain stretching to the horizon, a landscape apparently created by either mindless or rigidly efficient automata so unlike ourselves.

4.2 Come and see what man has done

This brings us to the power of Spielberg's film-making, and the consequences that have flowed from viewing Holocaust history and its representation through Spielberg's eyes. Discussing Spielberg's films in general, a number of critics have argued that the danger is that we begin to see the world through his eyes. As Bernstein (1994: 432) has noted, 'Spielberg's movie ... is already beginning to affect the way our culture understands, historically orders, and teaches how the Holocaust should be remembered.' He goes on to argue that such effects 'require a sharp-eyed and unembarrassed resistance'. We will consider how, in Poland, 'Holocaust tourists' begin to see everything through Spielberg's eyes.

Since 1993 *Schindler's List* has become a major shaper of the development of Holocaust tourism in Poland, both in terms of the reproducers and consumers of such sites. First, there has been the development of Schindler tours and, second, the realism trope of the film has entrenched both the way the public consumes and the way the museum authorities reproduce Holocaust sites.

The fact that *Schindler's List* was filmed in Krakow and at nearby Auschwitz-Birkenau was a golden opportunity for tour operators in that region of Poland. Theme parks based on movie studios and featuring movie sets had become big business in the tourist and entertainment industries in the USA, and in Europe recognised tourist honeypots, have been only too ready to develop film tourism when their city had been used in popular films. In Salzburg, for example, visits to places used in the filming of *The Sound of Music* (1965) have become part of the tourist trade. 'Retracing Schindler's Steps', as the adverts in Krakow announce, has now become part of the Krakow tourist scene. But these tours are unlike that based on *The Sound of Music*, where the film and reality are clearly separated out in the mind of the tour operators and the consumer. In that tour there is no attempt to retrace the real story of the Von Trapp family in the places where it took place. In the case of the Schindler tours, however, there is an ambiguous fusing of history trail and cinematic tourism. At all times on the tours the filmed location takes precedence over the authentic historical site.

The fusing of history and story reached its most complete when the tour arrived at the quarry where the Plaszow film set had been built. Here tourists were reassured that they were not stepping down from the tour bus on to actual Jewish gravestones but replicas created for the film. Although all of the huts had gone, bought by a French film company, the barbed wire fences and gates remained. Like the tombstones, they were presented as both the actual set used by Spielberg and as close as visitors could get to what the camp was really like. For the visitors it was so easy to cross from film to history. The quarry has now been flooded by natural processes and the tour no longer goes there. This means, in terms of Plaszow, all the tour operators are left with is the actual site of the Plaszow camp. As we have noted there is little there to see and what is there contradicts the film. In order not to shatter the film's precedence over history the tour takes you to the other side of the camp, well away from the commandant's house. The guides wave their hands vaguely towards the horizon, merely stating that this is the camp and wrongly pointing out Goeth's first house as the house Goeth had specially built, the one we see in the film. The latter house is certainly not shown because it contradicts the image we have of the house in the film. Here, decisively, entertainment takes on the status of history, while through the film, history has become entertainment.

Holocaust history as material for theme park has thus been brought one step nearer through *Schindler's List*. The realism trope that Spielberg adopted has aided those at museum sites such as Auschwitz who have always believed that the only way the public are prepared to consume such sites is through authentic camp furniture and artefacts. Like the tour operators they believe that their livelihoods depend upon there being something there and that that something must be seen as authentic or else the public will not come. This confirms Bresheeth's (1997) argument that the film will act in people's minds as a metatext of historical evidence, displacing the evidence and documentation on which it is based.

Since the release of *Schindler's List* the reconstruction of barracks, watch-towers and the gatehouse at Auschwitz and Auschwitz-Birkenau has accelerated in order to recreate the authentic look of the camp. With each reconstruction and with more people having seen the Holocaust through Spielberg's eyes, the demand for the authentic appears to grow. The blurring of historic site and theme park is being completed with the various reconstructions because the reconstruction is sanitised. The smoke from the crematoria and the smell of burning human flesh is not recreated, nor is the sea of mud that was most of the area of the camp. No wonder, then, that at Birkenau in 1996 some of my students overheard an American couple say, 'What they need now are some dummies around the place in SS uniform.'

4.3 *Ars mons ars*

Art demands of us an imaginative response and an open mind. Spielberg's Holocaust and Holocaust heritage landscapes may well be barriers to a fuller understanding of the Shoah. Art and landscape can tell more truthful tales but only if they are released from the realism trope. These sentiments are echoed by Zelizer (1997: 29) when she quotes Hayden White.

> It may be, as Hayden White has argued, that in discussing the Holocaust we have embraced a limiting paradigm that prefers one type of repre-sentation of the past over others, recognising that 'the kind of anomalies, enigmas, and dead-ends met with in discussions of the representation of the Holocaust are the result of a conception of a discourse that owes too much to a realism that is inadequate to the representation of events'.

If White is right, then how might we move away from that paradigm? I offer two cases from 'high'/popular culture of how this has been done. The first is Richard Jones's production of Wagner's *Ring* at Covent Garden in

1994–96. This was a multilayered and black comedic exploration of the *Ring*. Two aspects from a production that sought to see the work from a post-Holocaust perspective must suffice. First, Nigel Lowery's designs centre around the suburban bourgeois house and it is into these everyday, if somewhat surreal, landscapes that humans step in order to do crimes against their fellow humans. Second, in *Gotterdammerung*, Jones places soldiers who look like ordinary Tommies (British soldiers) in a beer hall setting where they use bullying tactics to ensure they all conform with zeal in the brutal victimisation of Brunnhilde. Here was German art, Browning's *Ordinary Men*, Goldhagen's *Hitler's Willing Executioners*, and Perry and Croft's *Dad's Army* potently combined for a British audience. Auschwitz/atrocity were made very much our patch, something Jones underlined at the start of *Gotterdammerung* by playing the first scene of the opera with the house lights up. We were implicated in everything we were going to see. We were not 'the people in the dark', the passive spectators of Schindler's heroic life up there on the screen. As Horowitz (1997: 138) argues, the audience of *Schindler's List* is never implicated in the moral economy of the film, never prodded to examine its own social and political ethics.

Another artist whose surface belies deeper explorations of the human condition is Hitchcock, particularly in his films *The Birds* (1963) and *Psycho*. Are these films exploring issues that *Schindler's List* fails to do effectively? In *The Birds* Hitchcock chooses to set the terrifying random attacks by the birds in a quiet coastal village against a backdrop of beautiful countryside. These are everyday landscapes but ones that we would rate highly in a landscape evaluation exercise. Here we expect peace and we find ourselves in the midst of terror. The discovery of the mutilated body of Dan Fawcett is all the more horrific because the exterior shots of the farm both before and after the discovery show a beautiful setting (Wood, 1989). The dissonant effect is that realised by Lanzmann in his film of the Holocaust, *Shoah*, where right from the opening the bucolic is juxtaposed with the barbaric. We begin to question everything that we take for granted. Wood has written explicitly about a connection between the death camps and *Psycho*. In 1945 Hitchcock himself accepted a commission to edit a documentary film about the camps that never went beyond the rough-cut stage. As Wood (1989) comments, *Psycho* explores two aspects that are central to our understanding of the Holocaust: the utter helplessness and innocence of the victims, and the fact that human beings, whose potentialities all of us in some measure share, were their tormentors and butchers. Hitchcock does not compartmentalise one from the other; in this highly successful Hollywood film he succeeds where Spielberg fails. As Horowitz (1997) points out, Spielberg never allows his film to develop a complicated sense of the Nazi perpetrator and hence never challenges his audience with questions about what allows ordinary people to commit extraordinarily brutal acts. But it would be a brave teacher who attempted to teach about the Holocaust using *Psycho* when the world knows what an accessible and authentic Holocaust history *Schindler's List* is.

In these examples myths and extraordinary events are set in ordinary places. Contrast this with Spielberg, who gave his most important landscape – the landscape of Plaszow with the dominant commandant's house – almost mythic status. Mass murder was conceived of, ratified, implemented and executed in ordinary landscapes. From leafy suburb to pastoral meadows might be one description of that murderous trajectory. It is only with our hindsighted representation that we map on to these landscapes the extraordinary barbarism that occurred there and expect to see the lie of the landscape reflect the crime. This expectation goes back to those first images on those suburban cinema screens in Britain in the late 1940s. Spielberg plays to those expectations rather than undermines them. But we must resist such attempts to make the place fit the event. Through that resistance we may continue to strive to discover what facilitates, what Lifton refers to as the 'coexistence of the killer self and the decent self' (cited in Horowitz, 1997).

Now do this . . .

1. The obvious directions to send you in are to the video store and to Poland. The latter is the ideal so you can encounter some of the places written about here and, in particular, places like Plaszow where you can 'see' if my arguments about Spielberg's landscapes hold up. The ideal is costly, though you can get to Krakow by bus for under £80 and stay in good, clean accommodation in the very centre of Krakow for £10 per night. You can include a full day trip to Oswiecim, the town where the former camp of Auschwitz is, for £20 and you get to arrive there by train. You should keep a journal of your trip.

2. But let's say that is unfeasible, then watch the video of *Schindler's List*. Again check my arguments as you watch the various landscapes Spielberg re-presents. You can follow a sequence of Schindler landscapes in the photographs provided on the following pages (Figures 4.1–4.10). The captions should let you come to your own conclusions. You could also read Keneally's novel *Schindler's Ark* and see how he uses the landscape of the ghetto, Schindler's factory and the Plaszow camp in a less didactic way than Spielberg does. You should also find Schindler to be a more ambiguous and ambivalent character in the novel.

3. Landscapes of the Holocaust have not been written about in great detail. We have already mentioned in the main body of the text the film *Shoah* directed by Claude Lanzmann. He describes it as 'a topographic film'. Its nine-and-a-half-hour length, with a lot of subtitling, makes it daunting. It is a film that you either love or hate. Most cities have a Jewish resource centre where you could borrow the video. The most accessible part to start with is the last section of Part II of the film, dealing principally with the testimony of Rudolf Vrba and Filip Müller on the fate of the Czech family camp. The enigmatic landscape of the

Auschwitz-Birkenau death camp is used to striking effect against the text of the testimony. You might like to sketch out a 'storyboard' of the shots of the landscape matched against the testimony, and then write about the ability of landscape both to support and underline the narrative and also to erode the narrative in terms of belief.

Figure 4.1 The Old Synagogue, which is on Szeroka Street in Kazimierz, appears in the background of a number of shots in the film of the ghetto square (Photo: Andrew Charlesworth)

Figure 4.2 Ciemna Street, Kazimierz: a number of scenes in the ghetto were shot here, including the encounter between Pfefferberg and Goeth (Photo: Andrew Charlesworth)

Figure 4.3 Schindler's factory in Lipowa Street, Podgorze: this is the actual factory and only needed a few adjustments on the outside to recreate Deutsche Emailwaren Fabrik (Photo: Andrew Charlesworth)

Figure 4.4 Podgorze from Lasota Hill: the actual ghetto filmed by Spielberg from this spot (Photo: Andrew Charlesworth)

Figure 4.5 The remains of the film set of the Plaszow camp in the Liban quarry (Photo: Andrew Charlesworth)

Figure 4.6 The film set of the Plaszow camp as seen from above the Liban quarry, April 1993; Goeth's house can be seen at the back of the set (Photo: Andrew Charlesworth)

Figure 4.7 Detail of the set with Goeth's house (Photo: Andrew Charlesworth)

Figure 4.8 The site of the Plaszow camp today (Photo: Andrew Charlesworth)

Figure 4.9 Amon Goeth's house as it is today (Photo: Andrew Charlesworth)

Figure 4.10 Goeth's view of the camp from his balcony (Photo: Andrew Charlesworth)

Further reading

Charlesworth, A. 1994: Contesting places of memory: the case of Auschwitz. *Society and Space* **12**, 579–93.

Cole, T. 1999: Oskar Schindler and Auschwitz, in Cole, T., *Images of the Holocaust*. London: Gerald Duckworth.

Hartman, G.H. 1996: The cinema animal, in Hartman, G.H. (ed.) *The Longest Shadow: In the Aftermath of the Holocaust*. Bloomington: Indiana University Press.

Young, J.E. 1993: *The Texture of Memory: Holocaust Memorials and Meaning*. New Haven: Yale University Press.

5

Landscape in the Jewish imagination

Leah Garrett

The Jewish people have always had a unique conception of both landscape and geography. Until 1948, and the establishment of the State of Israel, for the most part the Jews saw themselves as temporary exiles in other people's countries. In 587 BCE the Jewish people were exiled from the Land of Israel by the Babylonians. The cultural belief was that at some point God would return them there. The terms for the exile include 'diaspora' and 'Galut'. 'Diaspora' is a word which suggests that the Jews are away from their home, the Land of Israel. 'Galut' is a Jewish religious term which intimates that God played a role in the Jewish exile.

The notion of Galut was generated from the Bible where exile was one of the curses on the people of Israel for not following God's commandments:

> The Lord will scatter you among all the people from one end of the earth to the other, and there you shall serve other gods, wood and stone, whom neither you nor your ancestors have experienced. Yet even among those nations you shall find no peace, nor shall your foot find a place to rest. The LORD will give you there an anguished heart and eyes that pine and a despondent spirit. The life you face shall be precarious; you shall be in terror, night and day, with no assurance of survival.
>
> (Deuteronomy 28: 64)[1]

The quotation from the Bible suggests that God had played a role in the exile of the Jews, and therefore God would eventually bring them back to the Land of Israel. After the exile, the Jewish people slowly spread out around the world to places like Egypt, Europe and Asia, where they lived as a minority group among local populations. For Jews around the world, the idea of exile and return became a central vision of Jewish selfhood. Diaspora Jews used the motif of exile and punishment, with its implied redemption and return, as a way to find meaning in the diaspora. Often living in lands where they had few political or civil rights, and where they faced outbreaks of anti-Jewish violence, the idea that God was watching over the Jewish people gave the temporary exile a larger purpose and was a means to find comfort in their situation.

Moreover, Judaism became rooted in ideas of exile. Before the Jewish exile in 587 BCE and the destruction of the Second Temple in 70 CE, religious life was centred around the Temple in Jerusalem where Jewish priests would conduct animal sacrifices. Once living in the diaspora, the Jews adapted their religion so that it was mobile and could be brought anywhere they lived, rather than being centred in Jerusalem. The belief in a return to Jerusalem and a rebuilding of the Temple by God once the Messiah came, nevertheless remained a central feature of Judaism in exile, called Rabbinic Judaism. The great book of Judaism in exile, the Mishnah (200 CE), documented the laws of Jewish life in order to institute a set pattern of beliefs and practices for a people without their own land. In this book, much discussion is devoted to the religious practices of the Jews before 70 CE when their religion centred around 'the Temple' where, as mentioned above, animal sacrifices were the primary form of religious observance. Once the Jews were in exile, and the Temple destroyed, animal sacrifice was replaced by prayer. However, the Mishnah, written in exile for Jews in exile, laid out the laws of sacrifice as though the Temple still existed. This was done to remind the Jews of their Temple, and that some day the Messiah would come and it would be rebuilt. When this occurred, the Jews would need to know how to properly conduct religious services. The Mishnah documents this for them so it will never be forgotten.

The ways that Jews rooted themselves in lands that they considered to be exilic locations were manifold and included, to differing degrees: teaching their children the local languages along with Jewish ones, be it Spanish, Arabic, Polish or Russian; following the local laws; serving in the army (although in some cases this was forced, as in Russia in the nineteenth century); and interacting with their Christian or Arab neighbours. It also involved holding political offices such as in medieval Spain; adapting their cuisine, while keeping it kosher, to the local foods; assimilating, converting or intermarrying with locals (although this was a small number); having their music, literature and dress style take on aspects of the surrounding culture.

At the same time, they continued to keep a distinct culture, at least before the twentieth century. This could include following Jewish dietary and lifestyle laws, such as keeping kosher and resting on the Sabbath, and continuing to circumcise their sons even in nations such as Britain where it was rarely done. In addition it included following their religion; developing the Jewish languages of Yiddish (based on German), Ladino (based on Spanish) and Judeo-Arabic, while continuing to use Hebrew as the holy language; seeing their spiritual home as the Land of Israel; discouraging intermarriage in their children; giving their children Jewish names; sending their children to Jewish schools; and teaching their children a deep love for Judaism and Jewish culture.

Contemporary Jews who come from this tradition relate to landscape and geography in multiple ways. For Zionist Jews, or Jews who support a

Jewish homeland regardless of where they currently live, the establishment of Israel in 1948 means that the diaspora is over and that the Jews have returned home. For some ultra-orthodox Jews, in contrast, the Galut will only be over once the Messiah comes (the Jews do not believe that Jesus is the Messiah) and returns all the Jews of the world to the Land of Israel; for them, the State of Israel does not mark the end of the exile. For other Jews, the land where they live now – be it Britain, Ireland, America or Morocco – is their home, and the diaspora and Galut are cultural notions that are basic to Judaism, but their 'home' is where they currently live.

Whether or not Jews are Zionists, ultra-orthodox or secular, the idea of 'home' and 'away', or 'centre' (the Land of Israel) and 'diaspora' (England, America, Africa) has given them unique ideas of landscape and geography. For most Jews before the establishment of the State of Israel in 1948, life was conducted on a dual terrain: the real space where one lived in the present, and the mythical locale of the Land of Israel. (The Land of Israel is often called 'Eretz Yisrael' and refers to the biblical Land of Israel. In contrast Israel refers only to the nation established in 1948.) Some of the questions this brings up are as follows.

- Where and what did constitute home – one's present home or the mythical place of return to Eretz Yisrael?
- How does the imagined landscape of Eretz Yisrael relate to the real world the Jews are living in?
- How does the Jewish idea contrast with non-Jewish models?

This dual positioning meant that notions of landscape, geography, home, away, the road, public and private, were understood in a different way than for non-Jews. For example, for many non-Jews, 'home' means where one lives now – London, Wales or Belfast, say – and 'away' means at university, on holiday, at a neighbour's house. For the Jewish people until the twentieth century, and for many still, 'home' means *both* where one lives now *and* the imagined place of the Land of Israel, while 'away' can mean away from one's house or away from the Land of Israel. This Jewish idea of landscape is best expressed by the poet Judah Halevi (1080–1142) who wrote nearly 1000 years ago, 'In the East is my heart, and I dwell at the end of the West.' In other words, while living in the 'diaspora' where he dwells, his heart and soul are in the East, in the Land of Israel. This idea is reiterated every time Jews pray as they turn their bodies towards Israel and ask that God will return the Jews there. Or, at the end of the Passover meal, when they say 'Next year in Jerusalem.'

5.1 The Jewish idea of landscape

A central place to examine the Jewish idea of landscape is in Jewish litera-ture. For the Jews, the 'people of the book' who often saw themselves, and were treated as, temporary residents of others' lands, literature has always played an extremely large role in the culture. Without their own political system, government, prime minister, monarch or president, much of Jewish culture was tied not to the institutions of government, but was instead transportable as books. In place of a constitution such as the Americans have, the Jews had the Ten Commandments. In place of an established judicial system specific to the country where they lived, the Jews followed the laws written in books such as the Talmud (although they were also required to obey the local laws). In place of historical documents that describe the lives of kings, queens, presidents and military leaders, the Jews of the world have books that describe, often in wondrous terms, the lives, beliefs and actions of their great Rabbis. More so than with most peoples, to investigate the culture of the Jews means to turn to their literature.

In literature, geography is a construct. While London is a real, physical space in the world, London in a literary work is described according to the author's imagination. Charles Dickens's and Virginia Woolf's London differ not only because they describe a London of different eras, but because it is affected by their personal viewpoint. Although London will suggest the same area and will probably provoke in the reader a series of similar impressions, the authors are giving us descriptions of the city that are mediated by their personal viewpoints.

When we consider the landscapes of literature, it is very important to be aware of the way that power structures affect the author and the people the author describes, be they African-Americans in the American South, Indians in India during colonisation, non-whites in South Africa during apartheid or Jews in Europe. Instead of assuming (as we do in much European literature) that public spaces are unrestricted areas and that the landscape is equally free for all to partake of, we should remember that for many groups the lands they live in and move through are neither safe nor free. We need to be aware of the unique problems that certain travellers have to face and how this influences the stories they tell and how we should read them. bell hooks writes of being a black woman travelling alone through white America that 'to travel, I must always move through fear, confront terror' (hooks, 1992: 344) Traditional Jewish travellers (which is to say Jews who dressed 'Jewishly') moving alone through eastern Europe must also have felt themselves to 'move through fear, confront terror'. This basic fact of Jewish geography must be acknowledged to understand how landscapes were described.

The general trend of European literature has been instead to assume that all people could partake of bourgeois travel (or was only interested in describing the class, gender and race of people who could), and therefore often excluded other types of travel and travellers from consideration. For the Jews who were excluded from 'good' forms of travel, which the scholar James Clifford calls 'heroic, educational, scientific, adventurous, ennobling', Jewish travel tended to be more a matter of necessity than a free, positive choice. Instead of the Sentimental Tour of the eighteenth century, in Jewish literature we have travelling merchants on the move for economic gain. In place of tourism, adventure and science, we have Jewish travel resulting from necessity: the search for better economic opportunities, or forced migrations. In Yiddish literature of travel, the displaced family or the travelling salesman replaces the tourist. Because of this altered concept of movement, the landscape itself becomes not one's large home, but instead a place one must pass over out of necessity and often at some risk.

5.2 Landscapes of exile and return

To interpret Jewish images of landscape and geography, the imagined terrain of exile and return must be sketched; a European map must be replaced by a Jewish one in which both exile and the Land of Israel are home, although one is the physical home, and the other the spiritual one. Therefore a two-dimensional map is inadequate to portray the Jewish notion of geography before the twentieth century because home was not simply where one's house or family was. Home was both the here and now, and the 'not-yet-home' with one's sideward glance toward Eretz Yisrael. For some, this notion of 'not-yet-home' continues to this day, as in Simon Schama's *Landscape and Memory*, where he recounts the following conversation:

> I remembered someone in a Cambridge common room pestering the self-designated 'non-Jewish Jew' and Marxist historian Isaac Deutscher, himself a native of this country [Lithuania], about his roots. 'Trees have roots', he shot back, scornfully, 'Jews have legs.' And I thought, as yet another metaphor collapsed into ironic literalism, Well, some Jews have both and branches and stems too.
>
> (1995: 29)

Yet after a painful visit to the Lithuanian town of his family's origins and the destroyed Jewish cemetery, Schama changes his notion of Jews having 'branches' stating 'perhaps Deutscher was right, I thought. Trees have roots; Jews have legs' (1995: 36).

This is a vision of rootlessness, and either no home (as for Schama) or a dual home. Any map of Jewish literary consciousness up to 1948 must thus include a rendering of Galut geography where 'away' means being away from both one's house or family and away from Eretz Yisrael. Some examples of this mapping could be as shown in Figure 5.1.

In the map on the left in the figure, Eretz Yisrael is a large shadow over daily life in eastern Europe. In the middle map, life in eastern Europe is paralleled by life in Eretz Yisrael, but on a much larger scale. And in the map on the right, the two spheres of Eretz Yisrael and eastern Europe exist at the same time but in different locales.

Let me give you an illustration of how this Jewish mapping shows up in literature. The example is from a novella that the great writer Sholem

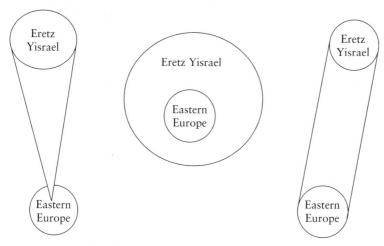

Figure 5.1 Jewish cultural visions of place

Yankev Abramovitsh (commonly known as Mendele Moycher-Sforim or Mendele the Book Peddler) (1835–1917) wrote in 1878 in Yiddish called *Kitser masoes Binyomin Hashlishi* (*The Brief Travels of Benjamin the Third*). Yiddish is a language that uses the same alphabet as Hebrew but has a grammatical system based on German (although approximately one-third of the words are Hebrew, Russian or local terms from the places where the Jews live). It developed in the thirteenth century, and was used primarily in eastern Europe and brought by Jewish immigrants at the end of the nineteenth century to places such as the United States, Canada, England and Australia. Where Hebrew was the Jewish holy language until the establishment of the State of Israel, when it became the daily language of Israelis, Yiddish was used in the home, at work, in school. Yiddish was also the language of a rich literature that was wiped out when the Nazis murdered many of the Yiddish-speaking Jews of the world. Nowadays, the Jews who still use Yiddish as a living language are predominantly ultra-orthodox. They believe that Hebrew should not be a day-to-day language as it is in Israel, because it is only for holy purposes and therefore, they instead use Yiddish as their secular language.

Mendele Moycher-Sforim is considered the 'grandfather' of Yiddish literature. Part of his greatness as a writer is his ability to honestly portray the daily life of shtetl Jews ('shtetl' is the term for the Jewish villages of eastern Europe before the Holocaust) in highly humorous ways. He wrote in a variety of styles. *Kitser masoes Binyomin Hashlishi* is a Yiddish retelling of Miguel Cervante's *Don Quixote*. In Mendele's version, Don Quixote and Sancho Panza become Benjamin the Third and Senderl. They are shtetl Jews who undertake their travels in order to find the lost tribes of Israel. In the following excerpt from the novella, we see a clear presentation of the Jewish concept of landscape, where the diaspora is a temporary home far from the Land of Israel as the real 'home'. The passage describes how the Jews of Benjamin's Polish town, Tuneyadevka, react to the arrival of a date from the Land of Israel:

> Once, it so happened, someone arrived in Tuneyadevka with a date. You should have seen the town come running to look at it. A Bible was brought to prove that the very same little fruit grew in the Holy Land. The harder the Tuneyadevkans stared at it, the more clearly they saw before their eyes the River Jordan, the Cave of the Patriarchs, the tomb of Mother Rachel, the Wailing Wall. They bathed in the hot springs of Tiberias, climbed the Mount of Olives, ate dates and carobs, and stuffed their pockets with holy soil to bring back to Tuneyadevka. There was many a heartfelt exclamation and damp eye on that day.

'For a moment', Benjamin has recalled of that occasion, 'the whole of Tuneyadevka was in the Land of Israel' (Abramovitsh, 1996: 307).

In the story, the date arrives at a time when the Jews of the town are undergoing increased anti-Jewish persecution. The date offers them a means to retreat into a fantasy world where they all live safely in the Land of Israel. The passage also clearly demonstrates how the landscape of Eretz Yisrael was laid over the day-to-day landscape of eastern Europe to such an extent that it became as 'real' as the 'real' world of eastern Europe. In the extract cited above, one sees how the Land of Israel of the shtetl Jew's imaginings was the land as described in the Jewish Bible, rather than the physical space as it existed during the time frame of the story.

Images of the 'road' in Jewish literature also clearly show the Jewish notion of landscape. In the Jewish landscape as it is represented in Yiddish literature, 'the road' snakes its way through the surrounding landscape and suggests two distinct ideas. The first is the 'territorial' road as the physical path that crosses the land where the Jews live. The second is the 'extra-territorial' eternal Jewish road of the Galut, and the road becomes a means to symbolise how the path of the Jews, like the path of the road, is marked by 'wandering'. For the Jews, the mythic road as Galut intersected with the territorial, physical road, making the Jew move through both historical and mytho-poetic time and space.

While Jews often portray their own history as that of a wandering people, this is different from the negative 'Christian' image of the Wandering Jew. The Wandering Jew was a Jerusalem shoemaker, Ahasuerus, who was cursed by Christ, and as a result became a repentant Christian forced to wander the earth until the Second Coming. The Wandering Jew is a 'dignified figure' but this dignity is a double-edged sword: the Wandering Jew's debasement can only become dignity through Christianity. The Wandering Jew is similar to the 'mammy' figure of the wise, gentle, black woman servant of the American South or the 'Noble Savage' of eighteenth-century European literature. This is a figure marking

out the total disenfranchisement of a people, and the need of the disenfran-
chiser to recreate what they have done into a positive image.

An emblematic road tale in Yiddish is Mendele Moycher-Sforim's *Fishke der Krumer* (*Fishke the Lame*) (1888),[2] which tells of a crippled man who is manipulated into a marriage, and then forced to go on the road with a pack of poor, scam-artist beggars. In both *Fiske der Krumer* and *Kitser masoes Binyomin Hashlishi* (Abramovitsh, 1996), the protagonists are wandering beggars, and the Jews of the towns they move through generally provide them with assistance of some type. By so doing, in this literature the indi-vidual shtetl becomes a Jewish world shtetl where Christians are occasion-ally encountered (usually in a comic way), but where all roads lead into and out of a predominantly Jewish space, and where the greatest dangers are from corrupt fellow Jews. In Yiddish literature, we find numerous examples of the writers making the lands of Poland, Russia and the Ukraine into Jewish lands with very few Christians. Moreover, the land itself is described in a 'Jewish' way, thus a tree may be written about as 'shaking like a lulav' (a lulav is a Jewish ritual object), or a Polish mountain may be described as looking like Mount Ararat from the Bible. In numerous writings of pre-twentieth-century Jewish literature, the landscape is transformed into a safe space for Jews, which is described using Jewish cultural terms. Perhaps the writers did this as a fantasy that the Jews had power over their own destiny in these lands, rather than being at the mercy of local Christians.

In European fiction, characters are generally defined by the author as figures representative of either the 'native' or the 'alien' to the land, and even in some texts the character will be both. For example, in Robert Louis Stevenson's *Kidnapped* (1886), the protagonist, David Balfour, at the begin-ning of the narrative is happily domesticated and a native at home in his lowland Scotland. He speaks the language, his world is peaceful, he takes for granted the landscape around him because he knows it so well. However, once he is kidnapped, and escapes by making his way to an island and then the mainland, he shifts into a figure of the alien even though the terrain he is travelling over is still Scotland. Now it is Highland Scotland and the language is no longer familiar (it is Gaelic rather than English), the terrain is new (at first he gets brutally sick on the island he has escaped to by eating raw shellfish, because everything is so foreign he does not realise his 'island' is separated from the mainland by a shallow channel he can walk over at low tide) and he is thrust into the role of an alien within his own country (of course, this is intensified by being on the run from kidnappers). Everything is strange, new and scary because his perspective has changed from that of a native to that of an alien.

However, regardless of the series of hardships David Balfour must face in *Kidnapped*, he believes that things will eventually be sorted out once he returns home because there is a fixed, safe order to his nation. As a member of this nation, the police or governmental officials will eventually make things right for him. While he may now be on alien terrain, the nation is his and he is a part of it. In European literature the dangers in travel tended to run the gamut from robbers (*Ivanhoe*, 1819) to abusive adults (*David Copperfield*, 1848), yet the protagonist remains for the most part a member of the nation rather than an Other to the nation. For Jews in eastern Europe, the notion of the native and the alien was utterly altered. There was none of the sense of security felt in *Kidnapped* by David Balfour, who knows that all will be made right in the end. For the Jew, the police and the officials were often representatives of dangers rather than one's fellow nationals.

What stands out about Jewish literature before the twentieth century is how infrequently external landscapes are described. In fact, there are remarkably few realistic descriptions of natural scenery of any type. The ability to present a positive picture of nature often relies on a pride in the land, and the natural world we do have described positively is not the here and now of eastern Europe, but the other place of Eretz Yisrael, which is envisioned in highly poetic, positive terms.

Following the European literary tradition, one would assume that the road would thus likely stand as the opposite in Jewish literature to images of the shtetl. Where the shtetl was the mythical space of the Jewish collective, when Yiddish writers instead chose as their setting the land beyond the shtetl, they would represent it in a more 'realistic' way and represent Jews in contact with non-Jews. The road would be the place on which to show the relationship between Jews and the broader world, and would be the arena in which to portray individuals in confrontation with outside socio-political forces. Instead, Yiddish writers often described the road in the same way as the shtetl, as a Jewish space.

Although the road in Yiddish literature was a Judaised space like the shtetl, it was different from the shtetl in a number of ways. Where the shtetl was described by male writers as the domestic or 'female', the road was the terrain of the male. This we see most emblematically in the Yiddish writer Sholem Aleichem's novel *Menakhem-Mendl* (2002), where the husband's letters are from a series of towns and cities beyond the shtetl, and the wife's letters are rooted in the static, yet safe, domestic shtetl. Moreover, the shtetl reflects a communal narrative, while tales of the road are often about Jewish travellers alone or in pairs.

While the idea of 'home' and 'away' changed with the establishment of Israel in 1948 when many Jewish Zionists made Israel the Jewish home, the event that most radically altered the Jewish conception of landscape was the Holocaust. By 1945, with the murder of six million Jewish women, men and children, and the destruction of the shtetls of eastern Europe, 'home' and 'away' took on radically different forms as demonstrated in the work of the great Hebrew writer Yehuda Amichai (2000), here in his poem entitled *Jewish Travel: Change is God and Death is His Prophet*:

Yehuda Halevi wrote, 'In the East is my heart, and I dwell at the end of the West.'

That's Jewish travel, that's the Jewish game of hearts between east and west,
between self and heart, to and fro, to without fro, fro without to,
fugitive and vagabond without sin. An endless journey, like the trip
Freud the Jew took, wandering between body and mind, between
mind and mind, only to die between the two.
Oh, what a world this is, where the heart is in one place and the body
in another (almost like a heart torn from a body and transplanted).
I think about people who are named for a place where they have
never been
and will never be. Or about an artist who draws a man's face
from a photograph because the man is gone. Or about the migration
of Jews, who do not follow summer and winter, life and death
as birds do, but instead obey the longings of the heart. That's why
they are so dead, and why they call their God *Makom*, 'Place'.
And now that they have returned to their place, the Lord has taken up
wandering to different places, and His name will no longer be Place
but Places, Lord of the Places.
Even the resurrection of the dead is a long journey.
What remains? The suitcases on top of the closet,
that's what remains.

(Amichai, 2000: 117–18)

In this quotation, Amichai first presents the Jewish landscape as I have described it earlier, where the Jews in the 'diaspora' live in one land, while yearning for another. He then shifts the poem to describe the Jewish landscape in a post-Holocaust, post-Zionist world where the binary of 'real' Europe and 'mythic' Eretz Yisrael shifts. Before the Holocaust, as I have discussed, 'real' Europe exists simultaneously with the imagined Eretz Yisrael of Jewish longing. After the Holocaust, as Amichai's poem documents, Europe becomes the mythic space, the landscape of remembrances peopled by the ghosts of the murdered. The 'suitcases on top of the closet' are all that remain when the Jews of Europe are dead. Now, in this new world, Israel becomes the 'real' land of wars, schools and living nationalism, while Europe is the place of shadows of the ghosts of the once living. It is a place of remembrances but devoid of Jews. After the Holocaust, the place where most Jews had lived before, eastern Europe, is for many a ghost town of memories of the dead. The Jewish life there has been wiped out and is turned from a home into a graveyard. Yiddish as well is wiped out.

Nowadays 'home' for many Jews is either Israel, where they feel they have returned, or places such as Britain and the United States. Many Jews consider these places a 'diaspora' while they hope to return eventually to the Land of Israel, while others believe these places are their permanent home.

5.3 Conclusion

In conclusion, the Jewish idea of landscape and geography is influenced greatly by the notion of 'diaspora' and 'home'. Nowadays millions of Jews live in Israel, a land many only dreamed about. There the ideal of Israel is confronted with a constant struggle to assert what Israel is in terms of its borders. The rhetoric of Zionism often intermingles with the old dreams of the Land of Israel, making many religious Israelis reluctant to return any of the land 'of the Bible' to the Palestinians. For Israeli Jews, the ideal meets the reality, and the landscape takes on both aspects: a space documented in the Bible and 'the Jewish nation'. The issues of nationalism are especially complicated because Israel has only been in existence for little more than half a century. In the lifetime of many of today's Jews, Israel has attempted to create roots in a place where few Jews lived before the first waves of mass Jewish immigration in 1900. This has meant that there is still a great deal of shakiness and uncertainty about the ramifications of the new, young, nation.

In the 'diaspora', the idea of the Land of Israel intersects for many with a pride in the land in which they live. Yet even in nations such as Britain and the United States, where many Jews have moved from being on the margins of society and facing regular anti-Semitism to become part of the mainstream, there are, for many, residual feelings of insecurity about whether or not they are fully accepted members of the society. This shift from marginalisation to centrality has altered again the Jewish concept of land and space.

The notion of the Land of Israel, which gave so many Jews in exile spiritual sustenance has become complicated by the reality of the State of Israel, a state that some Jews feel ambivalence towards because of its actions as regards the Palestinians. Some Jews in the 'diaspora' see the State of Israel as the Jewish homeland but have complicated feelings about the level of their commitment. Others feel a deep attachment to a nation in which they do not live but nevertheless call their own, and they show this by supporting Israel with money, intellectually and spiritually with little question. They think of themselves as having a stake in Israel, particularly since the Israeli 'law of return' means that any Jew may become a citizen there. There is no other nation in the world that gives instant citizenship to members of a specific religion. For the Jews, however, who regard themselves as sharing a culture, history and peoplehood beyond a religion, the 'law of return' supports the idea that all Jews are a common nation. This idea of nationhood developed and sustained the Jews over time when they had no political nation. Now with the existence of the State of Israel, the idea of 'nationhood' has taken on radically different dimensions.

In the last half-century or so, Jews throughout the world have altered their concepts of space, land, home and away, as deep roots have been established both in the 'diaspora' and in 'Israel'. Jews as a whole have become less religious, more secular and more interested in embracing the surrounding culture, and after the Holocaust many nations have become more accepting of them. In Israel, the creation of a 'Jewish nation' has brought attempts to the forefront to teach Israeli Jews to have deep ties to a nation that is still extremely young. In America, Britain and other places, where there has been a decline in Jewish marginalisation as many Jews have become part of the mainstream, deep roots have been established as well, although often with some residual insecurity about how accepted the Jewish people really are. This new 'rootedness' in both Israel and the 'diaspora' has changed Jewish landscapes as the surrounding world has become less the provenance of others to a place many Jews seek to claim as their own.

Now do this . . .

1. Try to draw in two dimensions, or sculpt in three dimensions, the Jewish conception of geography and landscape, or 'home' and 'away', both before the Holocaust and afterwards. Now draw or sculpt your own conception of 'home' and 'away' and compare it with the Jewish model.
2. Read Mendele Moycher-Sforim's novella *The Brief Travels of Benjamin the Third*, and discuss how the author represents the Jewish notion of landscape.
3. Write a one-page story that captures the diaspora idea by having the Jews of a small town find something that makes them turn their attention to the Land of Israel.
4. Read the following passage from the Israeli national anthem 'Ha Tikva', and discuss the idea of land and landscape that it presents, and what it says to Israelis about how they should view their country:

   > Our hope is not yet lost
   > The hope of two thousand years
   > To be a free people in our own land
   > The land of Zion and Jerusalem.

   Compare this with the British or American national anthem and how it describes the nation, and what it says about how either the British or the Americans should view their country.
5. Think about groups where you live, perhaps including your own, that are considered 'minority' cultures. Come up with a list of ways that the minority groups manage to keep a distinct culture. Come up with a list of ways that they have acculturated into the surrounding traditions.

Further reading

Abramovitsh, S. 1996: The Brief Travels of Benjamin the Third (trans. Gorelick, T. and Halkin, H.), in Miron, D. and Frieden, K. (eds) *Tales of*

Mendele the Book Peddler: Fishke the Lame and Benjamin the Third. New York: Schocken, 301–91.

Amichai, Y. 2000: Jewish travel: change is God and death is his prophet, in Bloch, C. and Kronfeld, C. (trans.) *Open Closed Open.* New York: Harcourt.

Davies, W.D. 1982: *The Territorial Dimension of Judaism.* Berkeley: University of California Press.

Eisen, A. 1986: *Galut: Modern Jewish Reflection on Homelessness and Homecoming.* Bloomington: Indiana University Press.

Howe, I. and Greenberg, E. (eds) 1990: *A Treasury of Yiddish Stories.* New York: Penguin Books.

Miron, D. 1996: *A Traveler Disguised: The Rise of Modern Yiddish Fiction in the Nineteenth Century* (2nd edn). Syracuse: Syracuse University Press.

Miron, D. 2000: *The Image of the Shtetl and Other Studies of Modern Jewish Literary Imagination.* Syracuse: Syracuse University Press.

Scheindlin, R. 1998: *A Short History of the Jewish People: From Legendary Times to Modern Statehood.* New York: Oxford University Press.

Telushkin, J. 1990: *Jewish Literacy.* New York: William Morrow & Co.

Notes to Chapter 5

1 Jewish Publication Society (trans.) 1985: *Tanakh: A New Translation of The Holy Scriptures According to the Traditional Hebrew Text.* New York: JPS, 320.
2 *Fishke der Krumer* came out as a Hebrew story in 1869, and was expanded into a novella that was published in 1888. It can be found in Mayzel, N. (ed.) 1928: *Ale Verk fun Mendele Moycher-Sforim,* Vol. 3. Warsaw. An excellent translation into English (by T. Gorelick and H. Halkin) is found in Miron, D. and Frieden, K. (eds) 1996: *Tales of Mendele the Book Peddler: Fishke the Lame and Benjamin the Third.* New York: Schocken, 3–298.

|6|

Landscape and identity

Catherine Brace

6.1 Introduction

In this chapter I want to consider the 'work' that landscape does (to borrow a phrase from Don Mitchell) in relation to the construction, articulation and maintenance of identity (Mitchell, 2000). Don Mitchell's conceptualisation of landscape as something that works in the service of individuals and human groups is useful because it forces us to remember that landscapes are not passive but operate as part of the intricacies of social relations, including identity formation. I will work from the position that all landscapes, whether real or imagined, are representational – in other words, they all form part of the medium through which we make sense of things and through which meaning is produced and exchanged (Hall, 1997). This is an important point because it means that we cannot privilege the material landscape as being somehow more important and meaningful than landscapes depicted in works of art, on film, in novels or even in music. All these are important when we come to think about how people make sense of who they are and the social relations that structure their lives.

In recent years geographers and others have paid a great deal of attention to the practices and politics of identity formation. Those words – practices and politics – indicate that identity is no longer something that is taken for granted but now lies at the heart of critical enquiry. There's also an increasingly large body of work that takes seriously the role of landscape in the formation and construction of identities. Much of this research has been informed by contemporary cultural geography, which has itself been involved in developing new ideas about what identity is and how it works. I begin this chapter by reviewing current thinking on identity formation before moving on to examine three main case studies that address different identity formations and the role of landscape in constructing these.

6.2 Identities

Geographers, historians and other academics have taken account of differences between human beings for many years in one way or another. Most commonly, scholars from a range of disciplines have used social class as a key means of grouping people together and even accounting for social difference. In the 1970s and 1980s social geographers started to pay attention to different human groupings such as race and ethnicity, but this work was still based on identity as something stable and coherent that was readily mapped on to particular places (Pratt, 2000). However, recent theoretical advances such as poststructuralism have called into question the idea that identities are fixed, immutable, stable and given. Rather, academics are much more likely to refer to identity as something that is constructed, created and recreated – all words that help us to see that our identities are *made* through different social processes and constantly on the move. Geographers and others have also been encouraged to think about the difference between groups and individuals in more complex ways, and have explored how identity is constructed around not just class or race but also gender, sexuality, disability, age and other markers of difference. The most recent developments suggest that, while these markers of difference are important, it is rare that only one of them dominates all the time in any one person (Castells, 1997).

It is important to remember that, although identity is talked about as something that is created, identity formation is not always – if ever – completely a matter of free will. There have been attempts to assess the relative importance of structures, or forces beyond our control that shape our identities, and agency, or the degree of control we can exert over who we are (Woodward, 2000). The relative contribution of these is sometimes very hard to determine. Academics have tried to indicate this by talking about identity formation as a *narrative* process – an ongoing story in which the plot is directed by social rules, practices, institutions, places, interactions with family, nation, the economy, and lots of other social and political institutions and practices that constitute our social world and that are temporally and spatially specific (Somers, 1994). So identity is complex, fluid and dynamic, always in a state of flux. But there is even more to it than this, for narratives of identity are not just constructed by individuals for individuals. As Peter Jackson points out, identities are 'subject to social regulation through cultural norms and expectations' and also the power of some groups to define the identity of others (Jackson, 1999: 133).

One of the most powerful arguments about identity rests on ideas connected with how we come to know ourselves and define others, and in particular how the process of marking oneself as having the same identity as one group of people also entails marking oneself as different from some others. This is what Mike Crang refers to as a relational concept of identity, which recognises that identity can be defined as much by what we are *not* as by what we *are* (Crang, 1998). Crucially, this is an uneven relationship, saturated with power. This idea has considerable potency because the Self can define the Other as something undesirable and unacceptable, which can in turn legitimate action. For an example we need only to think of how the construction of gay lifestyles as deviant and unnatural led to Clause 28 – a piece of British legislation that prevented the promotion of homosexual lifestyles by public bodies such as schools and local authorities. Crang argues that it is impossible to think about how people can have an identity and define themselves through characteristics that they share with others without also working out who is excluded and, if people are powerful enough, how they operationalise that exclusion (Crang, 1998). Later on in this chapter I will show how landscape works to include some groups and exclude others.

This interest in identity is of more than passing academic relevance. Some academics argue that real material changes in the nature of society and the economy in the latter half of the twentieth century have resulted in new identity formations and undermined some of the presumed certainties of cultural identity (Carter *et al.*, 1993). Others suggest that such certainties have never existed and that identities have always been forged out of power relations and conflicting identity claims. For example, some postcolonial studies attempt to expose the workings of power and identity in historical contexts (see, for example, Yeoh, 2000). Because we now recognise that identity is something much more complex than just straightforward social categories, is made and not given and cannot be taken for granted, we can also start to explore critically the ways in which some people or groups have tried to claim that their identity is natural, normal or right, and other identities are unnatural, different or deviant. Sometimes this is done very subtly – so subtly in fact that unequal power relations and their effects become embedded in our everyday lives and taken for granted. It is now widely recognised, for example, that gender differences between men and women are constructed out of the unequal power relations that exist between men and women through which men have been able to define women as weaker, less rational, nurturing and unstable (Blunt and Wills, 2000). This has had real material consequences on the lives and opportunities of women, yet gendered identities were taken for granted until the basis on which they were constructed was challenged and exposed. Gender differences are not natural and irrefutable, but constructed and maintained. I will say more about this in an example below.

W.J.T. Mitchell argues that we can only understand the relationships between landscape and identity if we change the word landscape from a noun to a verb – an 'object' word to a 'doing' word. This makes us ask not just what landscape *is* or *means* but what it *does*. It stops us from seeing landscape as an object or text, and makes us see it as a 'process by which social and subjective identities are formed' (Mitchell, 1994: 1). This is quite a conceptual leap but, once made, it opens up all kinds of possibilities.

Mitchell, for example, is especially interested in how some social groups come to have power over others, and argues that landscape doesn't just symbolise power relations but actually makes them work. In other words, landscape doesn't just show us what power relations exist, it actually *perpetuates* those relations; landscape is an instrument of cultural power (more on this later). In this sense, it is a form of communication: communicating aspects of identity and the power of some identities over others. In what follows, I explore a number of examples of recent research that has tried to make sense of the relationship between landscape and identities.

6.3 Landscape and gendered identities

I have already mentioned that some identity formations become hegemonic; in other words, they come to dominate because they are constructed in such a way that their dominance seems like the natural order of things. In this section I want to explore the relationship between landscape and the construction of gendered identities in two different pieces of work, one of which explores masculine identities, whilst the other attempts to reclaim landscape as a way of articulating empowered feminine identities.

Richard Philips argues that hegemonic masculinities become taken for granted, or naturalised, in and through everyday practices like – in the example of his research – reading adventure stories (Philips, 1995; 1997). He takes as his empirical focus adventure stories like *The Young Fur Traders* by R.M. Ballantyne, written in 1856. In this book the hero, Charley, and his friend Harry go to work in the wilds of Canada as apprentices to the Hudson Bay Company. Their journeys in Hudson Bay Company territory are also metaphorical journeys from boyhood to manhood. But the manhood that they achieve is very particular; they become 'uncompromisingly, uniformly masculine', muscular, rugged, brave and strong (Philips, 1995: 597). In other words, they embody an ideology of British masculinity – or to put it another way, they fulfil popular expectations of what the ideal man should be like. Philips argues that the landscapes of the book are absolutely crucial to the articulation of this ideology. The characters 'do not set out with manly qualities, but acquire them en route. Their adventurer's manhood is constructed, naturalised and normalised in and through the setting' (Philips, 1995: 589). What, then, are the characteristics of the setting, and how do they help articulate masculine ideologies?

The Hudson Bay Company territory in Canada is liminal space – in other words it is both literally and metaphorically marginal to the spaces of everyday life in which behaviour is rigorously controlled by social codes. This literal and metaphorical distance from centres of civilisation tests the heroes because they are removed from their usual range of experience, sources of support and rules of conduct. The Hudson Bay Company territory provides the ideal setting for the 'rites of passage' that are central to the achievement of appropriate masculine qualities. These include living rough, encountering danger in many forms, testing the spirit, body and resourcefulness, and earning the respect of those who epitomise the masculinity to which Charley aspires, like the other voyageurs who are 'healthy, hardy and good humoured, with a strong dash of recklessness' and with magnificent physiques (Ballantyne, in Philips, 1995: 601).

The landscape of *The Young Fur Traders* is a vast, unnamed wilderness in which, Philips argues, it is possible 'freely to invent and reinvent adventures and adventurers' (Philips, 1995: 598). This landscape of wild primeval forests and mountains provides the possibilities of reckless adventure that will enable Charley and Harry to discover their potential as men. Yet the landscape is not neutral but is coded as feminine, as is nature. As Philips argues, 'the metaphorical femininity of the landscape presents an other against which the hero can define his masculine self' (Philips, 1995: 601). This has wider ramifications, reinforcing constructions of women as more natural and irrational than men. In *The Young Fur Traders*, 'the "beauty" and "mystery" attract men, who "penetrate" her and find "perfect paradise" in her "green bosom"' (Philips, 1995: 601).

It is important to remember that, although *The Young Fur Traders* is a work of fiction with all the self-conscious creativity that this implies, it is no less powerful or important as a means of narrating and maintaining ideas about masculinity. It does not matter that the landscapes are imaginary, for they are sufficiently realistic to make Charley's adventures plausible and his resultant manliness credible. Through use of landscape and setting, the stories make the power of men seem like the natural order of things. Charley and Harry's encounter with and eventual triumph over adversarial landscapes legitimates their 'natural' authority over others.

By seeing adventure stories as perpetuating dominant masculine identities, Philips argues that we can start to destabilise or denaturalise the power of such identities. It is also important to remember that the stories do not just speak to masculine identities but also construct the identities of women and native Americans. The white, middle-class male is constructed as superior to not just other white males but to women and racial others as well (Morin, 1998).

This articulation of masculine power is common not just to adventure stories but all kinds of landscape representation in which the visual command of landscape is crucial. This can be seen not just in the creative arts like landscape painting, poetry or prose, but also in the discipline of geography. Indeed, anyone who has been on a geography field trip will know that *seeing* the landscape is equated with *knowing* it in some way. Because geography is regarded as a science, the act of seeing is privileged with being objective. The power inherent in the act of seeing has only recently been subject to critical enquiry. Historians of geographic thought and feminist geographers, for instance, have come to realise that the assumption of objectivity means that the power of the geographers' gaze to naturalise uneven gender relationships needs to be taken seriously. According to Gillian Rose, the result has been a new recognition that, in geographical discourse, landscapes are often seen in terms of the female body and the beauty of a feminised nature (Rose, 1993). Rose goes on to argue – making use of Berger (1972) – that:

> ... this feminisation of what is looked at does matter, because it is one half of what Berger characterises as the dominant visual regime of white heterosexual masculinism. ... This particular masculine position is to look actively, possessively, sexually and pleasurably, at women as objects.
>
> (Rose, 1993: 88)

In other words, when (male) geographers represent the landscape as feminine, and especially a female body, they are perpetuating both the link between women and nature and the power of men to *see* and *know*, to possess metaphorical, intellectual and sexual power over women. How can this power be disrupted?

Catherine Nash points out that simply exposing the masculinity of the landscape tradition in geography has not been sufficient to curtail its power. While feminist scholarship has highlighted the oppressive nature of images of feminised landscapes or women's bodies as terrain, this alone has not led to the demise of such images. Instead, Nash argues that 'it is necessary to engage with [oppressive images] to disrupt their authority and exclusive pleasures and open up the possibilities for difference, subversion, resistance and reappropriation of visual traditions and visual pleasure' (Nash, 1996: 149). She uses two works of art to make her argument, one of which I will focus on here. Diane Baylis's photograph *Abroad* (1992) shows a male torso captured in such a way that the legs and chest appear as interlocking hills, with body hair suggesting vegetation (Figure 6.1). It was produced as part of an exhibition that explicitly addressed female desire and visual pleasure. Nash explains that part of the power of the photograph to disrupt conventional links between feminised bodies, landscape and nature lies in its use of the rules of composition, framing and perspective, which have traditionally regulated landscape painting:

> The spatial organisation of the image creates a vanishing point and visual focus centred on the genitals. The body is truncated in order for the allusion to landscape to work and thus there is no returning gaze.
>
> (Nash, 1996: 159)

The viewer is encouraged to take aesthetic and sexual pleasure from gazing on the male body. This disturbs the conventional masculine gaze on the landscape in two ways. First, the photograph allows women to experience the pleasure of gazing, not by simply replicating the masculine gaze but by creating new ways of looking. Second, the photograph disrupts the assumption that men take exclusively heterosexual pleasure in gazing on an

Figure 6.1 *Abroad* (1992), Diane Baylis

exclusively feminised landscape by suggesting that men can also take sexual pleasure in the photograph. Making the male body a landscape also points to what Nash calls 'the arbitrary and constructed authority of figuring the female body as nature. It is easy in this instance to find curves in the male body to correspond to apparent rounded forms in the natural landscape' (Nash, 1996: 160). In other words, the photograph manages to undermine the seemingly definite, incontrovertible connection between nature and femininity, and empowers women to take active, sexual pleasure rather than be passive subjects of the male sexual gaze.

6.4 Landscape and national identity

Earlier on in this chapter I suggested that our sense of who we are is forged in part by reference to who we are not. In other words, we identify with some groups and not with others. Anthony Smith argues that, of all the senses of belonging and group identity that help to constitute the Self, 'national identity is perhaps the most fundamental and inclusive ... other types of collective identity – class, gender, race, religion – may overlap or combine with national identity but they rarely succeed in undermining its hold' (Smith, 1991: 143). How is this sense of connection to a group of people, most of whom we will never meet, made? One popular and compelling way of understanding the way people connect to the nation is through the idea, developed by Benedict Anderson (1983), that the nation is an 'imagined community'. He argued that the nation could usefully be seen as:

an imagined political community. ... It is *imagined* because the members of even the smallest nations will never know most of their fellow-members, meet them, or even hear of them, yet in the minds of each lives the image of their communion.

(Anderson, 1983: 6; original emphasis)

Anderson's view of the nation as an imagined community is now very widely used by academics as a convenient shorthand to indicate that a sense of national belonging is created and fluid, not given, fixed and unchanging. Anderson went on to say that the use of the word 'imagined' should not lead us to believe that there are 'true' or more authentic communities that can be compared to the 'imagined community' of the nation. Rather, 'communities are to be distinguished, not by their falsity/genuineness, but by the style in which they are imagined' (Anderson, 1983: 6). This 'imagined community' is created, recreated, maintained and reinforced in all kinds of cultural products from fiction and non-fiction (e.g. Jeremy Paxman's *The English*), films (e.g. the 'Carry On' films), ceremonies (e.g. the coronation), institutions (e.g. parliament), music (e.g. Britpop), paintings (e.g. Constable's *The Haywain*), parades (e.g. the Lord Mayor's Parade in London) and – crucial for this discussion – landscapes. Like masculinity, which I discussed earlier, the idea of the nation becomes so powerful that it is often taken for granted, considered in some way 'natural' and rarely questioned. The appearance of a homogenous, unquestioned and unquestionable national identity is achieved by a process of inclusion of ideas or images that give credence to a particular version of national identity and omission of ideas or images that challenge it. Later I will discuss some photographic work that highlights the way the so-called iconic landscapes of the nation serve to reinforce racial difference and exclusion. Here, I want to say a bit more about the relationships between landscape and national identity.

Landscapes are undoubtedly very important to the constitution of national identity; they 'give shape to the imagined community of the nation' (Daniels, 1993: 5). In his exploration of the links between landscape and national identity in the United States and England, Stephen Daniels contends that:

> ... national identities are co-ordinated, often largely defined, by legends and landscapes, by stories of golden ages, enduring traditions, heroic deeds and dramatic destinies located in ancient or promised home-lands with hallowed sites and scenery. ... Landscapes, whether focusing on single monuments or framing stretches of scenery, provide visible shape; they picture the nation. As exemplars of moral order and aesthetic harmony, particular landscapes achieve the status of national icons.
>
> (Daniels, 1993: 5)

These are very powerful arguments, for they speak to the ways in which landscapes give the nation – essentially an abstract concept – material form.

In work on American national identity, for example, Daniels shows how the Hudson River Valley in the eastern United States came to symbolise the 'epic' scales of national development in the 1820s. The flourishing industry and trade along the banks of the river spoke to a vision of the nation as forward-looking and progressive (Daniels, 1993). Landscapes work to express the proper order of things and naturalise the power of the nation, but they can only do this by implicitly excluding any hint of contradiction or contestation. Of course, that some visions of the nation achieve dominance over others indicates a power relationship at work; some groups and individuals have the power to create and sustain a dominant set of ideas about what the nation should be like while others are left powerless to resist.

Recent research on the construction of national identity in England has pointed to the ways in which rural landscapes came to symbolise Englishness in the period between the First and Second World Wars (Brace, 1999a). This was accompanied by and partly resulted from a popular 'discovery' of rural England by walkers, motorists and day-trippers and those reading the huge quantity of countryside writing produced at the time. Countryside books envisioned England visually, through line drawings, photographs and decorative dust jackets, and textually through anthologies of rural poetry and prose, topographical writing, countryside memoirs and guidebooks. Here I want to focus on the visually striking representations of English rural landscapes on the dust jackets of books produced by B.T. Batsford Ltd, and in doing so continue to think through one of the themes of this chapter, which is that landscape representations rarely if ever innocently picture reality. As I will show, Batsford dust jackets offered social and spatial narratives of Englishness with a precise moral and political purpose.

B.T. Batsford Ltd was formed in the mid-1800s and specialised in expensive, high-quality, lavishly illustrated, technical and scientific books, and volumes on the decorative and creative arts. In the 1930s, in common with a number of other publishers, Batsford started producing countryside writing in large quantities. The dust jackets that I am interested in were designed by Brian Cook, who later became a Conservative MP of the one-nation variety and was the nephew of the company's director Harry Batsford. Brian Cook's work dominated Batsford covers because the company was forced to lay off most of its staff in the Depression years of the late 1920s and early 1930s. Brian Cook undertook most of the illustrative work himself and many books were written by the director, Harry Batsford, and the chief editor, Charles Fry, sometimes using the pseudonym Charles Bradley Ford (Brace, 2001).

Like many other forms of representation, Cook's dust jackets privilege sight as a means of coming to know place. What is important about Cook's dust jackets is both the way visual components of the landscape are brought together, and the position from which they are viewed. Cook's dust-jacket art utilises the surveying gaze as a position from which to comment authoritatively on England and the proper order of things.

On the dust jacket for *The Legacy of England*, published in 1935 (Figure 6.2), the view is framed by trees and shrubbery on the left and the church on the right. The lane draws the viewer simultaneously into the picture and the heart of the village. But the position from which this is viewed is elevated, perched high above the rooftops, enabling not just the contemplation of the village but the surrounding countryside. Several of Cook's early dust jackets combine both artistic conventions of framing and composition with conventions of an outlook geography that takes as its starting point the view from an elevated position from which all salient features of the landscape can be observed, described and categorised (Matless, 1992).

The elevated position encourages the act of survey in two senses: to view and to take stock, both of which have a didactic function. Form and structure are made more apparent, giving the very best vantage point for the act of discovery and enlightenment that awaits the reader between the covers of the book. But as much as the elevated position offers the opportunity to be able to see more clearly, the act of seeing is remarkably proprietary and reactionary. The elevated position allows the appropriation of the English rural landscape – to see the order of things as they were, are and should be in a conservative vision of rural England. The villages look inward to the main street or the green, nestled in a valley, overseen by the manor, surrounded by fields, in an organic relationship with the landscape – constitutive of the scene rather than disrupting it (Brace, 1999b). There are few people, and even fewer signs of progress or modernity: no new roads, no pylons, no unsightly building. The elevated position also allows the viewer to be distant from dissenting voices or contested interpretations of either rural landscapes or the nation. Further, the surveying gaze indicates

Figure 6.2 *Legacy of England* (1935) dust jacket, B.T. Batsford Ltd

objective detachment, reinforcing the authority of the claims to knowledge embedded in the images.

The act of creative composition in the Cook dust jackets should not be underestimated. Brian Cook refused to work anywhere except in his studio using sketches and photographs collected during tours during which Harry Batsford and Charles Fry would collect material for their books (Brace, 2001). The result was often an amalgam of the most pleasing rural images. The cover for *The Landscape of England* (1933), for instance, comprised a view of the coastline at Coombe Martin in Devon with a Cotswold church and village nestling in the valley providing a focal point for the front of the book. The great majority of the jackets were designed from a number of different photographs and portions of photographs to provide suitable compositions for the three elements of the jacket: front, back and spine. Although the dust jackets create an imaginative geography, they still have the power to suggest the ideal condition of rural England. If anything, this power was enhanced by Cook's ability to select and reject components of the picture, producing composite yet still eminently believable and credible images.

Such representations of England as rural, timeless, harmonious and organic were a thinly veiled social and political critique of the contemporary state of the nation. They were set against the perceived threat to the English countryside from suburban and ribbon development, new roads and urban sprawl. The eminent architect, Clough Williams Ellis, was in terror of the 'suburban minded jerry-builder' who spread a discordant rash of bungalows and suburbs over rural England (Brace, 1999b). But there were also less visible threats to the English countryside and the Englishness it came to represent. These threats came from mass cultural productions and entertainment, which apparently eroded the English mind and culture, leaving English people distant from their so-called rural heritage and incapable of enjoying it without destroying it. In other words, Batsford dust jackets enact a powerful moral geography of England between the wars, which takes the English rural landscape as a symbol of English national identity.

In exploring these moral geographies of the English landscape further, David Matless (1995) argues that the landscape offered sites where good citizenship could emerge through an orderly encounter with the countryside. However, the good citizen only made sense in relation to the contrasting 'anti-citizen'. Matless has noted that with the expansion of car ownership, bus travel and communal charabanc trips into the countryside between 1918 and 1939, trippers from urban areas were seen to display 'conduct unbecoming'. Litter, noise, flower-picking and disobedient bathing contrasted with the behaviour of 'the right leisure user' (Matless, 1995: 94). Matless goes on:

> . . . the nation was seen to have a behavioural problem. Various stock litter-dropping noise-making figures emerge; thoughtless upper and

middle class 'motor-picnickers' not clearing their empties, loud working-class charabancers. Offenders are often labelled 'Cockney', regardless of their precise geographical origin. This cultural figure is picked upon as a grotesque, to be celebrated in its natural *urban* habitat but labelled *out of place* in the country.

(Matless, 1995: 95; original emphasis)

Batsford dust jackets symbolically exclude this disruptive element, envisioning an England free of day-trippers, whilst simultaneously encouraging an informed, appreciative encounter by what Matless calls 'the right leisure user'. Policy-making over leisure, which was in part aimed at creating good citizens, could be regarded as an 'act of cultural authority, assessing the kind of public which should move in particular public spaces' (Matless, 1997: 142). Such acts of cultural authority took place on the covers of Batsford books but also between the covers of other guidebooks, topographical writing and magazine articles, and throughout the genre of non-fictional rural writing to which Batsford books belonged.

This example of Batsford books and other forms of non-fictional rural writing demonstrated that the consumption of the spaces of rural England were crucially intersected with 'socio-cultural expectations' of how such consumption should take place (Cresswell, 1996). As Tim Cresswell argues, 'when different cultural values clash . . . normative geographies are defined by those with the power to do so' (Cresswell, 1996: 10). In this case these normative geographies were defined through the huge volume of non-fictional rural writing in the first half of the twentieth century. However, it is important to recognise that discourses of Englishness located in rural landscapes continue to exclude today. Steven Daniels argues that all discourses of national identity work on the basis of accepting some histories and geographies and rejecting others, even those of people who dwell within the boundaries of the nation (Daniels, 1993). The ways in which dominant discourses of Englishness continue to exclude is vividly realised in the work of the black photographer Ingrid Pollard. Her series of photographs entitled *Pastoral Interludes* consists of five tinted pictures of black figures, male and female, in rural landscapes, accompanied by text that 'speaks of a sense of dread in visiting the countryside, of not belonging, of the threat of violence, even death and the history of slavery which brought black people to Britain' (Kinsman, 1995: 301–2).

Using these photographs Paul Kinsman has argued that:

. . . the barriers of exclusion from full access to national life faced by black people range fully across the institutions and ideas which configure national identity, of which the landscape is only one. The access they were, and still are, denied, and which is beginning to be directly contested, is symbolic access to the icons of nationhood.

(Kinsman, 1995: 301)

The purpose of the pictures is to unsettle the popular understanding of the idealised rural landscape in which difference is systematically elided, symbolically by the exclusion of black conceptions of the nation and literally by land ownership and laws of trespass. But the landscapes also call attention to the dimensions of contemporary racism more generally for, as Kinsman points out, it is the marginal place ascribed to black people in Britain and the racism they experience every day in their lives that makes powerfully iconic landscapes insecure for them (Kinsman, 1995). For example, the ways in which black people are imagined to be 'urban' gives the impression that they are 'out of place' in rural spaces. Ingrid Pollard deliberately uses familiar rural imagery such as fields, stone walls and rolling countryside along with soft tinting to draw the viewer in, to almost lull them into a false sense of security, before powerfully disrupting the taken-for-granted view of rural England with angry and ironic captions. Pollard's work is interesting because it shows us that national identity is a discourse of exclusion that is naturalised through landscape representations.

6.5 Contested identities: Cornwall

One of the themes running through this chapter is that identity formation is often a contested activity and that landscape is mobilised to negotiate identity in a number of ways. There are many examples of research that point to the contested nature of identities – in other words how people subvert or resist the way their identities are characterised, or try to destabilise the power that hegemonic identities have (see the discussion of Diane Baylis's photograph *Abroad*, above). In this section I want to look at the some of the ways in which Cornish identity is negotiated. Cornwall is a very interesting example because it is seen to be both physically and economically marginal to the rest of England, and claims a distinctive history and culture. Because of this, Cornwall has had an ambiguous, and at times confrontational, relationship with England and the English state. However, as I will show, the picture is further complicated by disagreement over what makes Cornwall Cornish and how best to express the identity of the place.

In this section I will examine the construction and representation of Cornwall by the poet Arthur Caddick and the artist Peter Lanyon. Arthur Caddick (1911–87) lived and worked in Nancledra, near St Ives, Cornwall, between 1945 and 1981. Although Caddick was not Cornish, his writing made explicit the link between Cornish landscape and identity. Peter Lanyon, a Cornishman who lived most of his life in Penwith – the most westerly part of Cornwall – was one of the leading modern abstract artists of the twentieth century and used his art to express a sometimes highly political, multidimensional view of Cornish life.

Arthur Caddick moved to Penwith in west Cornwall with his wife and family in 1945 to pursue his life-long ambition to be a writer, arriving at a time when Cornish language, identity, culture and nationalism were topics of widespread debate (Brace, 1999c). Caddick participated in these debates through his poetry and prose in which he frequently insisted that Cornishness was not a matter of birth but a state of mind realised through contact with the culture and landscape of Cornwall. In his work Caddick argued that the unique qualities of the Cornish landscape inspired creative effort and invoked a particular sense of place. This, in his view, was the explanation for the attraction that the area held for the many artists who made Penwith their home, including internationally famous painters, sculptors, engravers, printers, potters and writers. As a Yorkshireman by birth, Caddick satirised those who insisted that only people born in Cornwall could feel or evoke the spirit of the place. In this he was at odds with the Cornish Gorsedd, a group of bards who supported the revival of the Cornish language and particularly Cornish ways of life. Here we start to see some of the complexity that surrounded the articulation of Cornish identity in the post-war period, for while Caddick set his face against England and celebrated Cornwall's marginality, the Gorsedd attempted to shift the focus from a metropolitan vision of England that positioned Cornwall on the margins to a sense of Celtic nationhood that positioned Cornwall as one of the six Celtic nations (Scotland, Ireland, Wales, Brittany, Cornwall, Man) with England on the margins of this Celtic world. The Cornish nationalist movement, Mebyon Kernow, went further, seeking political independence from England. Caddick satirised the efforts of both organisations mercilessly, principally on the grounds that he saw them as irrelevant to the problems of high unemployment and industrial and economic decline in post-war Cornwall.

Caddick's corpus, which includes both satirical and lyrical poems, is interesting for three main reasons. First, he privileged landscape above language as a key influence on identity formation. Second, he recognised the contingent nature of identity – that identity is made and not given. Third, Caddick's work shows us that the claims to knowledge that are often made simply on the basis of belonging to a particular group can be contested by those outside that group – in this case, Caddick actively contested the right of the Cornish Gorsedd to claim that only pure-bred Cornish could come to know the essence of the place.

Despite satirising the effort to revive the Cornish language and traditions, Caddick himself, in his lyrical poetry, still drew on well-understood imagery of an ancient, timeless landscape with deep historical roots and a distant mystical past. He reflected on the way the landscape inspired creative effort in the poignant poem *Lesson Learnt on Cornwall's Hills*:

> Through having passed half my life among them
> I have become one with giant outcrops
> Of gaunt granite at extraordinary angles,
> Hieroglyphics which record the ravages

Of time's unsentimental journey.
One, also, with the subtle delights
Of high places, the scent of heath, furze, bracken,
The flowering from gale-bent blackthorn branches
Of delicate white sprays
Before green leaves break open
And the omens sea-gulls cry aloud
As they follow the plough on inland fields
That a hurricane has crossed the horizon
To shroud the blue bay in a pall of cloud
And scrounge the shore with whip-lashed squalls of rain
I have stood in a luminous silence
Where no one who stands alone is lonely . . .

                              (Caddick, in Brace, 1999c)

In this poem, the configuration of soil, rock, plants, animals, sea, wind and rain make up Cornwall's particular character for Caddick. The idea of a place 'Where no one who stands alone is lonely' speaks to the profound connection between people and landscape, which reanimated him. He was attached elementally in more ways than one, reflecting that 'A man comes here from a metropolis and finds himself face to face with the silent, unrelenting scrutiny of the eternal elements' (Caddick, in Brace, 1999c).

For Caddick, the intangible creative force that Cornwall exercised was given material form by artists of all kinds in paint, clay, verse, prose, wood, iron and stone. The creative possibilities were endless in what he called the 'clearing house' for the spirit, where life was lived closer to the elements and distant from the ceaseless buzz of metropolitan England. Here we see Cornishness being constructed against the English 'Other'. Cornwall is constructed as set apart and different from the rest of England, and most particularly metropolitan England. To feel and understand something of Cornwall depended not on being able to trace your Cornish ancestry or speak the language but in the sense of being connected to a place unlike any other capable of inspiring creative effort. In arguing this, Caddick resisted the exclusionary practices of the Cornish Gorsedd and the nationalist movement, Mebyon Kernow, which he saw as marginalising both 'un-Cornish' with a strong attachment to the county and ordinary Cornish people themselves. Where the Gorsedd and Mebyon Kernow insisted that Cornish identity was constructed around language, Caddick instead highlighted the symbolic significance of landscape and climate, and his personal connection with the land (Brace, 1999c).

Arthur Caddick was a contemporary and friend of the artist Peter Lanyon, who was a key member of the St Ives School of modern art until he broke away from this group after a disagreement. David Crouch argues that Lanyon's art forms 'a distinctive cultural understanding of place which incorporates the politics of Cornish culture, work and dissension; about everyday knowledge of what was around him; and of mythic meanings of land and sea' (Crouch, 1999: 74). Crucial to Lanyon's artistic philosophy was the rejection of the landscape tradition that attempts the depiction of three-dimensional actual space through perspective. The static viewpoint only served to constrain the creative mind. Instead, Lanyon deliberately attempted a multidimensional engagement with place, pointing out that:

> I wasn't satisfied with the tradition of painting landscape from one position only. I wanted to bring together all my feelings about the landscape, and this meant breaking away from the usual method of representing space in a landscape painting – receding like a cone to a vanishing point. I wanted to find another way of organising the space in the picture. For me, this is not a flat surface. I've always believed that a painting gives an illusion of depth – things in it move backwards and forwards.
>
> (Lanyon in Crouch, 1999: 77)

After Lanyon broke away from the St Ives School in 1950, he started a new phase in his work in which he became more immersed in Penwith, the area of west Cornwall that was his home. Crouch argues that there is a certain amount of ambivalence in Lanyon's sense of Cornishness. On the one hand, in attempting to record and resist the post-war exploitation and cultural appropriation of Cornwall, he was capable of essentialising place. On the other, his work 'undermined fixed and stable essences about place', partly through incorporating into one canvas numerous places and times encountered from different positions and different speeds. In this he departed radically from the convention of painting a particular tract of land at one particular time from one fixed, static, often elevated viewpoint.

Incorporating speed, movement, feelings, knowledge, history and memory into a painting allowed Lanyon to arrive at a much more richly contextual understanding of the Cornish landscape and also to enter into the cultural politics of place, about which he felt strongly. This is demonstrated in his painting *St Just* (1951–53) (Figure 6.3). Lanyon was angry that the tin-mining district, at the centre of which lay the town of St Just, had been exploited and its wealth removed by mine owners who were indifferent to the area, its people or the great loss of life from mining accidents caused by negligence. As Crouch argues, 'Lanyon's anger is made explicit in the painting in the form of a crucifix which runs down the centre of the painting like a black mineshaft' with landscapes and mourners on either side (Crouch, 1999: 78).

Lanyon's art emphasises the highly complex, multifaceted encounter with place that we all have, but that is difficult to express within traditional conventions of landscape art. Like Lanyon, Caddick tried to arrive at a more nuanced expression of place in his poetry. Together, they blur the categories of insider and outsider by each demonstrating ambivalences and inconsistencies in their work. Ultimately, however, Caddick and Lanyon tell us

Figure 6.3 *St Just* (1951–53), Peter Lanyon

something about the politics of identity formation in Cornwall in the post-war period, and illustrate the larger point that identities are fluid and on the move, contingent and partial.

6.6 Conclusion

If nothing else, this chapter should have demonstrated that landscapes are not passive. There is a politics in the act of creating, modifying and moulding real and imagined landscapes, but there is also a politics of seeing such landscapes, in how the view is framed, in where the view is gained, and in who and what can be seen and not seen. What is of particular concern to geographers and others interested in identity formation is the way in which landscapes help to picture identity and how they can be used to fix meaning, or give the impression that meaning is fixed, natural and incontrovertible. Such interpretations of landscape depend on being able to see identity as made and not given, in flux and not stable, and affected in lots of different ways by the workings of power. In this chapter I have highlighted the work that landscape does to support gender difference and inequality, how it works as part of an exclusionary discourse of national identity that erases black voices, and how it features in contested discourses of regional identity. Much recent work has focused on destabilising the way landscapes are used to naturalise uneven power relationships of all kinds. The examples I have used here only scrape the surface of contemporary research, but are united by a belief that identity formation can be thought of as a narrative process in which landscapes play a part. The challenge for researchers and students alike is to find ever more sensitive ways of unpacking these narratives and the landscapes that are deeply embedded in them.

Now do this . . .

1. Visit your local art gallery or exhibition space
    How do people express their identities and their relationship with place through the creative and decorative arts? How is art used to challenge or reinforce hegemonic identities? How is identity expressed through types of artistic creation other than pictures? How, for example, is identity expressed in pottery, sculpture, the decorative arts and stained glass?
2. If you are in the vicinity, visit the Tate Gallery, St Ives, Cornwall, and the Penlee Gallery, Penzance, Cornwall
    The Tate Gallery at St Ives has permanent exhibitions of paintings, models, sculpture and pottery by local artists, some of whom formed part of the St Ives movement of modern art in the post-war era and include famous names such as Barbara Hepworth, Peter Lanyon, Alfred

Wallace, Patrick Heron and Ben Nicholson. The Penlee Gallery, Penzance, houses the work of the Newlyn Artists – a group of artists who arrived in Penwith in the late nineteenth century and included Walter Langley, Stanhope Forbes, Dame Laura Knight and Lamorna Birch.

Here are some questions to think about whilst visiting these galleries.

(a) How does the presence of the Tate in St Ives and the Penlee Gallery in Penzance 'fix' the identity of these towns as haunts for artists of all types?

(b)What different visions of Cornishness are expressed in the exhibits?

(c) What other identities are on display – what do the creations say about gendered, ethnic or sexual identities?

3. Read *Passage to Juneau* by Jonathan Raban (Picador, 1999)

In *Passage to Juneau*, the travel writer Jonathan Raban takes a journey in his yacht from Seattle, Washington State, to Juneau, Alaska. On the journey he reflects on the constitution of his own identity, in particular in relation to that of his father (who dies part way through the journey). However, the book is not self-indulgently introspective, for Raban has as his companions Captain Vancouver's account of his voyage along the same route in *Discovery*, a vessel of exploration, in 1792 and other eighteenth- and nineteenth-century accounts of exploration and discovery of the north-west coast of North America. Raban discusses the white colonisers' early encounters with indigenous American peoples and shows how a particular politics of identity ran through such encounters. He also shows how Captain Vancouver's crew interpreted the spectacular scenery of the Inside Passage – a sea route on the west coast of North America – by reference to prevailing contemporary tastes for romantic sublime landscapes.

Here are some questions to think about whilst reading the book.

(a) What does Raban have to say about the performance of contemporary Native American cultures?

(b) How have contemporary Native American identities been shaped by the enduring power of earlier representations by white settlers?

(c) What are the differences, according to Raban, between the attitudes of settlers and indigenous Americans to the landscape?

(d) How does the metaphor of travel help Raban come to terms with his own identity?

4. Watch *Ice Cold in Alex* (1958), starring John Mills, Anthony Quayle, Harry Andrews and Sylvia Sims, directed by J. Lee Thompson

This classic British war film, set in 1942 in Libya, sees a small group escape the siege of Tobruk and attempt to make their way across the desert to Alexandria and safety. In the course of the journey some of the party come to suspect that an itinerant South African soldier travelling with them might be a German spy. In the film, national anxieties about the war and prejudices against other nations are played out as the four struggle across the desert in an old military ambulance. The desert is more than a backdrop to their journey – it is crucial to the narratives about identity that are constructed in the film.

Here are some questions to think about whilst watching the film.

(a) How does the bleak, harsh landscape of the desert inform the exploration of personal, political and national issues of identity and difference?

(b) How is the 'enemy' constructed through individuals, and ideas about the German Other?

(c) How do the characters change through their encounter with the desert?

(d) How are gendered identities performed? How is gender difference portrayed?

Further reading

Brace, C. 1999a: Finding England everywhere: regional identity and the construction of national identity, 1890–1940. *Ecumene* 6 (1), 90–109.

Brace, C. 1999b: Gardenesque imagery in the representation of regional and national identity: the Cotswold garden of stone. *Journal of Rural Studies* 15, 365–76.

Brace, C. 1999c: Cornish identity and landscape in the work of Arthur Caddick. *Cornish Studies* 7, 130–46.

Nash, C. 1996: Reclaiming vision: looking at landscape and the body. *Gender, Place and Culture* 3 (2), 149–69.

Philips, R. 1995: Spaces of adventure and cultural politics of masculinity: R.M. Ballantyne and 'The Young Fur Traders'. *Environment and Planning D: Society and Space* 13, 591–608.

Woodward, K. 2000: *Questioning Identity: Gender, Class, Nation.* Milton Keynes: Open University Press.

|7|

Landscapes of rurality: rural others/other rurals

Keith Halfacree

. . . a cultural concern for the 'other' has been drawn by the magnetism of the rural, where there is a rich tapestry of myth and symbolism capable of hiding or excluding othered identities.

(Cloke, 1997a: 369)

In his book on the representation of the rural poor in English landscape painting, John Barrell (1980) shows that whilst the picture of rural Britain was usually dominated by those in the light, there were also those in darkness – the marginalised elements within rural society – to consider. We must always be aware *how* these marginalised groups were considered, represented (as stereotypes, romanticised, exoticised, etc.) and understood, and *why* this situation existed. For example, in eighteenth-century art the 'basic rule' was: 'the rich and their habitations must be illuminated, and the poor and theirs be left in the shadows of the "dark side of the landscape"' (Barrell, 1980: 22). Moreover, there were strong ideological underpinnings to explain this rule:

> This division has the advantage of marking the differences in status and fortune between rich and poor, while showing that the unity of the landscape and of the society it can be seen to represent is dependent on the existence of both, which combine in a harmonious whole. As the landscape could not be structured without the natural contrasts of light and shade, so the society could not survive without social and economic distinctions . . .
>
> (Barrell, 1980: 22)

Thus, an often exquisitely finished and seemingly clearly legible object could obscure a whole host of deeper issues and meanings, all of which remain to be uncovered.

This chapter seeks to explore the relevance of Barrell's account with respect to everyday lives within the *present-day* British rural landscape. It begins, as does Barrell, by noting the ambiguity of meaning that lies at the heart of the 'rural landscape', suggesting immediately the need to tease out this ambiguity. Whilst rural landscapes are manifested through and in various discourses and representations, the second section outlines the principal family – Barrell's 'basic rule' – of these representations through a discussion of the 'rural idyll'. Reflecting the duplicity of this representation, this section goes on to subject it to critical scrutiny and draws out its selective focus on those in 'the light'. This takes us into the third section, where a range of alternative rural experiences – rural others, previously hidden in 'the dark' – are briefly outlined. These varied experiences play themselves out across rural (and other) places, but they are not all equally apparent, partly on account of differential power. As Barrell observed, the interrelationship between light and darkness can be regarded as a metaphor for the structure of society. These issues of place and power are addressed in the fourth section, where it is suggested that it is often more useful to talk of other rurals rather than rural others, since this emphasises the integrating role played by space in terms of the play of representation and power. This suggested practice is demonstrated for two sites in which varied rural imaginations come together in an uneasy and often conflictual manner. The chapter concludes with a note of caution as regards exploring the 'dark side' of the contemporary British rural landscape.

7.1 The duplicity of the rural landscape

As noted in this book's Introduction, academics such as Denis Cosgrove and Stephen Daniels have done much to take geographers away from seeing landscapes in predominantly material terms and have instead drawn out their cultural dimensions. However, by recognising this irreducible cultural dimension to landscape, human geographers have also to recognise explicitly its selectivity in terms of what and how it presents the world. Thus, for Cosgrove (1984), landscape is a 'way of seeing' the world but, as such, it is also an illusory ideology, hiding the everyday realities of capitalism. He concludes by stressing that landscape is 'a *restrictive* way of seeing' (269; emphasis added), whilst Daniels (1989) talks of the *duplicity of landscape*, as it sits uneasily between ideology/illusion/manipulation and authenticity/reality/redemption. One of the core tasks of academics is to reveal this duplicity and, more specifically, to draw out ways of seeing that remain hidden or occluded (see also Williams, 1973). This latter task is highly pertinent with respect to exploring the rural landscape.

The rural landscape holds a special place within many cultures. This is not least due to its symbolic importance in relation to ideas of nationhood and identity, such as in Great Britain, which is the geographical focus of this chapter. This connection is demonstrated clearly in Catherine Brace's chapter in this collection (see also Matless, 1998). For example, John Short argues that:

In England the two meanings of country, as countryside and nation, are collapsed into one another; the essence of England is popularly thought to be the green countryside – the enclosed fields, the secluded/excluded parklands of the country houses, and the small villages. . . . *The countryside . . . is . . . the most important landscape in the national environmental ideology.*

(Short, 1991: 75; emphasis added)

As Short suggests, we are talking here of a certain kind of rural landscape – one that is vague, incommunicable, indivisible, ahistorical. This forms the core of Patrick Wright's (1985) notion of a Deep England national ideology, which emerged strongly in the 1920s and 1930s (see Brace, Chapter 6 of this volume). Wright illustrates this concept through reference to H.A.L. Fisher's 1933 essay on 'The Beauty of England', where England, landscape and rurality are intrinsically interwoven:

> The unique and incommunicable beauty of the English landscape constitutes for most Englishmen [*sic*] the strongest of all the ties which bind them to their country. However far they travel, they carry the English landscape in their hearts. As the scroll of memory unwinds itself, scene after scene returns with its complex association of sight and hearing, the emerald green of an English May, the carpet of primroses in the clearing, the pellucid trout-stream, the fat kine browsing in the park, the cricket matches on the village green, the church spire pointing upwards to the pale-blue sky, the fragrant smell of wood fires, the butterflies on chalk hills, the lark rising from the plough into the March wind, or the morning salutation of blackbird or thrush from garden laurels.

(Fisher, 1933: 15)

Or, there is W.G. Hoskins's (1955) study of *The Making of the English Landscape*. This book is mostly a historical account of the way the landscape of England has been shaped through the centuries. However, in the final chapter, 'The Landscape Today', Hoskins calls up similar symbolism to Fisher of a deep (rural) England, but one this time very much under threat:

> What else has happened to the immemorial landscape of the English countryside? Airfields have flayed it bare wherever there are level, well-drained stretches of land . . . Poor devastated Lincolnshire and Suffolk! And those long gentle lines of the dip-slope of the Cotswolds, those misty uplands of the sheep-grey oolite, how they have lent themselves to the villainous requirements of the new age! Over them drones, day after day, the obscene shape of the atom-bomber, laying a trail like a filthy slug upon Constable's and Gainsborough's sky. England of the Nissen hut, the 'pre-fab', and the electric fence, of the high barbed wire around some unmentionable devilment; England of the arterial by-pass, treeless and stinking of diesel oil, murderous with

lorries ... Barbaric England of the scientists, the military men, the politicians: let us turn away and contemplate the past before all is lost to the vandals.

(Hoskins, 1955: 231–2)

The importance of these imagined rural landscapes to national identity is not confined to England. In Wales, whilst competing with an industrial working-class discourse (Williams, 1985), 'From the Romantic period onwards, Welsh patriots saw the rural areas and the *gwerin* [folk or common people] as the bastions of national strength and morality' (Gruffudd, 1995: 221). This association was one reason why education on 'rural lore' and rural issues generally was promoted during the inter-war years within Wales; rurality was seen as a tool for national revival and as a means to resist Anglicisation (Gruffudd, 1996). In Scotland, too, the resistance of groups such as Settler Watch and Scottish Watch to the in-migration of English 'white settlers' to rural areas can be interpreted in part as a concern about potential loss of national identity (Jedrej and Nuttall, 1996).

The symbolic importance of rural landscapes and the 'work' that they do (see Brace, Chapter 6 of this volume) is therefore clear from the perspective of national identity. However, their significance does not end there and we shall see echoes of much of this imagery of national identity in the next section, reiterating their contemporary significance and relevance to many aspects of cultural life.

7.2 Representing the rural landscape: the 'rural idyll'

Introducing the rural idyll

Following a more poststructural line (see Brace, Chapter 6 of this volume), rural landscapes, as cultural objects, are manifested in and through discourses. Such discourses come to tell a story about the rural, which is also a story about society – they are allegorical. The way the rural landscape comes across in these stories is inevitably selective. Indeed, one can describe the rural landscape as having been transformed into a 'social representation': an 'organizational mental [construct] which guide[s] us towards what is "visible" and must be responded to, relate[s] appearance and reality, and even define[s] reality itself' (Halfacree, 1993: 29). Such representations comprise both concrete images and attached or associated concepts and emotions, as was clear from the representations of 'England' contained within both Fisher's and Hoskins's quotes.

The best-known contemporary family of representations of the rural, which overlaps considerably with Wright's Deep England, whilst being less directly tied to ideas of national identity, is that of the 'rural idyll' (see Figure 7.1). This landscape can be defined as:

... physically consisting of small villages joined by narrow lanes and nestling amongst a patchwork of small fields where contented ... cows lazily graze away the day. Socially, this is a tranquil landscape of timeless stability and community, where people know not just their next door neighbours but everyone else in the village.

(Halfacree and Boyle, 1998: 9–10)

Or, clearly echoing Hoskins:

The countryside as contemporary myth is pictured as a less-hurried lifestyle where people follow the seasons rather than the stock market, where they have more time for one another and exist in a more organic community where people have a place and an authentic role. The countryside has become the refuge from modernity.

(Short, 1991: 34)

Crucially, the rural idyll is not just significant as a way of representing the rural passively, since many people 'buy in' strongly and actively to this cultural imagination. Note, for example, its importance in marketing (Thrift, 1989) or in the popular media (Phillips *et al.*, 2001). The idyll can go on to be associated with human behaviour. For example, it is of importance when explaining the demographic trend – manifest strongly in Britain since the late 1960s – of the reversal of the population drift from the countryside towards the big cities. This trend of counterurbanisation has been explained in a number of ways, such as being the result of economic spatial restructuring. However, a role can be given to personal preference and, when this is investigated, migrants' idyll-ic representations of the rural

Figure 7.1 A British 'rural idyll'? (Photo: Keith Halfacree)

prove important. This was demonstrated in a case study of migration in the late 1980s to six villages in rural Lancaster and mid-Devon, in the north-west and south-west of England, respectively. Table 7.1 describes the 'physical' and 'social' features of the (rural) destination emphasised by the migrants in interviews. These are almost all features of the rural idyll (Halfacree, 1994; 1995). Similar views and associations have been described elsewhere in Britain (for example, Cloke *et al.*, 1998; Jones, 1993).

Table 7.1   Key 'physical' and 'social' features of the destination for urban-to-rural migrants

Physical features

- The area was more *open* and less crowded; one no longer felt hemmed-in by houses. There was a more human scale to things.
- It was a *quieter* and more tranquil area, with reduced traffic noise and less hustle and bustle.
- The area was *cleaner,* with fresh air and an absence of traffic pollution and smog.
- The *aesthetic quality* of the area was higher – views, green fields, aspect, beauty. There was stimulating, spiritual scenery.
- The surroundings were more *natural,* with an abundance of flora and fauna.

Social features

- The area allowed one to *escape* from the rat race and society in general. This was underpinned by a degree of utopianism.
- There was a *slower* pace of life in the area, with more time for people. There was a feeling of being less pressurised, trapped and crowded, and of being able to breathe.
- The area had more *community* and identity, a sense of togetherness and less impersonality. The general idea of small is beautiful came across here.
- It was an area of *less crime,* fewer social problems and less vandalism. There was a feeling of being safer at night.
- The area's environment was better for *children 's upbringing.*
- There were far *fewer non-white* people in the area.
- The area was characterised by *social quietude* and propriety, with less nightlife and fewer 'sporty' types.

(Source: Halfacree 1994: 180)

Critique of the rural idyll

The rural idyll is a duplicitous landscape, in that it represents a partial and misleading representation of the countryside. On the one hand, taking a historical perspective, we could discuss the ways in which the idyllic [*sic*] landscape of small fields and quiet lanes was created partly by the destruction of many small villages and houses, which 'spoilt the view' from the big house (Cosgrove, 1984). More generally, the enclosure of open fields and common pastures drove many people off the land (Short, 1991). On the other hand, taking a more contemporary perspective, we can outline the selectivity of this idyll today with respect to life within rural Britain.

Chris Philo adopted the latter strategy in a landmark review of rural geography that appeared as an extended book review in 1992. Philo, a cultural and historical geographer, was able to approach rural geography from the fresh perspective of a relative outsider. Whilst he saw much good work being done, he was also sharply critical, lamenting:

> ... rural studies in general and rural geography in particular have all too rarely taken as an explicit point of departure the variegated human constituents of rural areas ... nor sought at all systematically to reconstruct their associated geographies.
>
> (Philo, 1992: 200)

In all approaches to the subject, 'the treatment of rural people still all too rarely allows more than a "pallid skeleton" to emerge of these people and of their worlds'. Consequently:

> ... there remains a danger of portraying British rural people ... as all being 'Mr Averages': as being men in employment, earning enough to live, white and probably English, straight and somehow without sexuality, able in body and sound in mind, and devoid of any other quirks of (say) religious belief or political affiliation. This is to reduce the real complexity of the rural population to the 'same', and to turn a blind eye to the presence of all manner of 'other' human groupings within this population.
>
> (Philo, 1992: 200)

Instead of trying to understand all rural residents in terms of Mr Average, we need to recognise a number of *marginalised* groups. These groups – *rural others* – reflect diverse economic, social, cultural and other forms of oppression and discrimination. Such a postmodern agenda, with its irreducible emphasis on diversity and difference, broadens concerns primarily rooted in economic relations. Hence, for Cloke (1993: 120):

> ... to the 'less fortunate' we might want to add 'the different' and to the concern for housing and economy, we might want to add a concern over the need for a sense of mutual respect, welcome and caring.

Who, then, are recognised as 'the different' within rural geography? Who are the rural others?

7.3 Recognising rural others

Philo's paper opened the floodgates for studies that have sought to outline his 'neglected rural geographies' (see Cloke and Little, 1997; Milbourne,

1997; Table 7.2). Consideration of the dimensions of gender, race and nomadism relative to the landscape of the rural idyll illustrates this.

Table 7.2   The range of rural others

Group	One example
Women	See main text
Ethnic minorities	See main text
Travellers	See main text
Children/youth	C. Ward (1988)
The elderly	S. Harper (1997)
Gay people	D. Bell and G. Valentine (1995)
The disabled	R. Gant (1999)
Religious minorities	C. Philo (1997)
Psychos!	D. Bell (1997)
'Indigenous' people	S. Fielding (1998)
Homeless	P. Cloke, R. Widdowfield and P. Milbourne (2000)
'Low impact' settlers	S. Fairlie (1996)
Crofters	A. McIntosh, A. Wightman and D. Morgan (1994)
Animals	R. Yarwood and N. Evans (2000)
The poor/working class	P. Cloke (1997b)
(Small) Farmers?	L. Holloway (2000)
Hunters?	G. Cox and M. Winter (1997)
'Mr Average'????	???

N.B. Only one reference is given for each author per example.

A gendered landscape: uncovering women's domestic place

Typically of landscapes (see Brace, Chapter 6 of this volume), the rural idyll is strongly gendered. This has major implications concerning the extent to which women and their actions are 'visible' within the rural environment, the norms that flow from this visibility, and the resultant experiences rural women have. Although the gendered dimension of the rural idyll reflects the more general patriarchal structure of society, such a structure makes its presence especially strongly felt within the rural sphere. Moreover, given that rural society is often seen as the essence of British identity (see above), this blueprint has implications well beyond this sphere.

Complementing work by researchers such as Sarah Whatmore (1990), who exposed the 'invisibility' of farming women within studies of agriculture, the unequal and often equally hidden position of women within rural society generally has been uncovered. Especially informative has been the work of Jo Little (for example, Little, 1986; 1987; 1997; Little and Austin, 1996) and Annie Hughes (1997a; 1997b). Attention has been given, in particular, to the domestic character of the rural idyll and the consequences that this has for women's lives in rural areas. The 'sense of community' so central to the rural idyll is the product of an accepted order within the village, an order that stems from the family, and emphasises the home and domestic sphere. This geography places women firmly within the home, as the lynchpin of a stable, contented nuclear family. They have the so-called traditional gender role of the homemaker, whilst the man goes out to earn money to support the family. In summary:

> the rural idyll has traditionally included very conventional images and expectations of women's place in rural society; at the heart of the family, the centre of the community. There can be no doubt that the woman of the rural idyll is the wife and mother, not the high-flying professional, the single childless business entrepreneur.
>
> (Little and Austin, 1996: 106)

This selective place for women is boosted by organisations such as the Women's Institute (2001), often the only important women's organisation in many villages. Traditionally, their activities concentrated on learning domestic skills such as jam-making and baking, all of which bolstered the domestic association. Such an emphasis is still apparent, even though the organisation has branched out more generally into 'women's issues' in recent years. The following quote, taken from a newcomer to a village in mid-Wales, summarises the central significance of the Women's Institute and its conservative character quite nicely:

> The week that I moved here the old lady next door said that church was at 9.30am and 3.30pm on alternate Sundays and WI was the first Wednesday in the month. She finished by saying that she would pick me up for the WI. There wasn't any question about it. ... It was accepted. ... It was presumed that that is what women did ...
>
> (Quoted in Hughes, 1997b: 179–80)

There are, of course, consequences for rural women being placed so firmly within the home and in association with domestic work (Little, 1987). Women's experiences and spheres of influence are restricted, both physically and ideologically, by their roles as wives and mothers. For example, there is often a clear distinction made between the 'private' sphere of the home and the 'public' sphere of the village. Women may feel especially out of place in public places such as the pub, the village hall and the sports field. Even when they are found in such spaces they tend to be expected to undertake domestic tasks, such as providing refreshments for the village cricket team!

The strong association between rural women and the domestic sphere also makes it harder for women to obtain waged labour outside the home (Hughes, 1997a; Little, 1997). First, the need for such work will be poorly recognised, as it is not a component of the idyllic landscape. Second, engagement in work outside the home is likely to be disparaged, deterring women from seeking it. Third, the lack of an association between rural women and local waged labour means that when such employment does become available – increasingly the case – it taps into an inexperienced 'green' workforce. This may expose rural women to greater exploitation than their urban counterparts.

All is not doom and gloom for women in rural areas, however. For example, whilst the middle-class version of the rural idyll remains domestic, it has more space for women taking up paid work (Hughes, 1997a). It has moved on from confining women to the home. More generally, counter-urbanisation has seen something of a 'modernisation' of rural life and attitudes. Nonetheless, there is an association between moving to rural areas and leaving paid work (Hughes, 1997a; Little, 1997). Finally, there are initiatives in rural areas trying to improve women's opportunities. For example, the Women Returners' Network assists those who wish to return to the paid labour force, perhaps after child-rearing.

A racialised landscape: uncovering racism

Great Britain today is a very nostalgic society, yearning for an imagined better past. This nostalgia is reflected in everything from heritage tourism to postmodern architecture, all of which draw on versions of 'the past'. Indeed, reference to the past gives 'Englishness' part of its distinctive cultural character, as we saw in the first section. Raphael Samuel (1989) argued, however, that this form of Englishness is now associated with race as well as the rural landscape; in short, Wright's Deep England is populated by happy *white* faces. In contrast, the modern England of economic turmoil and strife is fundamentally urban, and populated partly by non-white people (Agyeman and Spooner, 1997). Crucially, however, this sense of Englishness looks around and 'sees' Deep England still with us in our rural areas, with the latter imagined in terms of the rural idyll. The 'countryside tradition' keeps the flame of 'Englishness' burning; it speaks of a timeless, unchanging place (Thrift, 1989).

Recognising this imagined geography helps us also to recognise the presence of racism within rural Britain. Rural racism had remained hidden for so long in part because of the lack of non-white people within rural Britain. However, its invisibility also reflects the rural idyll's emphasis on community and social harmony in the countryside, which leaves little space for conflictual divisions. Yet, in the last few years, a number of studies have exposed the 'whiter shade of pale' (Malik, 1992) at the heart of the rural idyll.

A first clue comes from Les Roberts (1992), former Director of Durham Rural Community Council. Not long after taking up this post, having worked previously in an urban environment, Roberts wrote powerfully and shockingly about the racist face of the British countryside. He observed, 'it is not for nothing that the British National Party targeted County Durham as its top priority recruiting ground for 1992' (1992: 5; see also Arnot, 1995). Elsewhere, a Commission for Racial Equality survey revealed a high level of racism in south-west England (Jay, 1992). The report detailed clear evidence of discrimination, violence, harassment and general ignorance of black peoples' cultures throughout the region. This was not confined to less intelligent people but was also expressed by many professionals, including teachers. The survey also found a lack of knowledge and concern about the problem of rural racism amongst official bodies, such as local councils.

A more complex expression of rural racism was described in Susan Smith's (1993) account of the Beltane festival held in the town of Peebles near Edinburgh. This local carnival and celebration of local tradition was revived in Victorian times. In 1991, however, there was an objection that one aspect of the festival was racist, namely the 'blacking up' and dressing in 'golliwog' costumes of some participants. Crucially, this objection was made by someone living outside Peebles (but who came from the town originally). The response to this objection was either denial or trivialisation. Denial typically took the form that there was no racism in rural Scotland; it was an aspect of urban life, especially English urban life. Those who trivialised the issue argued that the costumes were 'traditional' and should be left alone. They objected strongly to 'outsiders', especially urban residents, passing judgement on *their* traditions. Hence, in this context, rural racism represented an element of the celebration of locality and resistance to the will of the larger (urban) state.

The linking of racism to other aspects of rural life, as in Peebles, and its general integration into the rural idyll suggest just how hard it is to counter: the rural idyll's 'whiteness is blinding' (Agyeman and Spooner, 1997: 195). However, there are positive initiatives under way. For example, the Black Environment Network (2001) has since 1988 encouraged the engagement of black people with the countryside and brought multiculturalism onto the rural policy agenda (Agyeman and Spooner, 1997; Kinsman, 1997). A more artistic approach to addressing rural racism has been tried by the photographer Ingrid Pollard (Kinsman, 1995). Her photographs, as fully discussed in Catherine Brace's chapter in this volume, present black people in rural settings undertaking the same sorts of activities as white visitors, such as walking. She begins to subvert the conventional rural image with these pictures and the accompanying text, which exposes racism in the rural landscape. Nonetheless, as with the issue of gender, there is still far to go before the rural idyll is truly multicultural. There remains much 'race hate among the hedgerows' (Arnot, 1995).

A settled landscape: uncovering space

Geographers have in recent years emphasised the extremely dynamic nature of capitalism's spaces. For example, space economies are constantly being made and remade in a process of 'creative destruction'. Developing this idea, landscapes are rapidly and constantly being remade. As a result, space under capitalism becomes stripped of its meaning; it becomes an abstraction, readily emptiable and (potentially) easily reconfigured when the next opportunity for profit comes along. There is a place for everything, but this place has little permanence as, with the next round of restructuring, the people, factories, boomtowns, etc. may well be shifted elsewhere. This sense of impermanence is the essence of the concept of 'footloose' industry.

When this idea is applied to rural landscapes we can readily appreciate just how unstable and tenuous their supposedly 'timeless' idyllic representation really is. Creative destruction hovers constantly over the rural idyll's landscape, threatening to undermine and disrupt it. For example, think of the house-building industry's attempts to remodel the physical shape of the village by adding new estates (see Murdoch and Marsden, 1994). This industry potentially exposes the village not as a timeless place of community, kinship and belonging but as an abstract space for maximising profit. Certain socio-cultural groups, too, may also threaten the rural idyll by exposing its foundations on sand.

The mid-1980s saw the press pick up on a new type of semi-nomadic person besides the increasingly settled Gypsies within rural Britain. This group was soon dubbed New Age Travellers, although the label hid a wide variety of different people and lifestyles (see Earle *et al.*, 1994; Lowe and Shaw, 1993). Numbers grew rapidly so that by the summer of 1993 there were up to 20 000 on the road. These new travellers engaged in a wide variety of jobs: fruit picking and other casual farm work, vehicle repairs, making and selling handicrafts. They also developed something of a communal culture. Partly this was driven by economic necessity and the need for protection, but it also represented a less individualistic and privatised ethos. Indeed, this communal lifestyle is what attracted many to the travelling life, although 'the key attribute of travelling was . . . the ability to move on and into the countryside' (Davis, 1997: 125).

The new travellers posed a fundamental threat to the rural idyll and thus represented a very 'dangerous' rural other (Halfacree, 1996; see also Hetherington, 2000). Threat came, first, from the fact that there was no place within the rural idyll for such people. They were 'out of place' (Cresswell, 1996). They were not encompassed, even marginally, by its cultural imagination; they did not figure anywhere within its landscape. They thus threatened its ability to represent the British countryside by revealing it as a limited way of seeing. Yet, even if these travellers were incorporated into the dominant rural imagination, they still posed a threat. Through trespass, they challenged the character of rural space as a private commodity, a status implied by both the rural idyll and the forces of creative destruction. Through their nomadism, they suggested that the everything-has-its-place/everything-in-its-place *sedentary* character of the rural idyll was by no means either natural or timeless. The landscape of the British countryside is fluid and flexible, not fixed and firm. Consequently, although ideologically at odds with the profit logic of capitalism, new travellers threatened to strip away the duplicitous landscape of the rural idyll that hid the underlying reality of that logic. Thus, we can understand some of the draconian legislation passed by Parliament to discipline such people and practically exclude them from the British countryside, such as the Criminal Justice and Public Order Act 1994 (Halfacree, 1996; Sibley, 1997).

The last three subsections have demonstrated that the landscape of the rural idyll is gendered, racialised and settled. Moreover, this selectivity is not neutral but has often negative consequences for women, black people and new travellers, respectively. Bringing the experiences of these three groups of rural others into 'the light' also begins to speak to issues of marginality, exclusion and *power*.

7.4 The issue of power: recognising other rurals

Power, place and the rural

Uncovering different rural others helps us build up a much richer mosaic of rural experiences than is gained from simply focusing on Philo's Mr Average or, more implicitly, assuming that rurality is, by and large, 'the same' for everyone. Instead of just the landscape inscribed by the 'basic rule' of the rural idyll, we have a diversity of highly contrasting lives hidden behind a seemingly singular physical landscape. As Murdoch and Pratt (1993: 425; original emphasis) express it: '*the point is there is not one but there are many*'. However, this plural landscape remains two-dimensional if the issue of power is not given greater attention. As Catherine Brace makes clear in her chapter in this volume, landscapes are entwined with and help to perpetuate power relations. Cloke's 'the different' and 'the less fortunate' need to be seen as fundamentally linked; the processes of othering that establish the 'basic rule' that inscribes 'light' and 'dark' with regard to rural landscapes must be brought out.

Whilst highly sympathetic to Philo's call for greater recognition to be given to the diversity of rural lives, Jon Murdoch and Andy Pratt (1993) argued that there was a danger that this could overlook the playing out of power relations within rural areas. We must consider *which* rural experiences are the dominant ones in a particular place and at a particular time, *how* such dominance is achieved, and the *consequences* such dominance has for marginalisation. 'Giving voice' to rural others alone is not enough as 'an unreconstructed rural social science ... may simply lead to a "pick and mix" approach; a multitude of perspectives all as useful or useless as any other' (Murdoch and Pratt, 1993: 424). Barrell (1980: 33) saw a similar danger with respect to representing the poor in landscape paintings:

... one version of the Pastoral ... simply replaced another, and the
rural poor were no worse off when at the end of the eighteenth century
they were continually obliged to express their gratitude and obedience,
than when in the middle of the nineteenth their chief virtue was to be
seen but not heard.

(Barrell, 1980: 33)

Failing to address power when exploring rural others runs the danger of
replacing one version of our present rural representation with another
equally selective way of seeing. We more or less carry on as before: 'Middle-
class [Mr Average] power plays the lead [and] the "others" are bit part
actors in this scene' (Cloke, 1997a: 375).

Developing these insights, instead of talking about rural others it might
be better to talk of *other rurals*. Here, attention is switched from the idea of
just a diversity of different groups – a host of mutually exclusive geographies related to gender, race, nomadism, etc. – to an emphasis on how these
groups come together *with uneven power relations* in rural places.
Geography serves as an integrating medium. This reinforces again the point
that a seemingly singular physical rural landscape hides within it a host of
diverse experiences and understandings, but also that this hidden diversity is
linked through power relations. Landscape is both duplicitous *and* ideological.

A good way of recognising other rurals is through focusing on key places
or sites where a range of experiences come together and, very probably,
conflict. Such sites can be examples of somewhere generic or can be more
unique.

Rural sites: the village

A prime site for recognising other rurals is the village. One popular expression of this is the media's occasional dissection of village life. For example,
in a three-page investigation in the *Guardian* newspaper, the journalist
Decca Aitkenhead (1997: 1) asked: 'But what's it really like, this mysterious
life of a village?' and went to Castle Combe in the Cotswolds[1] in the west of
England to find out. Whilst dwelling on the main 'characters' to be found in
the local pub and elsewhere – such as Martin 'who appeared in the village
some years ago, has worked in every pub and hotel in the valley, and drinks
his wages on the market cross each night' (1997: 1) – Aitkenhead's account
suggests the range of meanings to be found in the village and points to some
enduring power relations: 'the real power in the valley still lies downstream,
in an old mill house, with a man called Paul Lysley' (1997: 2).

From a more academic perspective, detailed ethnographic research can
delineate the wide range of experiences present within the village. Such
work not only details the great range of rurals present but can also reveal
the operation of power relations between these experiences. Yet, generally

to date, such work has tended to focus on specific aspects of the rural land-scape. This has still proved highly productive. For example, in her study of the villages of East Harptree and Hawkesbury Upton, near Bristol in south-west England, Jo Little (1997; Little and Austin, 1996) painted a clear picture of women's everyday lives, whilst also showing how patriarchal power relations inscribed within the rural idyll blocked the fuller flowering of gender equality (see above). Similarly, Annie Hughes (1997a; 1997b) drew out her gender analysis from detailed fieldwork in two small villages in mid-Wales.

Michael Mayerfield Bell's (1994) focus on 'morality' and 'nature' in the village of 'Childerley' in Hampshire, south-west of London, also brought together a (limited) range of rurals. Bell demonstrated that although most of 'the residents of Childerley are white, mainly Tory, Christian and Protestant' (Murdoch and Day, 1998: 194) – classic Mr Average – there was also a range of other experiences present. Bell saw these differences largely in terms of class, which affected the cultural 'styles' that villagers adopted. These were simplified into two main families. Whilst poorer villagers dis-played a 'back door style', which was quite informal, communal and locally embedded, wealthier residents displayed a more formal, individualistic and geographically dispersed 'front door style'. Crucially, these styles were reflected throughout the lives of the residents, even influencing which pub was visited and subsequent behaviour in it. Whilst 'back door style' people prevailed in the Fox, for example, in the Horse and Hound a 'front door' orientation was evident:

> A visit to . . . the two pubs . . . makes clear the differences between the styles in degree of group orientation, formality, and interpersonal dis-tancing. In the public bar of the Fox, people tend not to stand or sit oppositionally. Most of the men . . . will huddle round the bar in a great mass. In this huddle with its constant surging motion, it is faces that one directs attention to, rising and almost floating above a dark, lower zone of bodies, barely distinguished from each other. . . . In contrast, in the Horse and Hound people sit directly opposite each other in small separate groups, backs facing backs at other tables. The group around the bar is much smaller, and there is less effort on the part of those sitting at the tables to be part of the goings on there.
>
> (Bell, 1994: 58–9)

The operation of power is revealed in Bell's study through the ways in which villagers sought to deny the reality of class through an appeal to a unifying discourse of the 'country person', with the rural landscape embodying 'nature' and 'real' communities. This is the equivalent of Barrell's integrating 'natural [but unequal] contrasts of light and shade'. As for Barrell, whilst this discourse seemingly united most of the villagers, it did so in ways that ultimately reflected class positions: 'moneyed villagers find in nature privacy and formality while the poorer villagers see informality, liveliness and animation. The villagers bring the natural realm into line with their social selves' (Murdoch and Day, 1998: 195).

Studying life in the village has also been used to investigate the relationship between 'locals' and 'newcomers' and the rural landscape. Specific attention has been given to the cultural consequences of the in-migration of English counterurbanisers to rural Wales (Boyle *et al.*, 1998; also in Scotland, see Allan and Mooney, 1998), notably that which has taken place into the Welsh-speaking, Welsh-identifying heartland of Y Fro Gymraeg. English in-migrants have been accused of undermining Welsh culture by not being able to speak Welsh (and not subsequently learning) and through their superior economic power, which drives up house prices and thereby encourages the out-migration of poorer, typically native-born residents. The norms and behaviour patterns of in-migrants are also often very different from those of established villagers. There is resentment both over in-migrants who 'hijack' local cultural institutions *and* over those who appear aloof from such institutions. English in-migrants are seen as lacking the necessary *cultural competence* to live within Y Fro Gymraeg's villages (Cloke *et al.*, 1997; 1998).

Detailed research into the villages of Y Fro Gymraeg can be used to tease out the contrasting rural landscapes of the different groups now resident in the village. English in-migrants' concern to obtain a better quality of life in an area perceived to conform to the rural idyll is not necessarily shared by established residents. Focus on other rurals draws out both the perceived and actual operations of power, which also serve to question the simplicity of initial categorisations, such as that between 'locals' and 'newcomers'.

Rural sites: Stonehenge

More unique places can also be explored for other rurals. Stonehenge in Wiltshire, south-west England (Bender, 1993; 1998; Hetherington, 1992) has long been recognised as an important site of pre-Roman civilisation, with the first element of the internationally famous henge built around 2100 BC in the early Bronze Age. The Stonehenge we know today took much of its present appearance in 1901, when it was fenced in response to the owner's concern over the numbers of visitors, with people driving right up to the stones. In 1983 it was taken over by English Heritage, the official body with responsibility for ancient sites. Presently, whilst English Heritage owns the inner triangle of the site, the surrounding 600 hectares belong to the National Trust – also for the nation – whilst land to the north is the property of the Ministry of Defence. The whole site has been declared a World Heritage Site in recognition of its international value.

Contemporary disputes over Stonehenge involve those who see it from a variety of overlapping perspectives (Bender, 1993; Hetherington, 2000). Kevin Hetherington (1992) distils these disputes into Stonehenge as a site of 'heritage' versus Stonehenge as a site of 'festival'. Some of the characteristics of this dualism are shown in Table 7.3 and illustrated in Figures 7.2 and 7.3. In summary, with Stonehenge as 'dead' heritage, all that has to be done is to package it and present it to the visitors who pay to gaze upon it and marvel at the past. In contrast, as a space of festival Stonehenge is very much alive and in the present, subject to spontaneous use and free access. Although representing Stonehenge through the language of heritage is far from uncontested (see Hetherington, 2000), it is through the conflicts over representing the site as a place of festival that other rurals make their clearest appearance.

Table 7.3 'Heritage' vs 'Festival' at Stonehenge

Heritage	Festival
Order	Disorder
Gaze	Use
Routine	Spontaneity
Continuity	Rupture
History	Present
Sediment	Change
'Home'	'Stranger'

(Source: Hetherington 1992)

The Stonehenge Free Festival emerged in the mid-1970s, with the upsurge of such events in the wake of hippy music, drug culture, alternative religious beliefs and ideas of medieval fairs (McKay, 1996; 2000). The first festivals had only a few thousand attending to listen to the sounds of bands

Figure 7.2 Stonehenge as heritage (Photo: Keith Halfacree)

Figure 7.3 Stonehenge as festival (Photo: Alan Lodge)

such as Hawkwind, but by 1984 numbers had risen to over 30 000. The festival was held at the mystical time of the Summer Solstice. Whilst on the one hand it was about music and general hedonism, it also fulfilled a number of other roles (Hetherington, 1992):

- place of exchange, including vehicle parts, scrap, crafts
- meeting place and somewhere to socialise and reminisce
- site of mystical significance
- key point of reference in a summer of travelling.

Consequently, the Stonehenge Festival became the most 'visible [annual] enactment of an alternative lifestyle' (Hetherington, 1992: 87). It was a clear space of transgression with respect to the norms of conventional society; a place where the accepted world was turned upside-down. A rural landscape was thus implicated within a process whereby established power relations were questioned, destabilised and even dethroned.

After years of uneasy co-existence, in 1985 English Heritage and the National Trust took out a court injunction to prevent the festival taking place. In spite of this injunction, and police saturation and fortification of the immediate area, some people did try in convoy to establish a festival, culminating in the infamous Battle of the Beanfield (NCCL, 1986). Police in riot gear broke up the convoy, some 500 people were arrested and many vehicles were destroyed or impounded. Every year until 1999, around the time of the Solstice, a four-mile exclusion zone was established around the stones, with razor wire, roadblocks, helicopters and searchlights dominating the surrounding landscape. The festival has never taken place again.

Tracing the deployment of very contrasting ideas of the rural – who it is for, what should go on there, who has right of access – within different readings of Stonehenge reveals the central importance of power relations in understanding the relative prominence and authority of specific readings of the rural landscape. The network linking the owners of the site with the police, the local state and the national state, firmed up considerably in the 1980s through public order legislation (Dixon, 1987) and was able to marginalise the alternative network headed by the various strands of festival-goers. In short:

> ... while the stones remained 'open' right through to the beginning of this century and people could come to them with their different under-standings, they are now 'closed' and Stonehenge has become a museum which attempts to 'sell', not always successfully, a particular sort of experience, a particular interpretation of the past. People with alternative views have to fight for right of entry and the right to express their views.
>
> (Bender, 1993: 264)

Nonetheless, qualifying Bender's pessimistic conclusion, this constellation of power is never fully settled. This is witnessed by continued disputes over the stones, as outlined colourfully on the Stonehenge Campaign (2001) website. Thus, on Solstice night 1999, when the exclusion zone around the stones was lifted after a successful legal challenge, around 500 'summer festival enthusiasts, travellers, and self-styled pagans and witches' broke down the fences and reached the stones (*Guardian*, 1999). In 2001, around 11 000 'witnessed the dawn' (*Guardian*, 2001). Who knows what may take place in years to come?

7.5 A cautionary conclusion

Paul Cloke (1997a) suggests in a recent editorial in the *Journal of Rural Studies* that interest in rural others is a key part of a more general 'cultural turn' within rural geography. Such work has opened up the cultural 'messiness' of the rural landscape and revealed its complexity. However, Cloke also expresses a few concerns and worries, which are adapted here.

- *Which others are considered?* Are we just concentrating on the more 'glamorous' at the expense of the more 'ordinary' resident? Are groups such as farmers, the poor, or even Mr Average himself not being as thoroughly researched as they might be? (Hence their inclusion in Table 7.2.)
- *How sensitive and committed are academics to the others they research?* There is a danger here of 'academic tourism', whereby the researcher goes in and 'does' the latest trendy rural group without really getting involved with the ethical issues that underpin research. Who is the research going to benefit? What will be its impacts on the people studied? Are stereotypes being reproduced through a lack of in-depth understanding?

- *Does an emphasis on the sheer diversity of rural others simply reflect a sense of hopelessness with regard to more traditional political goals?* Have we given up on changing society for the better and just sought to celebrate its diversity? Are we revelling in the duplicity of the landscape rather than seeking to change it? If so, is this enough?
- *Are we losing our sense of power relations within the complexity of detailing the diversity of rural others?* Are all rural others somehow 'equal' or are some more equal than others by virtue of the powers they command? Have we recognised adequately the ideology that underpins the 'basic rule' structuring the rural landscape?

The last of these issues has been addressed most fully in this chapter, where I suggested the value of looking through the lens of rural sites when studying rural others, such that the practising of power at the local level is a central theme. I called this the study of other rurals. The issues of choice of others, commitment and politics also inform this approach, however. Overall, it is clear that the rural landscape is extremely duplicitous, especially in relation to enabling us to 'see' the lives of marginalised groups, but also that these experiences *can* be brought out into the light such that they no longer remain a part of the 'dark side of the landscape'. Such was the intention of Barrell's book of this name, with which I started the chapter.

Now do this . . .

1. Representing the rural
   The way that the landscape of rural Britain is represented is a central theme of this chapter as we move away from the idea that landscape is a fixed, physical entity in favour of regarding it as fundamentally cultural. A key task is to recognise how different groups express their own interests, priorities and authority within the ways they represent the British countryside. These often varied representations comprise a diverse set of other rurals, some dominant and others much more marginal.

   Choosing *one* example from *each* of the following four categories, summarise and critically evaluate how they represent rural Britain today.

   (a) Pressure groups

   - Council for the Protection of Rural England – www.cpre.org.uk/
   - National Farmers' Union – www.nfu.org.uk
   - Country Land and Business Association – www.cla.org.uk/

   (b) Radical initiatives

   - Campaign Against Stevenage Expansion – www.case.org.uk
   - Steward Community Woodland – www.stewardwood.org

- Chapter 7 – www.tlio.org.uk/chapter7/

(c) Academic – choose *three* British rural papers from 1990s/2000s editions of:

- *Journal of Rural Studies*
- *Sociologia Ruralis*
- *Town and Country Planning*

(d) Fiction

- Television – an episode of a rural drama such as *Midsomer Murders, Wycliffe, Heartbeat* or *Emmerdale*
- Radio – a week of *The Archers* on Radio 4
- Novels – a modern-day work of fiction set in rural Britain

2. Reading memories of rural childhood
   One way of accessing the lives and experiences of the rural others that lie behind seemingly singular landscapes is to draw on personal memories of these landscapes. Memories of one's own childhood, in particular, can be used. For example, as a working-class child growing up in the 1970s about 1.75 kilometres from the village of Huntsham, near the market town of Tiverton in Devon, I used to play sometimes on the site of an old saw mill in the village. Although dilapidated, many of the sheds and much of the equipment was still there, providing plenty of diversions for creative entertainment! Looking at the site now (see Figure 7.4), it has been tidied up and redeveloped as social housing for elderly people in the village. Its former geography as a place of play seems to have been entirely erased. However, contemplating this place brings to mind a variety of landscapes still echoed there. Besides that of play, these include the following landscapes.

   - *Forestry and primary production*: their decline is symbolised by the closure and demolition of the mill itself and, less directly, by the retired former primary-sector workers living in the new social housing.
   - *Counterurbanisation*: many of the houses formerly lived in by the social housing residents are now occupied by newcomers to the village, who typically work away from the village and have gentrified their properties. Huntsham has become a desirable place to live.
   - *Game shooting*: the derelict saw mill site was used for many years as the meeting place for the local pheasant shoot, which met every Saturday during the season. This calls to mind (my stepfather was a gamekeeper) the spaces and meanings inscribed into the rural land-scape by these leisure users, and even the ruralities of the pheasants themselves.
   - *School journeys*: it was from the bus stop to the right of the site entrance that my sister and I caught a bus for the journey to school.

The school bus weaved its way through local lanes, past farms and small hamlets, picking up children all the way until we reached the small primary school – now closed due to declining numbers – at Shillingford, 11 kilometres away by road.

This brief personal tale reveals how a seemingly static physical landscape, at least in snapshot, hides a host of meanings and understandings for one individual, which speak not just of that individual's life but also of broader social, cultural and economic changes affecting rural places and rural lives.

Figure 7.4 The old saw mill site at Huntsham, Devon (Photo: Keith Halfacree)

Consider the rural landscapes of childhood present in your own region. Get into small groups to tease out the diversity of these experiences. How have these been sustained, enhanced or erased through differential power relations? What do they tell us about recent rural change?

3.   The cultural products of other rurals
      Popular music-based festivals, whilst by no means all rurally located, now form an integral part of the summer rural landscape. The festivals can be said to position and read the rural landscape in a number of different ways, including the following.

      • *Landscapes of hedonism*: the countryside is read as a place for an escape from the modern world and the nine-to-five daily grind. The rural becomes a site in which a more passionate reality can be played out, with music and other forms of cultural expression moving from the margins of everyday life to its centre. The primary focus is on pleasure and enjoyment.

- *Landscapes of alternatives*: the countryside is read as a place not just of escape but as a site where an alternative everyday reality can be glimpsed. The musical events are a taster for what this alternative could be. This kind of reading might well be tied in with the 'new traveller' lifestyle discussed in this chapter.
- *Landscapes of profit*: a very different reading is to see the rural landscape as primarily a source of profit. Here, the ability to pack thousands of paying visitors into a highly delimited space and then to take more money off them through supplying food, water, merchandising, etc. predominates.

Using George McKay's (2000) book on the Glastonbury Festival and other sources, such as the Internet and personal experiences, trace the relative fates of the three kinds of landscapes at this event. Would you regard Glastonbury today as a product of rural others, or has it been subsumed by dominant capitalist power relations into a kind-of 'Glastonbury plc'? To what extent have the three types of landscape managed to co-exist at the site? What evidence is there of conflict between them?

Further reading

The Bibliography at the end of this book provides plenty of opportunity for further reading on the theme of 'uncovering rural others/other rurals'. The following are five key readings to get you started.

Cloke, P. 1997a: Country backwater to virtual village? Rural studies and 'the cultural turn'. *Journal of Rural Studies* 13, 367–75.

Cloke, P. and Little, J. (eds) 1997: *Contested Countryside Cultures: Otherness, Marginalisation and Rurality*. London: Routledge.

Milbourne, P. (ed.) 1997: *Revealing Rural 'Others': Representation, Power and Identity in the British Countryside*. London: Pinter.

Philo, C. 1992: Neglected rural geographies: a review. *Journal of Rural Studies* 8, 193–207.

Short, J. 1991: *Imagined Country*. London: Routledge.

However, this further investigation is not just about reading. As suggested in the 'Now do this . . .' exercises, you should consider critically relevant 'rural' television and radio programmes, video and Internet resources, and so on. Last, but certainly not least, go out into the countryside yourself and with a critical eye see if you can find out more about the contemporary manifestations of the dark side of the landscape and of rural others/other rurals.

Note to Chapter 7

1   The choice of the Cotswolds for this dissection is especially ironic, given Catherine Brace's (1999b) recognition of a congruity between this area's regional identity as a 'garden of stone' and English national identity in the first half of the twentieth century.

Afterword: gazes, glances and shadows

Gillian Rose

As these essays make very clear, 'landscape' is an extraordinarily rich term in both academic and non-academic discourse. Central to many people's senses of belonging, exile and loss, its conceptual history and cultural workings have been explored by many scholars from a range of disciplinary backgrounds. As a geographer, my own initial engagement with academic discussions of landscape was to explore, in a polemical fashion, the masculinism of my discipline's way of seeing landscapes (Rose, 1993). I had in mind the geography field trips of my undergraduate degree, during which I was told by my lecturers what the scene I could see through the windows of the tour bus 'really meant'. That hill was evidence of a particular event in a glacial period; that empty factory evidence of a certain phase of early post-industrialisation; that graffiti evidence of alienated youth; that lake of medieval peat digging. A scene was turned into a landscape by the authoritative eye of the lecturer, who made it coherent by offering a narrative explanation that distanced us, its viewers/listeners, from any but the visual qualities of the scene. That coach window both limited and framed the view, and removed its smells, textures and tastes. Sensorily limited and reduced to evidence for explanations, these field trip landscapes became the passive carriers of my lecturers' knowledge. The lecturers' analytical insights laid the landscapes bare; while the lecturers made knowledge, the landscapes were transmuted into proofs. With the help of the writings of some of the earliest and, it has to be said, most extreme radical feminists, I interpreted this construction of landscape as part of a masculinist drive for indisputable, rational knowledge, which produced a passive, feminised landscape. Even then, though, I felt things were more complicated. At the time, I spent a little while exploring the ambivalent attitude towards landscape that it was possible to find in some accounts of doing geography fieldwork. Laid out before the all-commanding eye of the geographer 'she' might be, but the landscape could also look back, it seemed, be too enticing, too seductive; she might threaten that rational gaze with a beguiling sensuosity. And it's such complications that most intrigue me about this collection of essays. It is precisely the complexity of landscapes – their diversity of form, effect and affect – that make 'landscape' such a productive term to work with. This 'Afterword' considers some of the themes that recur within and some of the engagements between the chapters in this book. I want to begin, though, by returning to what for me was the starting point of my academic interest (as a geographer) in landscape: the work of Steve Daniels and Denis Cosgrove.

In a seminal text on landscapes, Cosgrove and Daniels (1988) remark that landscapes can be articulated in a variety of media – they can be written, filmed, painted, grown or built – and they also comment that a landscape is 'a pictorial way of representing, structuring or symbolising surroundings' (Cosgrove and Daniels, 1988: 1). That is, they consider landscape to be a way of imagining an environment that draws on a specific western visual tradition of representation: landscape painting (see also Cosgrove, 1984). In that tradition, a landscape is designed to be comprehended from a single viewpoint by a single viewer. This viewer may be someone reading a poem, watching a film or strolling through a park; whatever its medium, a landscape offers a coherent vista to a spectator.

This coherence is achieved in a number of ways. Foremost among them, as Denis Cosgrove (1984) has demonstrated, is landscape perspective. Perspective is a technique for producing a representation of three-dimensional space on a two-dimensional surface. It consists of imagined lines radiating from the point at which the spectator looks and from what is termed a 'vanishing point' on the image's horizon. This geometrical grid orders the space of the landscape view around the eye of the spectator, and this is not only a matter of technical skill but also of social power. Not all eyes see landscape in this ordered way. Cosgrove (1984), like W.J.T. Mitchell (1994), is unequivocal in locating the eye that can see, and thus make, landscapes in the bodies of the powerful, especially the landowning men of the upper classes. This is because the way a landscape view offers itself to the spectator parallels the very real power landowners had and have over their land. Cosgrove pays attention to the landowning classes in fifteenth-century Italy and eighteenth-century England, and other writers have considered how landscape has become part of a dominant way of seeing that legitimates a range of powerful socio-cultural positions in other times and places: class, gender, race, national identity and so on. Like Catherine Brace in this collection, I find Don Mitchell's (2000) notion of landscape 'working' to reinforce particular social identities very useful. Landscapes are not passive; they work, they perform, they have effects. The sets of lines that structure a perspectivally organised landscape image are two-way; they suggest that while an eye in a classed, racialised and gendered subject must see in such a way to produce a landscape, so the landscape image may itself have an effect back on that eye, reiterating – even recalibrating if necessary – that vision.

This understanding of landscape as itself an actor, in a relation with the people viewing it, is one of the most challenging parts of the recent literature on 'visual culture'. 'Visual culture' is rather a problematic term, I think, too baggy to mean very much other than any approach to visual images that places them in their contexts of production, meaning and use. There are, of course, many ways to define what 'context' means, and many ways to understand the processes of image-making, meaning-making and ways of seeing. The most common way to connect context and image is drawn from cultural studies: an image is read in terms of the signs left on it by wider systems of meaning. Hence a particular landscape can be read for signs of its Englishness, for example. This approach can reduce the image to nothing more than a reflection of those wider systems, however, and thus ignore the mediation of those systems by the image itself. The intersection of this broad acknowledgement that visual images do not exist in isolation from other social understandings and practices with more traditional forms of art history is the point at which a sense that visual images may have their own role to play in the mediation of 'context' is most strong. At this point, landscape is not seen simply as an effect of other processes: social relations, ideologies, discourses, representations. Instead, its visuality is seen as looking back, if you like, and having an effect itself.

If landscape is understood as having some sort of agency, however – as being at least partly active in relation to a particular viewer – then certain methodological implications follow. Careful attention should be paid to the formal visual qualities of a landscape image, for it is the visuality of an image that is the seat of its actancy. How exactly is a particular image organised? What does it display and what does it hide? What are its colours, spaces, volumes, dynamics? How are these arranged and what are their effects? In answering these sorts of questions, some of the conventional tools of art history – a careful look, the concern to describe the visual qualities of an image, the vocabulary of colour, form and composition – continue to prove useful. These tools may be obvious to those taught in art history departments, but they are not at all familiar to social scientists who, through cultural studies, are now also engaging with the meanings and effects of landscape images. These are the tools that need to be deployed, though, if the potency of visual images is to be adequately addressed.

Much work in 'visual culture' approaches visual images as symptoms of wider meaning systems, as I've said. 'Culture' is seen as expressing itself through visual images. However, there is another line of argument that connects 'culture' – or rather, cultures – to visual images in a different way. This is a body of work – also to be found in cultural studies – which argues that the meaning of images is made when they are seen by particular audiences. This argument says that spectators bring their own subjectivities, histories and geographies to a landscape, and that it is their viewing of it that gives it its significance (or, indeed, irrelevance). The exploration of how particular audiences engaged with specific landscapes is an important one. Clearly, different audiences may see landscapes in films, say, in different ways. How would the audience for a Bollywood movie react if *Tom Jones*

(1963) was screened instead? What do (different) Native Americans think about John Wayne westerns? How do (specific) Italians feel about being represented by *Mediterraneo* (1991), *Il Postino* (1996), Roberto Benigni and *Cinema Paradiso* (1988)? Taking the question of audiences seriously also demands, I think, taking the look of the academic seriously – because we are also an audience for the image, and cannot wish away our own gazes at landscape while we interpret others'. Quite how to be reflexive about our own practice is a difficult question, though. It seems to me that it's actually rather difficult to describe the full effects of what we're doing when we interpret an image, let alone to explain those effects by referring to big social categories such as 'class' or 'race'. And, of course, exploring audience reactions is practically difficult and, indeed, with some historical materials, almost impossible. But this is not only an empirical question, it is a theoretical one, about where the meanings of visual images are made. A commitment to audiences has to entail thinking through these issues.

I've offered here a discussion of landscape images that has suggested both that images themselves may have some sort of agency – their visual components may have certain effects – and that audiences too are a crucial site of meaning-making. Specific relations between audiences and images thus need careful analysis. And here I would suggest another role for a geographical perspective on landscape images: thinking about the spaces of landscape viewing. For specific audiences and images are brought together in particular places: conjunctions between spectators and landscapes happen in certain sorts of places. Thinking about how the interaction between certain seers and seens takes place may provide a framework for analysing that interaction. Thus art galleries, cinemas, the tops of mountains and the tops of skyscrapers are places defined in part by the qualities of the ways of seeing they induce. Landscapes themselves perhaps need to be placed in this way for the potential of landscape as an interpretative category to be fulfilled.

Now do this ...

1. Methodology
    Choose one chapter from this book and re-read it, thinking about the methods the author uses to interpret the landscape in question. How carefully do they describe its form? What context do they provide? How do they connect that context to the landscape?
2. Audiencing
    Take a specific landscape, one that's familiar to you. Think about how you could explore the way different people might see it differently. What different sorts of people would you be interested in? How would you describe their differences? How would you record their reactions to the landscape? How would you interpret those reactions?

3. Reflexivity

Think about a landscape image that's important to you. Describe it as fully as you can. Then try to think about how your particular (cultural) identity – as classed, racialised, gendered, among many other things – makes a difference to how you see it and feel about it. Are these categories – of class, gender and so on – adequate to the task? If not, why not?

Further reading

Cosgrove, D.E. 1984: *Social Formation and Symbolic Landscape*. London: Croom Helm.

Cosgrove, D.E. 1985: Prospect, perspective and the evolution of the land-scape idea. *Transactions of the Institute of British Geographers* (new series) **10**, 45–62.

Cosgrove, D.E. and Daniels, S. 1988: Introduction, in Cosgrove, D.E. and Daniels, S. (eds) *Iconography of Landscape*. Cambridge: Cambridge University Press.

Mitchell, D. 2000: *Cultural Geography: A Critical Introduction*. Oxford: Blackwell.

Mitchell, W.J.T. 1994: Introduction, in Mitchell, W.J.T. (ed.) *Landscape and Power*. Chicago: Chicago University Press, 1–4.

Rose, G. 1993: *Feminism and Geography: The Limits of Geographical Knowledge*. London: Routledge.

Landscape glossary

Compiled by Jessica Munns, with contributions from the authors

Agriculture: Human systems of cultivation of the land and domestication of animals; activities carried out by peoples who have combined into settled communities.

Ambivalence: The simultaneous existence of two conflicting feelings about a person, object or idea.

Apollo: Son of Zeus and Leto, and twin brother of Artemis in Greek mythology. Apollo was the god of prophecy, colonisation, medicine, archery, poetry, dance, music and intellectual inquiry. Apollo was also known as Phoebus ('radiant' or 'beaming') because he was a god of light, sometimes identified with Helios, the sun god.

Arcadia: A mountainous region in Greece (in the centre of the Peloponnese peninsula) named after Arcas, the reputed son of Zeus and the nymph Callisto. According to legend, Arcadia was the home of Pan. Following Homer, Virgil, Sidney and various other artists, Arcadia signifies a vision of harmony between nature and culture.

Arethusa: In Greek mythology, a nymph, one of the Nereids, associated with Arcadia and Sicily. The river god Alpheus desired her, but Arethusa fled to Sicily where she was changed into a fountain ('La Fonte Aretusa' in Syracuse) by Artemis. Alpheus looked for her beneath the sea and eventually united his waters with hers.

Artemis: Legendary daughter of Leto and Zeus, and twin sister of Apollo. Artemis was the goddess of fertility, the wilderness, the hunt and wild animals, and was armed with a bow and arrows made by Hephaestus. Often depicted with a crescent moon above her forehead, she was occasionally identified with Selene (goddess of the moon).

Backward glance: A motif associated with the Orpheus and Eurydice myth, which signifies a heightened self-consciousness about the mourning process.

Calliope: In Greek legend, the eldest of the nine Muses. Calliope ('beautiful voice') is the Muse of eloquence and epic poetry; her emblems are a stylus and wax tablets. Calliope is also mother of Orpheus and Linus.

Circonia: The Latin word for stork.

Cultural competence: The ability of an individual or group to fit in with the dominant cultural practices and ways of understanding present in a specific place.

Cultural landscape: Traditionally, the term 'cultural landscape' denoted a concern with mapping the physical expressions of a culture *in the landscape*, whereby visible elements of material culture, such as houses, barns and field boundaries could be used to define cultural hearths and processes of cultural diffusion. The focus was principally rural and premodern. More recently, geographers have reconceptualised the term 'cultural landscape', considering landscapes not only as physical products but also as socially produced in time and space. Thus the 'cultural landscape' itself is seen as a specific 'way of seeing' the world, within which a host of symbolic and ideological codes are embedded. Landscapes, then, are not merely the outcome of physical and cultural processes, but are themselves constitutive of social and cultural life.

Culture: A defining characteristic of human social life combining abstract ideas and material artefacts.

Dialectical temporality: The intellectual engagement of existential paradoxes that unfold in space and time.

Diaspora: A term for a people in exile from their original homeland. Used for the Jewish diaspora from the Land of Israel in 587 BCE. Does not carry the religious connotations of the other term for the Jewish exile, 'Galut'.

Dionysus: Legendary god of wine, agriculture and fertility, and patron of the Greek stage. Commonly known by his Roman name, Bacchus, Dionysus was also associated with mystery religions, such as the rites performed at Eleusis, and embodied the spirit of physical and spiritual intoxication.

Discourse: A narrative (story) and its associated representations and practices through which aspects of the world are made meaningful and intelligible. Defined by Harvey (1996: 78) as 'the vast panoply of coded ways available to us for talking about, writing about and representing the world'.

Doris: In Greek mythology, a sea goddess; daughter of Oceanus and Tethys, and wife of the sea god Nereus, her half-brother. Doris had 50 daughters, called the Nereids.

Dryad: A nymph, or female spirit of nature, in Greek legend, who presides over groves and forests. Each Dryad is born and lives along with a particular tree.

Dystopia: A hypothetical place, state of mind or situation in which the conditions and quality of life are difficult (if not impossible) to endure.

Eclogue: Derived from the Greek word *eklegein* ('to choose'), an eclogue is a short poem, usually involving dialogue, set in an Arcadian landscape.

Elegiac: Sad; mournful; plaintive.

Elegy: A poem about the loss of an event or a person, place, thing or symbolic idea that expresses lamentation, praise and consolation.

Epic: A long narrative poem that concerns a single heroic figure (or group of such figures) and historical events, such as wars or mythic quests, which are integral to a culture's beliefs and values.

Eschatology: Theories and religious beliefs about death.

***Et in arcadia ego*:** Originally an epitaph ('even in Arcadia, there (am) I') the phrase has become an artistic theme concerning the individual's confrontation with mortality within an idealised landscape.

Eurydice: Legendary, beloved companion and wife of Orpheus who, on the day of their marriage, died from the bite of a serpent and descended to Hades.

Experiential: Acquired from or pertaining to experience.

Furies: Mythical children of Gaia and Uranus, and Roman goddesses of vengeance; equivalent to the Greek Erinyes. The Furies are usually characterised as three sisters: Alecto, Tisiphone and Magaera. Greek poets imagined the Furies pursuing sinners on earth whereas Virgil placed them in the underworld.

Galut: Religious term for the Jewish exile, which implies that God played a role in the exile. Galut is a Hebrew word originating in the Bible. The term suggests that God caused the Jews to be exiled from the Land of Israel as a punishment. However, God will eventually return the Jews to the Land of Israel when the Jewish Messiah comes.

Grand Manner: An architectural style based on classical design principles, which gained popularity in late Victorian and Edwardian England. Specifically, its source lay in the English Baroque architecture of the late seventeenth and early eighteenth centuries, whose language of form could offer a supposedly 'English' style for modern buildings. Dominant features included elaborate decoration, expansive curvaceous forms, a sense of mass and the importance of the creation of sweeping vistas. Also significant was the attempt to translate design principles honed in the setting of English country houses to crowded urban settings, resulting in the placing of key features, such as domes, above the principal façades rather than over the main halls.

Grief: Intense, internalised suffering caused by loss, misfortune or injury either physical or psychological.

Hades: In Greek mythology, the son of Cronus and Rhea; ruler of the underworld, which also takes his name. Often depicted on an ebony throne, Hades wears a helmet, given to him by the Cyclopes, that makes him invisible.

Hamadryad: According to Greek myths, a Dryad that lives inside the tree with which it was born.

Hebrus: The legendary river that carried Orpheus's head to the island of Lesbos.

Hegemony/hegemonic: A concept elaborated by the Italian Marxist Antonio Gramsci to understand the capacity of a dominant group to exercise control in subtle, non-visible ways rather than by force or coercion. This idea is frequently used to understand the power relationships inherent in the process of identity formation. Gramsci associated hegemony most particularly with the arena of 'civil society', with reference to a host of institutions having an intermediary function between the state and society. Landscapes, it is argued, can also function as part of the range of hegemonic practices involved in diffusing the 'worldview' of society's ruling elite. By naturalising asymmetrical power relations through literally the 'lie of the land', landscapes can serve to legitimate existing regimes of economic and political control.

Historical discourse: A narrative (either personal or public in scope) concerning the representation of events.

Historical imagination: The act or power of creating images of what could or might have been present within the context of actual events.

Historiography: The theory of historical discourse.

The Holocaust: The word that has become the shorthand term for Nazi racial policy conceived and implemented by Germans and their collaborators. This policy was based on the premise that for social and more fundamentally genetic engineering to be successful one needed genetic selection and breeding in equal measure with the mass murder of those constructed as impure. To create a pure Aryan race those thought to be genetically inferior or tainted were to be eliminated, be they the mentally and physically handicapped Germans, German social misfits, Roma, Sinti (Gypsies) and Jews.

Iconic landscape: A landscape that has a powerful symbolic meaning to groups or individuals. Iconography, or the description and interpretation of visual images in order to disclose their hidden symbolic meaning, became recognised as a method for interpreting landscapes in the 1980s. It has helped geographers and others to recognise that human landscapes are shaped by, and themselves shape, broader social and cultural processes such as identity formation.

Iconography: The study of the use of signs and symbols in art to refer to more than themselves. These are often but not exclusively taken from nature – a lily as the sign of the annunciation, a rose as a sign of a beautiful woman.

Ideology: An imprecise term with a range of different meanings. Conventional meanings include, first, those ideas that underpin the collective consciousness of a social group at a particular time and, second, a collective consciousness that is 'false' in that a particular social group cannot apprehend the real conditions of their existence. This is, then, a *discourse* that serves to conceal real conflicts of interest, often but not exclusively class based, to the benefit of a dominant group or groups. With reference to landscapes, ideology may be thought of as those symbolic qualities that are encoded within particular designs to legitimate the sectional interests of particular, usually elite, groups.

Imperial Baroque: The coincidence of the turn to the architectural design principles of the Grand Manner, especially for public buildings, with the era of 'high imperialism' surrounding the cultural politics of late nineteenth- and early twentieth-century Britain. The sweeping classical façades, exuberant decoration and sense of power associated with Baroque, gained the style favour within the mindset of Britain's ruling elite.

Intertextuality: A concept drawn from literary theory, which has been applied to the reading of landscapes. It cautions that in attempting to read 'landscapes as texts', we cannot approach such landscapes directly without other textual filters. In other words the text we are seeking to read (a landscape) has a series of meanings constituted by other texts of which we are consciously or unconsciously aware. There is, therefore, an intertextual subjectivity to the reading of landscapes, which destabilises the notion that there can be an objective or direct reading of a 'real' landscape.

Israel: Term for the nation created in 1948 in Palestine. Israel connotes the idea of a Jewish homeland. Israel is currently comprised of two main populations: Jews and Palestinians.

Landscape: A natural environment that has been shaped by human means to a specific purpose. The term came into general usage in England in the late seventeenth century.

Landscape of memorialisation: A natural environment that has been shaped by human means in order to commemorate an event or a person, place, thing or symbolic idea.

Locale: The physical and temporal setting in which social interaction takes place.

Locus amoenus: Latin phrase meaning 'lovely place'.

Maenads: Female devotees of Dionysus in Greek mythology; also called Bacchae and Bacchantes. The Maenads are often depicted as crowned with vine leaves, clothed in fawn skins and dancing in wild abandonment.

Metatext: The dominant way of seeing the world, or parts of the world, displacing other possible visions.

Modern Movement: The key architectural movement of the first-half of the twentieth century, also known as the 'International Style'. Its origins are traced to European architects working before the First World War, such as Garnier, Loos, Gropius and also Frank Lloyd Wright in the USA. Particularly significant was the German design school known as the Bauhaus, which was founded by Gropius and later directed by Mies van der Rohe. Modernism in architecture eschewed what were seen as the decadent, bourgeois styles of the nineteenth century, especially with their attention to 'superfluous' and intricate ornamentation. The key principles were that form should reflect function, and especially acknowledge the 'truth' of the new industrial building materials of the age, such as glass and steel. Purity of form was highly prized, with angular shapes unrelieved by decoration or ornamentation. The ideology of the founders was stimulated directly by a strong socialist agenda.

Monument: A structure that sustains the memory of an event or a person, place, thing or symbolic idea.

Mourning: The emotions and external actions or social behaviours associated with the expression of grief.

Naiads: Legendary nymphs of bodies of fresh water; one of the three main classes of water nymphs, including Nereids (nymphs of the Mediterranean Sea) and Oceanids (nymphs of the oceans).

Narrative: To narrate a story, or account of events, through words and also through visual elements, increasingly used more generally to describe the ways in which 'master' narratives shape our understanding.

Nereids: Nymphs of the Mediterranean Sea, according to Greek mythology.

Oeagrus: A legendary Thracian king and the reputed father of Orpheus.

Ontological: Of or pertaining to the investigation of existence.

Oppositional cultural work: The facilitation of public debate and dialogue concerning opposing views on controversial topics central to a culture's identity.

Orpheus: Son of Calliope and either Oeagrus or Apollo; husband of Eurydice. One of the Argonauts, Orpheus was the greatest musician and poet of Greek legend.

Othering: The processes through which an 'Other' – understood as being somehow different from the Self – is defined, usually in negative ways facilitating discrimination.

Palimpsest: A surface that has been written upon more than once, the previous text or texts having been imperfectly erased and thus still visible.

Pan: Mythological Greek god of shepherds and flocks in Arcadia, and son of Hermes. Often depicted as a satyr with a reed pipe, a shepherd's crook and a branch of pine or crown of pine needles, Pan belonged to the retinue of Dionysus.

Paradigms of loss: Analytical models used for interpreting the expression of grief and the practice of mourning.

Pastoral: A mode (not a genre) drawn from Classical Greek and Roman literature and visual art, depicting the life of shepherds as idyllic; taken over by Christianity and associated with Christ as the 'good shepherd'. Pastoral modes were revived during the Renaissance and used with both pagan and Christian connotations (sometimes simultaneously).

Pastoral elegy: A poem that creates an idealised landscape to mediate the emotional and psychological tensions associated with the loss of an event or a person, place, thing or symbolic idea.

Persephone: Goddess of the underworld and of the harvest in Greek mythology; daughter of Zeus and Demeter. Persephone was abducted by Hades who made her his Queen.

Postmodernism: The rejection of singular and unified stories of how the world is and how we can obtain knowledge about it, and a consequent embracing of the partiality, fluidity and contingency of all knowledge.

Poststructuralism: Broadly speaking, a theory of how we make knowledge and meaning through the socially constructed medium of language. This includes the way we make knowledge about ourselves and others, and articulate different identities. Poststructuralism has helped scholars to recognise that language is not politically neutral, and that the ways in which groups and individuals are described can have significant consequences.

Psychoanalysis: A method of investigating and treating neuroses and other disorders of the mind.

Representation: The socially grounded and legitimised presentation of aspects of reality as a set of objects and meanings, so as to facilitate communication and, often, domination.

Semiotics: The study of signs and their meanings in a culture.

Shoah: This is another word for Holocaust, used by some because Holocaust can mean 'burnt offering' in the sense of sacrifice. That might imply something sacred rather than profane, and that Jews offered themselves up for sacrifice. Shoah means 'catastrophe' without any religious connotations.

Shtetl: The Jewish villages of eastern Europe before the Holocaust. Many were in the 'Pale of Settlement' – the area in Russia where the Jews were forced to live. Shtetls often had some Christians, but were overwhelmingly Jewish, poor and Yiddish-speaking.

Sicania: Sicily.

Sithonia: The second peninsula of Halkidiki, Greece.

Structures of signification: Those signs and symbols that are encoded into landscape designs in order to convey purposeful meanings. Such structures may be explicit, as in the design of utopian planning schemes, or hidden by the naturalising role of landscapes as a way of communicating asymmetrical power relations. Uncovering such 'structures of signification' is a central part of any critical reading of landscapes, whereby their ideological mystification has to be peeled away.

Sympathetic nature: The idea or principle of emotional and psychological correspondence between the natural and human worlds.

Textuality: A concept drawn from literary theory, which has been applied to the reading of landscapes. In positing that landscapes can be read as texts, this approach stresses that such 'texts' are far from innocent or unproblematic windows through which to view reality. Rather, landscapes are conceptualised as configurations of symbols and signs, which can be decoded, or interpreted, by deploying a textual metaphor that allows them to be read as a social document. In this way, the layers of ideological sediment that overlay all landscapes can be acknowledged and, as readers of such landscapes, we can develop a more critical stance upon their function as sources for the naturalisation of relations of social power.

Tragic joy: An ambivalent combination of anxiety, elation and sorrow.

Trope: From the Greek 'to turn', a term for any figurative or rhetorical device. Can also be described in terms of the process of creativity; referring to the producer (author, painter, film-maker) not the consumer. For the author it is their writing strategy and may be unconscious. For Hayden White (quoted in Barnes and Duncan, 1992: 4) it is 'the shadow from which all realistic discourse tries to free itself'. Though, as White points out, this flight is futile. We all create in a certain way and find we cannot escape that way of constituting the object.

Utopia: Any place, state, situation of or visionary system for ideal perfection.

Work of mourning and memorialising: The social behaviours associated with the expression of grief that facilitate the generation of recorded memories about an event or a person, place, thing or symbolic idea.

Zionism: A movement and ideology devoted to establishing and supporting a Jewish nation. Founded at the end of the nineteenth century by the Hungarian Jew Theodor Herzl. It succeeded in its mission by establishing the state of Israel in 1948. To be a Zionist nowadays is to support Israel.

Bibliography

Abramovitsh, S. 1996: Tales of Mendele the Book Peddler: Fishke the Lame and The Brief Travels of Benjamin the Third (trans. Gorelick, T. and Halkin, H.), in Miron, D. and Frieden, K. (eds) *Tales of Mendele the Book Peddler*. New York: Schocken.

Agyeman, J. and Spooner, R. 1997: Ethnicity and the rural environment, in Cloke, P. and Little, J. (eds) *Contested Countryside Cultures*. London: Routledge, 197–217.

Aitkenhead, D. 1997: Country folk, an everyday story. *Guardian* (second section), 25 August.

Aleichem, S. 2002: *The Letters of Menakhem-Mendl and Sheyne-Sheyndl and Motl, the Cantor's Son* (trans. Halkin, H.). Newhaven: Yale University Press.

Allan, J. and Mooney, E. 1998: Migration into rural communities: questioning the language of counterurbanisation, in Boyle, P. and Halfacree, K. (eds) *Migration into Rural Areas*. Chichester: Wiley, 280–302.

Allen, T. 1995: *Offerings at the Wall: Artifacts from the Vietnam Veterans Memorial Collection*. Atlanta: Turner.

Alsayyad, N. 1992: *Forms of Dominance: On the Architecture and Urbanism of the Colonial Enterprise*. Aldershot: Avebury.

Amichai, Y. 2000: Jewish travel: change is God and death is his prophet, in Bloch, C. and Kronfeld, C. (trans.) *Open Closed Open*. New York: Harcourt.

Anderson, B. 1983: *Imagined Communities*. London and New York: Verso.

Architect, 1877: Bank building at Shanghai, China, 6 October 1877, 185.

Arnheim, R. 1958: *Film as Art*. London: Faber & Faber.

Arnot, C. 1995: Race hate among the hedgerows. *Observer*, 9 April.

Baker, A.R.H. 1992: Introduction: on ideology and landscape, in Baker, A.R.H. and Biger, G. (eds) *Ideology and Landscape in Historical Perspective: Essays on the Meanings of Some Places in the Past*. Cambridge: Cambridge University Press, 1–14.

Baker, A.R.H. (forthcoming): *History and Geography: A Brief Critique of the Theory and Practice of Historical Geography and Geographical History*. Cambridge: Cambridge University Press.

Baker, A.R.H. and Biger, G. (eds) 1992: *Ideology and Landscape in Historical Perspective: Essays on the Meanings of Some Places in the Past*. Cambridge: Cambridge University Press.

Barnes, T. and Duncan, J. (eds) 1992: *Writing Worlds: Discourse, Text and Metaphor in the Representation of Landscape*. New York and London: Routledge.

Barrell, J. 1980: *The Dark Side of the Landscape: The Rural Poor in English Painting 1730–1840*. Cambridge: Cambridge University Press.

Bartov, O. 1997: Spielberg's Oskar: Hollywood tries evil, in Yosefa, L. (ed.) *Spielberg's Holocaust: Critical Perspectives on Schindler's List*. Bloomington: Indiana University Press, 41–60.

Bazan, A. 1967: *What is Cinema?* Vol. 1 (ed. and trans. by Gray, H.). Berkeley: University of California Press.

Bell, D. 1997: Anti-idyll. Rural horror, in Cloke, P. and Little, J. (eds) *Contested Countryside Cultures*. London: Routledge, 94–108.

Bell, D. and Valentine, G. 1995: Queer country: rural lesbian and gay lives. *Journal of Rural Studies* 11, 113–22.

Bell, M. 1994: *Childerley*. London: University of Chicago Press.

Bender, B. 1993: Stonehenge – contested landscapes (medieval to present-day), in Bender, B. (ed.) *Landscape. Politics and Perspectives*. Oxford: Berg, 245–79.

Bender, B. 1998: *Stonehenge. Making Space*. Oxford: Berg.

Bender, B. and Winder, M. (eds) 2001: *Movement, Exile and Place*. Oxford: Berg.

Berger, J. 1972: *Ways of Seeing*. London: BBC.

Bergère, M. 1996: The geography of finance in a semi-colonial metropolis: the Shanghai Bund (1842–1943), in Diedericks, H. and Reeder, D. (eds) *Cities of Finance*. Amsterdam: Royal Dutch Academy, 303–17.

Bermingham, A. 1987: *Landscape and Ideology: The English Rustic Tradition, 1740–1860*. London: Thames and Hudson.

Bernstein, M.A. 1994: The 'Schindler's List' effect. *American Scholar* 63 (3), 431–33.

Berque, A. 1995: *Les Raisons du Paysage de la Chine Antique aux Environments de Synthèse*. Paris: Hazan.

Bishop, E. 1994: *Elizabeth Bishop: The Complete Poems, 1927–1979*. New York: FSG.

Black Environment Network 2001: homepage at www.realworld.org.uk/ben.html (accessed June 2002).

Black, I.S. 1996: Symbolic capital: the London & Westminster Bank Headquarters, 1836–38. *Landscape Research* 21, 55–72.

Black, I.S. 1999a: Imperial visions: rebuilding the Bank of England, 1919–1939, in Driver, F. and Gilbert, D. (eds) *Imperial Cities:*

Landscape, Display and Identity. Manchester: Manchester University Press, 96–113.

Black, I.S. 1999b: Rebuilding *The Heart of the Empire*: bank headquarters in the City of London, 1919–1939. *Art History* **22**, 593–618.

Black, I.S. 2000: Spaces of capital: bank office building in the City of London, 1830–1870. *Journal of Historical Geography* **26**, 351–75.

Black, I.S. 2002: Reordering space: British bank building overseas, 1900–1940, in de Graaf, T., Jonker, J. and Mobron, J. (eds) *European Banking Overseas, 19th–20th Centuries*. Amsterdam, Aksant, 77–108.

Blunt, A. 1994: *Writing Women and Space: Colonial and Postcolonial Geographies*. London: Guilford Press.

Blunt, A. and Wills, J. 2000: Embodying geography: feminist geographies of gender, in *Dissident Geographies: An Introduction to Radical Ideas and Practice*. Harlow: Prentice Hall, 90–127.

Bordwell, D. 1985: *Narration in the Fiction Film*. Madison: University of Wisconsin Press.

Bordwell, D. 1996: Contemporary film studies and the vicissitudes of Grand Theory, in Bordwell, D. and Carroll, N. (eds) *Post Theory: Reconstructing Film Studies*. Madison: University of Wisconsin Press, 3–36.

Bordwell, D., Staiger, J. and Thompson, K. 1985: *The Classical Hollywood Cinema*. New York: Columbia University Press.

Boyer, M.C. 1994: *The City of Collective Memory: Its Historical Imagery and Architectural Entertainments*. Cambridge MA: MIT Press.

Boyle, P., Halfacree, K. and Robinson, V. 1998: *Exploring Contemporary Migration*. Harlow: Addison, Wesley, Longman.

Brace, C. 1999a: Finding England everywhere: regional identity and the construction of national identity, 1890–1940. *Ecumene* **6** (1), 90–109.

Brace, C. 1999b: Gardenesque imagery in the representation of regional and national identity: the Cotswold garden of stone. *Journal of Rural Studies* **15**, 365–76.

Brace, C. 1999c: Cornish identity and landscape in the work of Arthur Caddick. *Cornish Studies* **7**, 130–46.

Brace, C. 2001: Publishing and publishers: towards an historical geography of countryside writing, c.1930–1950. *Area* **33** (3), 287–96.

Branigan, E. 1992: *Narrative Comprehension and Film*. New York: Routledge.

Braudy, L. 1977: *The World in a Frame*. Garden City, New York: Anchor Books.

Bresheeth, H. 1997: The great taboo broken, in Loshitzky, Y. (ed.) *Spielberg's Holocaust: Critical Perspectives on Schindler's List*. Bloomington: Indiana University Press.

Brode, D. 1995: *The Films of Steven Spielberg*. New York: Citadel Press.

Bumstead, H. 2000: Personal interviews, July. San Marino, California.

Carter, E., Donald, J. and Squires, J. (eds) 1993: *Space and Place: Theories of Identity and Location*. London: Lawrence and Wishart.

Caruth, C. (ed.) 1995: *Trauma: Explorations in Memory*. Baltimore: Hopkins.

Castells, M. 1997: *The Power of Identity*. Oxford: Blackwell.

Charlesworth, A. 1994: Contesting places of memory: the case of Auschwitz. *Society and Space* **12**, 579–93.

Cheyette, B. 1997: The uncertain certainty of *Schindler's List*, in Loshitzky, Y. (ed.) *Spielberg's Holocaust: Critical Perspectives on Schindler's List*. Bloomington: Indiana University Press, 226–38.

China Mail, 1886: The new buildings of the Hongkong and Shanghai Bank, 9 August.

Cloke, P. 1993: On 'problems and solutions'. The reproduction of problems for rural communities in Britain during the 1980s. *Journal of Rural Studies* **9**, 113–21.

Cloke, P. 1997a: Country backwater to virtual village? Rural studies and 'the cultural turn'. *Journal of Rural Studies* **13**, 367–75.

Cloke, P. 1997b: Poor country. Marginalisation, poverty and rurality, in Cloke, P. and Little, J. (eds) *Contested Countryside Cultures*. London: Routledge, 252–71.

Cloke, P. and Little, J. (eds) 1997: *Contested Countryside Cultures: Otherness, Marginalisation and Rurality*. London: Routledge.

Cloke, P., Goodwin, M. and Milbourne, P. 1997: *Rural Wales. Community and Marginalization*. Cardiff: University of Wales Press.

Cloke, P., Goodwin, M. and Milbourne, P. 1998: Inside looking out; outside looking in. Different experiences of cultural competence in rural lifestyles, in Boyle, P. and Halfacree, K. (eds) *Migration into Rural Areas*. Chichester: Wiley, 134–50.

Cloke, P., Widdowfield, R. and Milbourne, P. 2000: The hidden and emerging spaces of rural homelessness. *Environment and Planning A* **32**, 77–90.

Cole, T. 1999: Oskar Schindler and Auschwitz, in Cole, T., *Images of the Holocaust*. London: Gerald Duckworth.

Cosgrove, D.E. 1982a: Problems of interpreting the symbolism of past landscapes, in Baker, A.R.H. and Billinge, M.D. (eds) *Period and Place: Research Methods in Historical Geography*. Cambridge: Cambridge University Press, 220–30.

Cosgrove, D.E. 1982b: *Geography and the Humanities*. Loughborough University of Technology, Department of Geography Occasional Papers 5.

Cosgrove, D.E. 1984: *Social Formation and Symbolic Landscape*. London: Croom Helm.

Cosgrove, D.E. 1985: Prospect, perspective and the evolution of the landscape idea. *Transactions of the Institute of British Geographers* (new series) **10**, 45–62.

Cosgrove, D.E. 1989: Geography is everywhere: culture and symbolism in human landscapes, in Gregory, D. and Walford, R. (eds) *Horizons in Human Geography*. Basingstoke: Macmillan Education.

Cosgrove, D.E. 1993: *The Palladian Landscape: Geographical Change and its Cultural Representations in Sixteenth-Century Italy*. Leicester: Leicester University Press.

Cosgrove, D.E. 1998: *Social Formation and Symbolic Landscape* (2nd edn). Madison: University of Wisconsin Press. (First published 1984, London: Croom Helm.)

Cosgrove, D.E. and Daniels, S. (eds) 1988: *The Iconography of Landscape: Essays on the Symbolic Representation, Design and Use of Past Environments*. Cambridge: Cambridge University Press.

Cosgrove, D.E. and Jackson, P. 1987: New directions in cultural geography. *Area* **19**, 95–101.

Cox, G. and Winter, M. 1997: The beleaguered 'Other': hunt followers in the countryside, in Milbourne, P. (ed.) *Revealing Rural 'Others'*. London: Pinter, 75–87.

Crang, M. 1998: *Cultural Geography*. London: Routledge.

Cresswell, T. 1996: *In Place/Out of Place*. Minneapolis: University of Minnesota Press.

Crinson, M. 1996: *Empire Building: Orientalism and Victorian Architecture*. London: Routledge.

Crouch, D. 1999: Everyday abstraction: geographical knowledge in the art of Peter Lanyon. *Ecumene* **6** (1), 72–89.

Crouch, D. 2000: Introduction, in Cook, I., Crouch, D., Naylor, S. and Ryan, J.R. eds. *Cultural turns/Geographical turns*. London: Prentice Hall, 70.

Curtius, E. 1973: *European Literature and the Latin Middle Ages*. Princeton: Princeton University.

Daniels, S. 1989: Marxism, culture and the duplicity of landscape, in Peet, R. and Thrift, N. (eds) *New Models in Geography 2*. London: Unwin Hyman, 196–220.

Daniels, S. 1993: *Fields of Vision: Landscape Imagery and National Identity in England and the United States*. Cambridge: Polity Press.

Daniels, S. and Cosgrove, D.E. 1993: Spectacle and text: landscape metaphors in cultural geography, in Duncan, J. and Ley, D. (eds) *Place/Culture/Representation*. London: Routledge, 57–77.

Davies, W.D. 1982: *The Territorial Dimension of Judaism*. Berkeley: University of California Press.

Davis, J. 1997: New Age Travellers in the countryside: incomers with attitude, in Milbourne, P. (ed.) *Revealing Rural 'Others'*. London: Pinter, 117–34.

Dennis, R. 2001: Reconciling geographies, representing modernities, in Black, I.S. and Butlin, R.A. (eds) *Place, Culture and Identity: Essays in Historical Geography in Honour of Alan R.H. Baker*. Quebec: Les Presses de l'Université Laval, 17–43.

Desser, D. (ed.) 1997: *Ozu's Tokyo Story*. New York: Cambridge University Press.

Dixon, D. 1987: Protest and disorder: the Public Order Act 1986. *Critical Social Policy* 7, 90–8.

Dodgshon, R.A. 1989: 'Pretense of blude and place of thair dwelling': the nature of Highland clans, 1500–1745, in Houston, R.A. and Whyte, I.D. (eds) *Scottish Society 1500–1800*. Cambridge: Cambridge University Press, 169–98.

Domosh, M. 1988: The symbolism of the skyscraper: case studies of New York's first tall buildings. *Journal of Urban History* 14, 320–45.

Domosh, M. 1989: A method for interpreting landscape: a case study of the New York World Building. *Area* 21, 347–55.

Domosh, M. 1992: Corporate cultures and the modern landscape of New York City, in Anderson, K. and Gale, F. (eds) *Inventing Places: Studies in Cultural Geography*. Melbourne: Longman Cheshire, 72–86.

Domosh, M. 1996: *Invented Cities: The Creation of Landscape in Nineteenth-century New York and Boston*. New Haven and London: Yale University Press.

Doneson, J.E. 1997: The image lingers, in Loshitzky, Y. (ed.) *Spielberg's Holocaust: Critical Perspectives on Schindler's List*. Bloomington: Indiana University Press, 140–52.

Duncan, J. 1990: *The City as Text: The Politics of Landscape Interpretation in the Kandayan Kingdom*. Cambridge: Cambridge University Press.

Duncan, J. and Duncan, N. 1988: (Re)reading the landscape. *Environment and Planning D: Society and Space* 6, 117–26.

Duncan, J. and Duncan, N. 1997: Deep suburban irony, in Silverstone, R. (ed.) *Visions of Suburbia*. London: Routledge.

Earle, F., Dearling, A., Whittle, H., Glasse, R. and Gubby 1994: *A Time to Travel?* Lyme Regis: Enabler Publications.

Edholm, F. 1988: 'Shoah': a film by Claude Lanzmann. *History Workshop* 25, 204–6.

Eisen, A. 1986: *Galut: Modern Jewish Reflection on Homelessness and Homecoming*. Bloomington: Indiana University Press.

Eisenstein, S. 1999: Beyond the shot, in Braudy, L. and Cohen, M. (eds) *Film Form in Film Theory and Criticism*. New York: Oxford University Press.

Empson, W. 1950: *Some Versions of Pastoral*. London: Chatto & Windus.

Everson, P. and Williamson, T. 1998: *The Archaeology of Landscape*. Manchester: Manchester University Press.

Fairlie, S. 1996: *Low Impact Development: Planning and People in a Sustainable Countryside*. Chipping Norton: Jon Carpenter.

Fielding, S. 1998: Indigeneity, identity and locality: perspectives on Swaledale, in Boyle, P. and Halfacree, K. (eds) *Migration into Rural Areas*. Chichester: Wiley, 151–65.

Fisher, H. 1933: The beauty of England, in Council for the Preservation of Rural England, *The Penn Country of Buckinghamshire*. London: CPRE.

Fitter, C. 1995: *Poetry, Space, Landscape: Toward a New Theory*. Cambridge: Cambridge University.

Ford, L.R. 1992: Reading the skylines of American cities. *Geographical Review* **82**, 180–200.

Freud, S. 1953: Mourning and melancholia, in Rickman, J. (ed.) *A General Selection from the Works of Sigmund Freud*. London: Hogarth, 142–61.

Gaiman, N. 1993: *The Sandman*, Vol. 6. New York: DC Comics.

Gallagher, T. 1986: *John Ford: The Man and His Films*. Berkeley: University of California Press.

Gant, R. 1999: 'Enabling' technology for disabled people: telecommunications for community care in rural Britain, in Walford, N., Everitt, J. and Napton, D. (eds) *Reshaping the Countryside: Perceptions and Processes of Rural Change*. Wallingford: CABI Publishing, 135–45.

Garrett, L. 2003: *Journeys Beyond the Pale: Yiddish Travel Writing in the Modern World*. Madison: University of Wisconsin Press.

Geist, K. 1997: Buddhism in 'Tokyo Story', in Desser D. (ed.) *Ozu's Tokyo Story*. New York: Cambridge University Press, 101–17.

Gombrich, E.H. 1972: *Art and Illusion*. Princeton: Princeton University Press.

Goss, J. 1988: The built environment and social theory: towards an architectural geography. *Professional Geographer* **40**, 392–403.

Groth, P. 1999: Making new connections in vernacular architecture. *Journal of the Society of Architectural Historians* **58**, 444–51.

Gruffudd, P. 1995: Remaking Wales: nation-building and the geographical imagination, 1925–50. *Political Geography* **14**, 219–39.

Gruffudd, P. 1996: The countryside as educator: schools, rurality and citizenship in inter-war Wales. *Journal of Historical Geography* **22**, 412–23.

Guardian 1999: Solstice sun rises on anarchy, 22 June.

Guardian 2001: Stonehenge solstice revellers see the light, 22 June.

HSBC 2000: *The HSBC Group: A Brief History*. London: HSBC Group plc.

HSBCa: HSBC Group archives, London: *The Hongkong and Shanghai Banking Corporation: The Official Opening of the New Building at Shanghai*, 23 June 1923.

HSBCb: HSBC Group archives, Hong Kong: *The Hongkong and Shanghai Banking Corporation: The Official Opening of the New Building*, 10 October 1935.

Haber, J. 1994: *Pastoral and the Poetics of Self-Contradiction*. Cambridge: Cambridge University Press.

Halfacree, K. 1993: Locality and social representation: space, discourse and alternative definitions of the rural. *Journal of Rural Studies* **9**, 23–37.

Halfacree, K. 1994: The importance of 'the rural' in the constitution of counterurbanization: evidence from England in the 1980s. *Sociologia Ruralis* **34**, 164–89.

Halfacree, K. 1995: Talking about rurality: social representations of the rural as expressed by residents of six English parishes. *Journal of Rural Studies* **11**, 1–20.

Halfacree, K. 1996: Out of place in the countryside: travellers and the 'rural idyll'. *Antipode* **29**, 42–72.

Halfacree, K. and Boyle, P. 1998: Migration, rurality and the post-produc-
tivist countryside, in Boyle, P. and Halfacree, K. (eds) *Migration into
Rural Areas*. Chichester: Wiley, 1–12.

Hall, S. (ed.) 1997: *Representation – Cultural Representations and
Signifying Practices*. London: Sage.

Harper, S. 1997: Contesting later life, in Cloke, P. and Little, J. (eds)
Contested Countryside Cultures. London: Routledge, 180–96.

Harris, D. 1999: The postmodernization of landscape: a critical historiography. *Journal of the Society of Architectural Historians* 58, 435–43.

Hartman, G.H. 1996: The cinema animal, in Hartman, G.H. (ed.) *The
Longest Shadow: In the Aftermath of the Holocaust*. Bloomington:
Indiana University Press.

Harvey, D. 1996: *Justice, Nature and the Geography of Difference*. Oxford:
Blackwell.

Harvey, D.W. 1979: Monument and myth. *Annals of the Association of
American Geographers* 69, 362–81.

Hassrick, P.H. 1989: *Charles M. Russell*. Norman: University of Oklahoma
Press.

Heath, S. 1981: *Questions of Cinema*. Bloomington: Indiana University
Press.

Hetherington, K. 1992: Stonehenge and its festival, in Shields, R. (ed.)
Lifestyle Shopping. London: Routledge, 83–98.

Hetherington, K. 2000: *New Age Travellers: Vanloads of Uproarious
Humanity*. London: Cassell.

Hirsch, E. 1995: Landscape: between place and space, in Hirsch, E. and
O'Hanlon, M., *The Anthropology of Landscape*. Oxford: Clarendon
Press.

Holdsworth, D.W. 1993: Revaluing the house, in Duncan, J. and Ley, D.
(eds) *Place/Culture/Representation*. London: Routledge, 95–109.

Holdsworth, D.W. 1997: Landscape and archives as texts, in Groth, P. and
Bressi, T.W. (eds) *Understanding Ordinary Landscapes*. New Haven and
London: Yale University Press, 44–55.

Holloway, L. 2000: 'Hell on earth and paradise all at the same time': the
production of smallholding space in the British countryside. *Area* 32,
307–15.

Hooke, D. 1998: *The Landscape of Anglo-Saxon England*. Leicester:
Leicester University Press.

hooks, b. 1992: Representing whiteness in the black imagination, in
Grossberg, L. and Nelson, C. (eds) *Cultural Studies*. New York: Routledge.

Horowitz, S.R. 1997: But is it good for the Jews? Spielberg's Schindler and
the aesthetics of atrocity, in Loshitzky, Y. (ed.) *Spielberg's Holocaust:
Critical Perspectives on Schindler's List*. Bloomington: Indiana
University Press, 119–39.

Horton, A. 1981: *The Films of George Roy Hill*. New York: Columbia
University Press.

Horton, A. (ed.) 1996: *Buster Keaton's Sherlock Jr*. Cambridge: Cambridge University Press.

Horton, A. 1998: Cinematic makeovers and cultural border crossings: Kusturica's 'Time of the Gypsies' and Coppola's 'Godfather' and 'Godfather II', in Horton, A. and McDougal, S.Y. (eds) *Play it Again, Sam: Retakes on Remakes*. Berkeley: University of California Press, 172–90.

Horton, A. 1999a: *Writing the Character Centered Screenplay*. Berkeley: University of California Press.

Horton, A. 1999b: *The Films of Theo Angelopoulos: A Cinema of Contemplation*. Princeton: Princeton University Press.

Horton, A. 2003: *Screenwriting for a Global Market*. Berkeley: University of California Press.

Hoskins, W.G. 1955: *The Making of the English Landscape*. London: Hodder & Stoughton.

Houlbrooke, R. (ed.) 1989: *Death, Ritual, and Bereavement*. London: Routledge.

Howard, W. Scott. 2002: 'The Brevities': formal mourning, transgression and postmodern American elegies, in Foster, E. (ed.) *The World in Time and Space*. Jersey City: Talisman, 115–39.

Howe, I. and Greenberg, E. (eds) 1990: *A Treasury of Yiddish Stories*. New York: Penguin Books.

Hughes, A. 1997a: Rurality and 'cultures of womanhood'. Domestic identities and moral orders in village life, in Cloke, P. and Little, J. (eds) *Contested Countryside Cultures*. London: Routledge, 123–37.

Hughes, A. 1997b: Women and rurality: gendered experiences of 'community' in village life, in Milbourne, P. (ed.) *Revealing Rural 'Others'*. London: Pinter, 167–88.

Hugill, P. 1995: *Upstate Arcadia: Landscape, Aesthetics, and the Triumph of Social Differentiation in America*. Lanham: Rowman & Littlefield.

Hunt, J. 1976: *The Figure in the Landscape: Poetry, Painting, and Gardening During the Eighteenth Century*. Baltimore: Hopkins.

Ingold, T. 1993: The temporality of landscape. *World Archaeology* **25**, 152–74.

Irving, R. 1981: *Indian Summer: Lutyens, Baker and Imperial Delhi*. New Haven and London: Yale University Press.

Izumida, H. 1991: Scottish architects in the Far East: 1840–1870, in Howard, D. (ed.) *Scottish Architects Abroad*. Edinburgh: Architectural Heritage Society of Scotland, 93–8.

Jackson, P. 1999: Identity, in McDowell, L. and Sharp, J.P. (eds) *Feminist Glossary of Human Geography*. London: Arnold, 132–4.

Jacobs, J.M. 1996: Negotiating the heart: place and identity in the post-imperial City, in Jacobs, J.M., *Edge of Empire: Postcolonialism and the City*. London: Routledge, 38–69.

Jakle, J.A., Bastian, R.W. and Meyer, D.K. 1989: *Common Houses in*

America's Small Towns: The Atlantic Seaboard to the Mississippi Valley. Athens: University of Georgia Press.

Janowitz, A. 1990: *England's Ruins: Poetic Purpose and the National Landscape.* Oxford: Blackwell.

Jay, E. 1992: *'Keep Them in Birmingham'. Challenging Racism in South-west England.* London: Commission for Racial Equality.

Jedrej, C. and Nuttall, M. 1996: *White Settlers. The Impact of Rural Repopulation in Scotland.* Luxembourg: Harwood Academic Publishers.

Jones, G. 1993: *British Multinational Banking 1830–1990.* Oxford: Oxford University Press.

Jones, G. 2000: *Merchants to Multinationals: British Trading Companies in the Nineteenth and Twentieth Centuries.* Oxford: Oxford University Press.

Jones, N. 1993: *Living in Rural Wales.* Llandysul: Gomer.

King, A.D. 1984: *The Bungalow: The Production of a Global Culture.* London: Routledge.

King, A.D. 1990: *Urbanism, Colonialism and the World Economy: Cultural and Spatial Foundations of the World Urban System.* London: Routledge.

King, F. 1987: *The History of the Hongkong and Shanghai Banking Corporation. Volume I: The Hongkong Bank in Late Imperial China 1864–1902.* Cambridge: Cambridge University Press.

King, F. 1988: *The History of the Hongkong and Shanghai Banking Corporation. Volume III: The Hongkong Bank Between the Wars and the Bank Interned.* Cambridge: Cambridge University Press.

Kinnaird, V., Morris, M., Nash, C. and Rose, G. 1997: Feminist geographies of environment, nature and landscape, in Women and Geography Research Group (ed.) *Feminism and Geography: Diversity and Difference.* Harlow: Addison, Wesley, Longman, 146–89.

Kinsman, P. 1995: Landscape, race and national identity: the photography of Ingrid Pollard. *Area* **27**, 300–10.

Kinsman, P. 1997: Re-negotiating the boundaries of race and citizenship: the Black Environment Network and environmental and conservation bodies, in Milbourne, P. (ed.) *Revealing Rural 'Others'.* London: Pinter, 13–36.

Kniffen, F.B. 1936: Louisiana house types. *Annals of the Association of American Geographers* **26**, 179–93.

Kniffen, F.B. 1965: Folk housing: key to diffusion. *Annals of the Association of American Geographers* **55**, 549–77.

Kracauer, S. 1978: *Theory of Film: The Redemption of Physical Reality.* London: Oxford University Press.

Lambert, E. 1976: *Placing Sorrow.* Chapel Hill: University of North Carolina.

Lambot, I. and Chambers, G. 1986: *One Queen's Road Central: the Headquarters of Hongkong Bank since 1864.* Hong Kong: Hongkong Bank.

Lang, A. 1899: *The Homeric Hymns*. New York: Longman.

Lanzmann, C. 1985: *Shoah*. London: Academy Video.

Lee, M.O. 1989: *Death and Rebirth in Virgil's Arcadia*. Albany: State University of New York.

Lees, L. 2001: Towards a critical geography of architecture: the case of an ersatz colosseum. *Ecumene* **8**, 51–86.

Leighly, J. (ed.) 1963: *Land and Life: A Selection from the Writings of Carl Ortwin Sauer*. Berkeley and Los Angeles: University of California Press.

Little, J. 1986: Feminist perspectives in rural geography: an introduction. *Journal of Rural Studies* **2**, 1–8.

Little, J. 1987: Gender relations in rural areas: the importance of women's domestic role. *Journal of Rural Studies* **3**, 335–42.

Little, J. 1997: Employment marginality and women's self-identity, in Cloke, P. and Little, J. (eds) *Contested Countryside Cultures*. London: Routledge, 138–57.

Little, J. and Austin, P. 1996: Women and the rural idyll. *Journal of Rural Studies* **12**, 101–11.

Loshitzky, Y. 1997a: Introduction, in Loshitzky, Y. (ed.) *Spielberg's Holocaust: Critical Perspectives on Schindler's List*. Bloomington: Indiana University Press.

Loshitzky, Y. 1997b: Holocaust Others: Spielberg's 'Schindler's List' versus Lanzmann's 'Shoah', in Loshitzky, Y. (ed.) *Spielberg's Holocaust: Critical Perspectives on Schindler's List*. Bloomington: Indiana University Press, 104–18.

Loughrey, B. 1984: *The Pastoral Mode*. London: Macmillan.

Lowe, R. and Shaw, W. 1993: *Travellers*. London: Fourth Estate.

Malik, S. 1992: Colours of the countryside – a whiter shade of pale. *Ecos* **13** (4), 33–40.

Maltin, L. 2000: *Leonard Maltin's 2000 Movie & Video Guide*. New York: Penguin.

Margolis, H. (ed.) 1999: *Jane Campion's The Piano*. Cambridge: Cambridge University Press.

Mast, G. and Kawin, B. 2000: *A Short History of the Movie*. Boston: Allyn & Bacon.

Matless, D. 1992: Regional surveys and local knowledges: the geographical imagination in Britain, 1918–1939. *Transactions of the Institute of British Geographers*, **17** (4), 464–80.

Matless, D. 1995: 'The Art of Right Living' – landscape and citizenship 1918–1939, in Pile, S. and Thrift, N. (eds) *Mapping the Subject – Geographies of Cultural Transformation*. London: Routledge.

Matless, D. 1997: Moral geographies of English landscape. *Landscape Research* **22** (2), 141–56.

Matless, D. 1998: *Landscape and Englishness*. London: Reaktion.

McBride, J. 1997: *Steven Spielberg*. London: Faber & Faber.

McIntosh, A., Wightman, A. and Morgan, D. 1994: Reclaiming the Scottish Highlands. Clearance, conflict and crofting. *The Ecologist* **24** (2), 64–70.

McKay, G. 1996: *Senseless Acts of Beauty*. London: Verso.

McKay, G. 2000: *Glastonbury. A Very English Fair*. London: Victor Gollancz.

Meinig, D.W. 1979: Reading the landscape: an appreciation of W.G. Hoskins and J.B. Jackson, in Meinig, D.W. (ed.) *The Interpretation of Ordinary Landscapes: Geographical Essays*. Oxford: Oxford University Press, 195–244.

Milbourne, P. (ed.) 1997: *Revealing Rural 'Others': Representation, Power and Identity in the British Countryside*. London: Pinter.

Miron, D. 1996: *A Traveler Disguised: The Rise of Modern Yiddish Fiction in the Nineteenth Century* (2nd edn). Syracuse: Syracuse University Press.

Miron, D. 2000: *The Image of the Shtetl and Other Studies of Modern Jewish Literary Imagination*. Syracuse: Syracuse University Press.

Mitchell, D. 2000: *Cultural Geography – A Critical Introduction*, Oxford: Blackwell.

Mitchell, W.J.T. 1986: *Iconology: Image, Text, Ideology*. Chicago: University of Chicago Press.

Mitchell, W.J.T. 1994: *Landscape and Power*. Chicago: Chicago University Press.

Mitford, J. 2000: *The American Way of Death Revisited*. New York: Random House.

Morgan, D. 1999: *Monty Python Speaks!* New York: Avon Books.

Morin, K.M. 1998: British women travellers and constructions of racial difference across the nineteenth-century American West. *Transactions of the Institute of British Geographers* NS **23**, 311–30.

Muir, R. 1998: Landscape a wasted legacy. *Area* **30**, 263–71.

Muir, R. 1999: *Approaches to Landscape*. London: Macmillan.

Murdoch, J. and Day, G. 1998: Middle class mobility, rural communities and the politics of exclusion, in Boyle, P. and Halfacree, K. (eds) *Migration into Rural Areas*. Chichester: Wiley, 186–99.

Murdoch, J. and Marsden, T. 1994: *Reconstituting Rurality*. London: UCL Press.

Murdoch, J. and Pratt, A. 1993: Rural studies: modernism, postmodernism and the 'post-rural'. *Journal of Rural Studies* **9**, 411–27.

Murphy, W.T. 1997: 'Nanook of the North', in *Films: International Dictionary of Films and Filmmakers* (3rd edn). New York: St James Press.

NCCL (National Council for Civil Liberties) 1986: *Stonehenge*. London: NCCL.

Nash, C. 1996: Reclaiming vision: looking at landscape and the body. *Gender, Place and Culture* **3** (2), 149–69.

Nichols, B. 1981: *Ideology and the Image*. Bloomington: Indiana University.

Noble, A.G. 1984: *Wood, Brick and Stone: The North American Settlement Landscape*. Vol. I: *Houses*; Vol. II: *Barns and Farm Structures*. Amherst: University of Massachusetts Press.

Olsen, D.J. 1986: *The City as a Work of Art. London. Paris. Vienna*. New Haven and London: Yale University Press.

Olwig, K. 1996: Recovering the substantive nature of landscape. *Annals of the Association of American Geographers* **86**, 305–19.

Ovid 1958 edition: *The Metamorphoses*. New York: Viking.

Palowski, F. 1994: *Retracing Schindler's List*. Krakow: Argona-Jordan Art.

Philips, R. 1995: Spaces of adventure and cultural politics of masculinity in R.M. Ballantyne and 'The Young Fur Traders'. *Environment and Planning D: Society and Space* **13**, 591–608.

Philips, R. 1997: *Mapping Men and Empire: A Geography of Adventure*, London: Routledge.

Phillips, M., Fish, R. and Agg, J. 2001: Putting together ruralities: towards a symbolic analysis of rurality in the British mass media. *Journal of Rural Studies* **17**, 1–27.

Philo, C. 1992: Neglected rural geographies: a review. *Journal of Rural Studies* **8**, 193–207.

Philo, C. 1997: Of other rurals?, in Cloke, P. and Little, J. (eds) *Contested Countryside Cultures*. London: Routledge, 19–50.

Philo, C. 2000: More words, more worlds. Reflections on the 'cultural turn' and human geography, in Cook, I., Crouch, D., Naylor, S. and Ryan J.R. (eds) *Cultural Turns/Geographical Turns*. London: Prentice Hall.

Pratt, G. 2000: Subject formation, geographies of, in Johnston, R.J., Gregory, D., Pratt, G. and Watts, M. (eds) *Dictionary of Human Geography*. Oxford: Blackwell.

Pregill, P. and Volkman, N. 1999: *Landscapes in History: Design and Planning in the Eastern and Western Traditions* (2nd edn). Chichester: Wiley.

Pringle, T. 1988: The privation of history: Landseer, Victoria, and the Highland myth, in Cosgrove, D. and Daniels, S. (eds) *The Iconography of Landscape*. Cambridge: Cambridge University Press, 142–61.

Pugh, S. 1988: *Garden-Nature-Language*. Manchester: Manchester University Press.

Ragon, M. 1983: *The Space of Death: A Study of Funerary Architecture, Decoration, and Urbanism*. Charlottesville: University of Virginia.

Ramazani, J. 1994: *Poetry of Mourning*. Chicago: University of Chicago.

Ritvo, H. 1992: *An English Arcadia: Landscape and Architecture in Britain and America*. San Marino: Huntington.

Roberts, L. 1992: A rough guide to rurality. *Talking Point* **137**.

Rose, G. 1992: Geography as a science of observation: the landscape, the gaze and masculinity, in Driver, F. and Rose, G. (eds.) *Nature and Science: Essays in the History of Geographical Knowledge*. Historical Geographical Research Series, 28.

Rose, G. 1993: Looking at landscape: the uneasy pleasures of power, in Rose, G., *Feminism and Geography: The Limits of Geographical Knowledge*. London: Routledge.

Rosenmeyer, T. 1969: *The Green Cabinet*. Berkeley: University of California.

Ruskin, J. 1971: Of the Pathetic Fallacy, in Adams, H. (ed.) *Critical Theory Since Plato*. New York: HBJ, 615–23.

Sacks, P. 1985: *The English Elegy*. Baltimore: Hopkins.

Samuel, R. 1989: Introduction: exciting to be English, in Samuel, R. (ed.) *Patriotism. Volume 3. National Fictions*. London: Routledge, xviii–lxvii.

Sauer, C.O. 1925: The morphology of landscape, *University of California Publications in Geography* 2, 19–54. (Reprinted in Leighly, J. (ed.) 1963: *Land and Life: A Selection from the Writings of Carl Ortwin Sauer*. Berkeley and Los Angeles: University of California Press, 315–50; pages quoted are from the Leighly volume.)

Scarry, E. 1985: *The Body in Pain*. New York: Oxford University.

Schama, S. 1995: *Landscape and Memory*. New York: Knopf.

Scheindlin, R. 1998: *A Short History of the Jewish People: From Legendary Times to Modern Statehood*. New York: Oxford University Press.

Schumann-Bacia, E. 1991: *John Soane and the Bank of England*. Harlow: Longman.

Scruggs, J. and Swerdlow, J. 1985: *To Heal a Nation*. New York: Harper & Row.

Seymour, S. 2000: Historical geographies of landscape, in Graham, B. and Nash, C. (eds) *Modern Historical Geographies*. London: Longman.

Shandler, J. 1997: Schindler's discourse: America discusses the Holocaust, in Loshitzky, Y. (ed.) *Spielberg's Holocaust: Critical Perspectives on Schindler's List*. Bloomington: Indiana University Press, 153–70.

Short, J. 1991: *Imagined Country*. London: Routledge.

Sibley, D. 1997: Endangering the sacred. Nomads, youth cultures and the English countryside, in Cloke, P. and Little, J. (eds) *Contested Countryside Cultures*. London: Routledge, 218–31.

Smith, A.D. 1991: *National Identity*. London: Penguin.

Smith, S. 1993: Bounding the Borders: claiming space and making place in rural Scotland. *Transactions of the Institute of British Geographers* 18, 291–308.

Somers, M. 1994: The narrative constitution of identity: a relational and network approach. *Theory and Society* 23, 605–49.

South China Morning Post 1934: The Bank, 17 October.

Spencer, J. 1973: *Heroic Nature: Ideal Landscape in English Poetry from Marvell to Thomson*. Evanston: Northwestern University.

Sterritt, D. 1993: *The Films of Alfred Hitchcock*. New York: Cambridge University Press.

Stonehenge Campaign 2001: homepage at www.geocities.com/soho/9000/stonecam.htm (accessed May 2002).

Sturken, M. 1997: *Tangled Memories: The Vietnam War, the AIDS Epidemic, and the Politics of Remembering.* Berkeley: University of California.

Telushkin, J. 1990: *Jewish Literacy.* New York: William Morrow & Co.

Thomson, D. 1995: *A Biographical Dictionary of Film* (3rd edn). New York: Alfred Knopf.

Thrift, N. 1989: Images of social change, in Hamnett, C., McDowell, L. and Sarre, P. (eds) *The Changing Social Structure.* London: Sage, 12–42.

Tilly, C. 1994: *A Phenomenology of Landscape.* Oxford: Berg.

Toliver, H. 1984: Pastoral contrasts, in Loughrey, B. (ed.) *The Pastoral Mode.* London: Macmillan, 124–9.

Urgnat, R. 1974: *Jean Renoir.* Berkeley: University of California Press.

Virgil 1984 edition: *The Eclogues.* London: Penguin.

Ward, C. 1988: *The Child in the Country.* London: Bedford Square Press.

Wasko, J. 1995: *Hollywood in the Information Age.* Austin: University of Texas Press.

Watson, T. 1895: *Poems.* Westminster: Constable.

Whatmore, S. 1990: *Farming Women: Gender, Work and Family Enterprise.* London: Macmillan.

Whitman, W. 1973: *Leaves of Grass.* New York: Norton.

Williams, G. 1985: *When was Wales?* Harmondsworth: Penguin.

Williams, R. 1973: *The Country and the City.* London: Hogarth Press.

Willis, C. 1995: *Form Follows Finance: Skyscrapers and Skylines in New York and Chicago.* Princeton: Princeton Architectural Press.

Withers, C.W.J. 1996: Place, memory, monument: memorialising the past in contemporary Highland Scotland. *Ecumene* 3 (3), 325–44.

Women's Institute 2001: homepage at www.womens-institute.co.uk/ (accessed May 2002).

Wood, R. 1989: *Hitchcock's Films Revisited.* London: Faber & Faber.

Woodward, K. 2000: *Questioning Identity: Gender, Class, Nation.* Milton Keynes: Open University Press.

Wright, P. 1985: *On Living in an Old Country.* London: Verso.

Yarwood, R. and Evans, N. 2000: Taking stock of farm animals and rurality, in Philo, C. and Wilbert, C. (eds) *Animal Spaces, Beastly Places. New Geographies of Human-animal Relations.* London: Routledge, 98–114.

Yeoh, B.S.A. 2000: Historical geographies of the colonised world, in Graham, B. and Nash, C. (eds) *Modern Historical Geographies.* Harlow: Prentice Hall.

Yip, C. 1983: Four major buildings in the architectural history of the Hongkong and Shanghai Banking Corporation, in King, F. (ed.) *Eastern Banking: Essays in the History of the Hongkong and Shanghai Banking Corporation.* London: Athlone Press, 112–38.

Yoch, J.J. 1989: *Landscaping the American Dream: The Gardens and Film Sets of Florence Yoch, 1890–1972.* New York: Harry N. Abrams, Inc.

Young, J.E. 1993: *The Texture of Memory: Holocaust Memorials and Meaning.* New Haven: Yale University Press.

Zeiger, M. 1997: *Beyond Consolation*. Ithaca: Cornell University.

Zelizer, B. 1997: Every once in a while: 'Schindler's List' and the shaping of history, in Loshitzky, Y. (ed.) *Spielberg's Holocaust: Critical Perspectives on Schindler's List*. Bloomington: Indiana University Press, 18–40.

Index

Page numbers in *italic* indicate the presence of an illustration.